BEYOND NEWS

Columbia Journalism Review Books

Columbia Journalism Review Books

Series Editors: Victor Navasky, Evan Cornog, Mike Hoyt,
and the editors of the *Columbia Journalism Review*

For more than fifty years, the *Columbia Journalism Review* has been the gold standard for media criticism, holding the profession to the highest standards and exploring where journalism is headed, for good and for ill.

Columbia Journalism Review Books expands upon this mission, seeking to publish titles that allow for greater depth in exploring key issues confronting journalism, both past and present, and pointing to new ways of thinking about the field's impact and potential.

Drawing on the expertise of the editorial staff at the *Columbia Journalism Review* as well as the Columbia Journalism School, the series of books will seek out innovative voices as well as reclaim important works, traditions, and standards. In doing this, the series will also incorporate new ways of publishing made available by the Web and e-books.

Second Read: Writers Look Back at Classic Works of Reportage,
edited by James Marcus and the Staff of the
Columbia Journalism Review

The Story So Far: What We Know About the Business of Digital Journalism, Bill Grueskin, Ava Seave, and Lucas Graves

The Best Business Writing 2012, edited by Dean Starkman,
Martha M. Hamilton, Ryan Chittum, and Felix Salmon

The Art of Making Magazines: On Being an Editor and Other Views from the Industry, edited by Victor S. Navasky and Evan Cornog

The Best Business Writing 2013, edited by Dean Starkman,
Martha M. Hamilton, Ryan Chittum, and Felix Salmon

The Watchdog That Didn't Bark: The Financial Crisis and the Disappearance of Investigative Journalism, Dean Starkman

BEYOND
NEWS

—

THE FUTURE OF
JOURNALISM

—

MITCHELL STEPHENS

Columbia University Press   New York

Columbia University Press
Publishers Since 1893
New York   Chichester, West Sussex
Copyright © 2014 Columbia University Press
All rights reserved

Library of Congress Cataloging-in-Publication Data

Stephens, Mitchell.
Beyond news : the future of journalism / Mitchell Stephens.
pages cm
Includes bibliographical references and index.
ISBN 978-0-231-15938-8 (cloth : alk. paper)
—ISBN 978-0-231-53629-5 (ebook)
1. Journalism—History—21st century.
2. Journalism—Technological innovations.
3. Online journalism. 4. Reporters and reporting.
I. Title.

PN4815.2.S48   2014
070.4—dc23   2013038840

Columbia University Press books are printed on permanent
and durable acid-free paper.
This book is printed on paper with recycled content.
Printed in the United States of America
c 10 9 8 7 6 5 4 3 2 1

Cover design: Lisa Hamm

References to Internet Web sites (URLs) were accurate at the time of writing.
Neither the author nor Columbia University Press is responsible for URLs
that may have expired or changed since the manuscript was prepared.

Publication of this book
is supported by
a grant from
Figure Foundation.

To my father, Bernard Stephens—dedicated to social justice
and to journalism

CONTENTS

INTRODUCTION

Quality Journalism Reconsidered

Most Americans today think of journalists the way most journalists think of themselves: as reporters of news. Indeed, many practitioners and patrons of traditional journalism in the United States would accept the standard for the profession that Bill Keller enunciated in 2009: "By quality journalism I mean the kind that involves experienced reporters going places, bearing witness, digging into records, developing sources, checking and double-checking."[1] Keller was then the top editor of the *New York Times*.

This book argues that this view of journalism, which arrived in the nineteenth century, is outdated in the twenty-first. It proposes an alternative understanding of quality in journalism. And, in so doing, it also suggests an alternative response to journalism's crisis.

Yes, the crisis. In recent decades, things have not been going well for journalists. Although the population has continued to grow, total newspaper circulation in the United States has dropped more than 25 percent since 1990, according to the Pew Research Center. The evening newscasts of the three traditional broadcast television networks in the United States—once the dominant news sources in the country—have lost more than half their audience since 1980. Meanwhile, two of the country's major news magazines no longer publish regularly, and the third, *Time*, watched its newsstand sales plummet 27 percent in 2012 alone.[2]

Large numbers of talented, hardworking people have as a result lost their jobs. Newspapers in the United States employed about 30 percent fewer journalists in 2012 than they did at the beginning of the twenty-first century, according to that Pew report.[3] Online and cable news operations have grabbed audiences but not replaced enough jobs—at least not enough that pay. A particularly chilling consequence of these cutbacks has been a drop in the number of professional reporters patrolling city halls, statehouses, and the sites of our recent or lingering wars.[4]

In their gloom, journalists and those who value them have been repairing to conferences to rend their clothes, wail their wails, and curse the Fates. Some, overcoming a much-prized dispassion, pen apocalyptic screeds and mouth dreadful prophecies.

These defenders of the craft—in their anxiety, in their distress—are wont to declare news itself to be in crisis.[5] In this, however, they are wrong. News for the most part is in fine shape.

News can be defined as new information about a subject of some public interest that is shared with some portion of the public.[6] It is hard not to notice that the amount of new information of public interest being shared continues to swell even as jobs handling it vanish. Indeed, the recent arrival of the most powerful information technology in human history has, as one might have expected, been a boon for news. The World Wide Web remains very young, but already it gathers accounts of an extraordinarily wide variety of events from an extraordinarily wide variety of sources and disseminates them in a wide variety of formats fast and far. Amazingly fast: newsworthy events nowadays—statements, contretemps, disasters—are all over the Web before they are over.[7] And impressively far: our computer-Internet-cell-Web devices, despite the efforts of some governments to restrict them, now zip words and images in and out of almost every country on earth. We have not before seen a news medium like this.

This does not mean the news that comes to us on our laptops, smart phones, tablets, or, soon, wearable devices is always edifying, constructive, or reliable. News in print or on television, after all, has often enough failed to embody those virtues. And the Web's manifold strengths as a news medium do not mean all news will be equally well served by it. As amateurs and algorithms collect and distribute more news, issues of accuracy, accountability, bias, depth, and professionalism loom larger. We have to be alert, as we must be with any medium, for blind spots. Once, it should be remembered, journalism reviews devoted themselves to cataloging the many egregious oversights of newspapers and newscasts—with their sometimes narrow-minded and conventional "gatekeepers."

The Web's weak points, at first glance, appear to fall into two categories. One is a failure to report regularly on news that grew up with and, perhaps, grew old with newspaper beat systems: varieties of local news in particular. The second is a reluctance to deploy teams of experienced reporters, of which the Web so far has few, and to devote space, of which it has plenty, to original investigations.

However, the multitudes that have by now obtained Internet connections have access to a bountiful supply of news. The gates have flung open. And the flow of news on the Web and its cousins seems, if anything, likely to continue to broaden, deepen, and accelerate. Entrepreneurs and nonprofits have even begun having a go at some of those blind spots. The future of news, in other words, appears reasonably secure.

It is the future of journalism that is looking grim.

Defining exactly what journalism is has proven surprisingly difficult.[8] It is, in some sense, a specialized enterprise—usually performed for pay—but define it too narrowly, and you risk depriving nonspecialists, amateurs, of its privileges and responsibilities.[9] It is clearly about news, but again too narrow a focus on reporting and distributing the news—Bill Keller's focus in 2009—can limit this enterprise's possibilities. Here is my definition: journalism is the activity of collecting, presenting, interpreting, or commenting upon the news for some portion of the public.

For approximately the past century and a half, journalists have emphasized the collecting and presenting of news. Since the middle of the nineteenth century, they have made their living—indeed, constructed grand enterprises—either through the sale of news or through the sale of ads next to news. (Chapter 2 of this book considers how this combination was accomplished, chapter 3 why this era is ending.) It does not look as if similar numbers of journalists will be able to make their living this way in the future.

In an effort to coax some money out of their growing numbers of online-only customers, many news organizations have begun constructing often partially permeable "pay walls."[10] Nevertheless, the flood of information on current events now sloshing around the Internet can be sipped, drunk, or bathed in on thousands of news sites, blogs, feeds, apps—mostly for free. This has understandably strained profit margins and flummoxed business models—including pay walls—at many of those news sites, blogs, feeds, and apps. There is not much of a living in hawking that which is given away free. That is like running a ferry after they've built the bridge. It is like selling ice after everyone has a refrigerator. Ask encyclopedia salesmen today, if you can find one.

Radio and television newscasts had overcome this problem with advertising. However, unlike the supply of programs on radio or TV back in their heyday as advertising media, the supply of news-rich pages on the Internet is now so large that it is hard to charge much for ads on those pages.[11] Even the supply of online audio and video news, which can be preceded by short commercials, seems to be heading in the direction of unlimited as audio and video become ever easier to record, edit, upload, and access. The success of digital news itself consequently undercuts the economics of digital journalism: because it is so plentiful, it is worth less to audiences and advertisers. Now that information pours out of spigots, the point is, painstakingly gathered facts on current events—what happened, who said what, when—have lost much of their value. (The problem traditional news organizations now face in trying to sell accounts of public events, even if they may have reported them somewhat more skillfully, is discussed in chapter 3.)

Probably the Associated Press (AP), Reuters, Bloomberg, and a few additional news organizations will be able to make a go of supplying written or video accounts of such events to websites fast and in bulk. However, it is difficult to see many others basing a business on the fruits of such run-of-the-mill reporting—on merely collecting and presenting routine news. After more than a century and a half of selling the latest facts, journalists need to sell something else.

With a desperation characteristic of people whose livelihoods are at stake, journalists have been forced in recent years to rethink how "quality journalism" might be distributed: newspapers and magazines contemplate abandoning print; radio news programs produce podcasts; television news networks have begun to think of themselves as video-report suppliers. And it is difficult to find a news operation today that does not arm its reporters with a variety of recording devices and that is not splashing news up on Facebook, Twitter, and some spiffy new app for Apple's latest insanely desirable iDoohickey. Journalists today are even rethinking how "quality journalism" might be funded: perhaps through nonprofits, if not pay walls.

Few today, however, are rethinking what, in these changing times, "quality journalism" might be. Yet definitions of quality, like technologies, are vulnerable to obsolescence. Consider—to jump fields and centuries—the case of Ernest Meissonier.

Meissonier, who died in 1891, was for a time the most respected painter in Paris and therefore the world.[12] "He is the incontestable master of our epoch," gushed another master painter, Eugène Delacroix, who proclaimed to Charles Baudelaire that, "amongst all of us, surely it is he who is most certain to survive."[13]

Meissonier excelled at precision and accuracy: "I paint like everyone else," he once explained. "Only I look always."[14] Meissonier's work was based, in other words, on intensive observation—of the exact positions adopted, for example, by a moving horse: "What efforts, what sketches, what lengths of precious time, what fatigue he incurred," one contemporary exclaims, "to faithfully translate the living animal!"[15] Critics raved about Meissonier's "scrupulous exactitude."[16] His painstakingly precise re-creations of great events dominated the most important expositions and commanded the highest prices.

Meissonier's masterwork, which took him twelve years to complete, was a depiction of Napoleon and his army at Friedland in 1807. It was sold to an American for 380,000 francs in 1876.[17] *Friedland* is currently on display in New York's Metropolitan Museum of Art and features quite a few well-realized horses.

Ernest Meissonier saw himself as part of a "tradition of . . . honesty, conscientiousness and truthfulness."[18] By the end of the nineteenth century, however, such efforts to get every detail just right were starting to seem a waste of time, and the tradition Meissonier exemplified was starting to seem something of a bore. A new technology was helping to change understandings of what painting might be.

Photography demonstrated, to begin with, that the "truthfulness" offered by Meissonier's paintings was limited—even when it came to horses' gaits. The American photographer Eadweard Muybridge, employing speeded-up cameras and a system of trip wires, had managed to photograph horses in motion. Muybridge, who was quite aware of Meissonier's work, confirmed the painter's depiction of the walk, but Muybridge's photos showed different leg positions during the trot and, in particular, the gallop than Meissonier had been able to paint by merely looking—however intently.[19] Horses legs simply moved too fast for naked eyes—even Meissonier's eyes—to follow. "If I could only repaint *Friedland*," Meissonier, who was quite aware of Muybridge's work, was reported to have said.[20] His later paintings restrict themselves to horses that are walking or standing still.[21]

And this new technology not only beat realistic painters at their own game but did so, as shutter speeds continued to accelerate, without all the "efforts," "sketches," and "fatigue." The camera, with its revelations, initially contributed to a fever for facts from which realistic painters such as Meissonier benefited. But soon enough photography devalued precisely that at which Meissonier specialized: it made producing painstakingly accurate re-creations of just about anything easy and therefore cheap.

Attitudes were in time adjusted accordingly. In the late nineteenth and early twentieth centuries, the notion that quality in art was dependent upon precision and verisimilitude faded. After Meissonier's death, his reputation tumbled to the point where one major two-volume history of French art in the nineteenth century did not even mention his name. The Louvre eventually exiled a marble statue of Meissonier from its halls.[22]

Have technologies today, in particular technologies introduced in the past couple of decades, done the same with the painstaking gathering of information on current events? Through blogs, emails, and tweets, audiences can receive firsthand reports on newsworthy happenings as those events trot or gallop along. Through video and live cameras, they can often even "observe" those events themselves. Have technologies today, therefore, beaten traditional news reporting at its own game? By making it so easy for audiences to find out what happened, have they reduced the value of telling them what happened? Have they, in other words, outdated the view of quality in journalism that many traditional journalists still hold: the veneration of witnessing, digging, finding sources, and checking?

Bill Keller, striking something of an apocalyptic tone himself, lamented the "diminishing supply" of his version of "quality journalism."[23] But "diminishing supply" can sometimes be a sign of diminishing need. The Web grants us all the ability to dig, find sources, and check—to *search*, in a word. It often grants us the ability to witness. Is it possible the supply of the kind of journalism in which this is done for us, like the supply of realistic painting after photography, *should* diminish? Maybe we don't require as many of Keller's "experienced reporters" as we did before much of the world presented itself to us online.

Without making light of the professional crisis journalism has experienced, we might discern an opportunity here for journalism. The Web allows our best journalists to surrender the prosaic task of telling everyone what just happened. It allows them to leave the speeches and press conferences in part to the cable networks and YouTube; to leave the interviews with police and survivors to diligent wire-service reporters; to fob off surveillance of some lesser boards and councils on civic-minded individuals with an urge to tweet and post. It would be a blow to what sometimes seems a colonial conception of reporting, but our best journalists might even surrender some of the responsibility for filling in Americans on what has been going on in India, Egypt, or Iraq to cosmopolitan residents of India, Egypt, or Iraq. It might no longer be quite so necessary to parachute in a jaded American with a notepad. The Web allows our best journalists—it requires them, I will argue—to return to an older and higher view of their calling: not as reporters of what's going on, but as individuals capable of providing a wise take on what's going on.

Certainly—at difficult times, in hard-to-reach places—"bearing witness" can reveal and expose. Certainly, facts must be checked, worried over. Certainly, much still can be uncovered by "digging into records" and "developing sources." Nothing said here is meant to imply that journalists should forgo human rights reporting, investigative reporting, enterprise reporting, or exclusives.

However, merely noting who said what at some public event—mere "stenographic" reporting, to use the most dismissive of the terms that has been applied to it—today shares some of the flaws of a Meissonier painting: it is occasionally less starkly truthful than simply watching or listening to recordings of that event, and it is less revealing than freer, more far-reaching discussions of that event online by well-informed individuals with an insight or point of view to share.

Ernest Meissonier's work was connected, of course, to a movement that extended well beyond painting: a movement that Honoré de Balzac proclaimed in the preface to one of his books in the 1830s: "The author firmly believes that details alone will henceforth determine the merit of works."[24] Details dominated much nineteenth-century fiction—realistic, naturalistic, even coarse, and often morally or politically troubling details. Though his work was not coarse or troubling, Meissonier, like Balzac, was a details man. So, for another example, was the English physician John Snow, who in the middle of that century located cholera deaths and wells on a map to demonstrate that the disease spread through contaminated drinking water.[25] The pursuit of details, of facts, was crucial to the advance of nineteenth-century science and medicine. And as that century progressed, increasing numbers of journalists became details men and women, too. (Chapter 2 considers how and why American journalists convinced themselves that their highest purpose was collecting facts.)

Despite the great accomplishments of what Balzac had called the impulse to "venerate the fact,"[26] literature, painting, and in some sense science would move on in the next century. They would cease to imagine the world as composed of discreet, independently verifiable details that could be captured by sufficient observation, "conscientiousness[,] and truthfulness." Novelists, painters, and in some sense scientists left realism behind in the twentieth century.

Most journalists in the United States did not. To the contrary: their embrace of realism—of facts, of details, conscientiously and truthfully rendered—became ever more passionate in the twentieth century.[27]

As early as 1859, the poet Charles Baudelaire was mocking the view that "art is, and cannot be other than, the exact reproduction of Nature."[28] The Impressionists later in that century were much inclined toward nature, but they didn't necessarily look for it where the Meissoniers of the world had found it. "Nature is not on the surface," Paul Cezanne proclaimed. "It is in the depth."[29] In the first decades of the twentieth century, paintings would appear that showed aspects of nature, human faces in particular, from multiple perspectives at once or that showed nothing easily recognizable as nature. In 1919, Virginia Woolf, writing about fiction, was attacking the "materialists" and noting how "life escapes" their "magnificent apparatus for catching" it.[30] Painting and literature turned from diligent attempts to capture material details to offering impressions and perspectives; they turned from the objective to the subjective. Physics turned, in important ways, from a universe filled with the fixed and knowable to a view of even the physical world, at great enough speeds or small enough sizes, as relative and uncertain.

Journalism missed that turn. In the United States, only a limited number of journalism critics[31] and a small minority of journalists in the twentieth century questioned the merit and scope of the "scrupulous exactitude" reporters were getting better and better at pursuing.[32] In 1922, even Walter Lippmann, among the wisest of journalists and journalism critics, thought "reality" could be easily located, although, not surprisingly, he had some difficulty settling on exactly where it might be found—"outside" us, not in the subjective "pictures in our heads" or, as he writes some pages later, in "the interior scene" rather than the "façade" we present to the world.[33]

By the start of the twenty-first century, journalists had grown a little more humble. "Journalism does not pursue truth in an absolute or philosophical sense," acknowledged one distinguished group, the Committee of Concerned Journalists, itself administered by the Project for Excellence in Journalism. But in its "Principles of Journalism" this group did insist that journalism "can—and must—pursue" truth "in a practical sense." It asserted, in a somewhat clumsy wording, that "this 'journalistic truth' is a process that begins with the professional discipline of assembling and verifying facts." And the Committee of Concerned Journalists was not at all humble in its view of the importance of such verified and assembled facts: "Democracy depends on citizens having reliable, accurate facts put in a meaningful context."[34]

Some of the words used here—*practical, process, context*—bespeak an awareness that piling detail upon detail does not a world make. That is encouraging. But in their pursuit of "excellence," such committees of journalists still have some difficulty surrendering the nineteenth- and twentieth-century notion that journalists are primarily collectors of facts.

The continued clinging to this notion is odd because newspapers, newsreels, and newscasts, though allergic to modernism and postmodernism, rank high among the forces that spurred modernism and postmodernism in the twentieth century. They helped outmode simpler conceptions of reality through their relentless interrogations, their compulsive cynicism, their mixings of high and low, their unavoidable heterogeneity, and their incessant reminders of the importance of the way something is communicated.

"Is the press a messenger?" asked the Viennese critic Karl Kraus in 1914. "No it is the event itself." Kraus's characteristic bitterness after the start of the First World War exceeded even his characteristic irony. The press, he complained, is "the most murderous weapon" progress wields, for it destroys the assumption that an occurrence might have an existence independent of the way we talk about it—the assumption, even, that the occurrence proceeds the way we talk about it: "Deeds are stronger than words," Kraus wrote, "but the echo is stronger than the deed. We live on the echo, and in this topsy-turvy world the echo arouses the call."[35]

The press spent much of the twentieth century demonstrating the power of "the echo," yet many journalists refused to take the lesson. Stiff-necked and unblinking in their own focus on events, lost in their own chase after deeds, spellbound by the perpetrators of such deeds, they failed to note the debt those events and deeds owed to culture, to language, to dissemination. They continued to believe that the facts they were "assembling and verifying" had an existence entirely independent of the process of assembling, verifying, investigating, sorting, and presenting in "a meaningful context."

Walter Cronkite always closed the *CBS Evening News*, probably the leading news source in the United States in the late 1960s and 1970s, by announcing, "And that's the way it is." He did not say—and I have seen no evidence that he thought—"and that's one perspective on the way it is." And Cronkite certainly did not say—and I would be surprised if he or most of his contemporaries in journalism thought—"and that's the way our coverage helps make it seem to be."[36]

In the nineteenth century, the best journalists had seen themselves as and were often welcomed as participants in literature and philosophy.[37] In the twentieth century, many of them seemed at war with literature and philosophy. Indeed, journalists would sometimes be dismissed as philistines, for they had become champions of precisely the era and ideology that contemporary artists and thinkers were aggressively positioning themselves against: journalism in the United States in particular, outside of the arts pages at least, became the last redoubt of realism—

of the insistence that there was, if you could get the facts right, a "way it is." "Objectivity" was American journalism's religion. Its practitioners transformed themselves into such fierce defenders of realism that they sometimes came through with parodies of avant-garde art or experimental prose and dismissals of literary theory as "mumbo-jumbo."[38] Indeed, Tom Wolfe—before he switched to novels among the most adventurous and creative of journalists—became one of the leading critics of the turn away from realism in literature and art.[39]

Many of the ways and means of realism remained beneficial, of course, for journalism: going places is good, digging and checking are good, as are thoroughness, industry, and fairness. Let us not underestimate the accomplishments of the realism that lived on in journalism in a century desecrated by some terrible and mighty events and deeds. The list of exposés managed by reporters in the United States in the twentieth century—with their doggedness in pursuit of old-fashioned, nineteenth-century-style facts—is long and impressive: it includes Lincoln Steffens on municipal corruption, John Hersey on the horrific consequences of the atomic bomb dropped on Hiroshima, Rachel Carson on the dangers of pesticides, Seymour Hersh on an American atrocity in Vietnam, and Bob Woodward and Carl Bernstein on foul doings in the Nixon White House. Tom Wolfe also had a point in arguing that, with many novelists having departed for more subjective realms, journalists had something of an exclusive on some contentious and colorful goings-on in the last half of the twentieth century.[40] The "magnificent apparatus" for capturing facts constructed by traditional journalism in the United States has often performed impressively.

And this "apparatus" has often enough seemed sufficient. It was hard to argue that journalists needed a Pablo Picasso or a Virginia Woolf, let alone a Werner Heisenberg, to tell us about the latest presidential campaign. But wouldn't that coverage have benefited, as it attempted to disentangle that which had been spun, from a little more facility with perspective, a somewhat more extensive acquaintance with the wanderings of the human mind, and a surer grasp of the limits of certainty? As the founder and editor of the *Talking Points Memo* journalism website, Josh Marshall, noted during the 2012 U.S. presidential primaries,

"Campaigns have a way of not working by logical principles or, perhaps we should say, Newtonian physics."[41] And didn't Woolf do rather well with the First World War? Didn't Picasso do rather well with Guernica? For details alone—even if "reliable," "accurate," and placed in "a meaningful context"—have serious limitation even as guides to the world of current events. The case can be made that politics sometimes "escapes" this journalism, as does much of the rest of "life."

In his journal, even Delacroix, though one of Ernest Meissonier's biggest admirers, confided his suspicion that "there is something else in painting besides exactitude and precise rendering."[42] There is something else in journalism, too.

Jill Abramson succeeded Bill Keller as the top editor of the *New York Times* in 2011. In 2010, she had offered her own explanation of what "quality journalism" provides: "trustworthy information about the world we live in—information that is tested, investigated, sorted, checked again, analyzed and presented in a cogent form."[43] This explanation is, with one exception, compatible with Keller's understanding of "quality journalism." But that exception is significant. Abramson includes a word not used by her predecessor: *analyzed.* That is a word with which a more up-to-date conception of journalism might begin.[44]

The definition of journalism introduced in this book is careful to acknowledge that journalism might be more than "exactitude and precise rendering." That definition includes interpreting or commenting upon the news—as bloggers today and printers at the time of the American Revolution would expect it to include; as our editorial writers, columnists, and contributors to opinion journals and others serious magazines would expect it to include. For even at the height of American journalism's fidelity to realism, even in the middle of the twentieth century, some examples of first-rate interpretation and comment could be found—on certain pages, in certain publications. (Chapters 4 and 6 include examples.)

The Committee of Concerned Journalists, Bill Keller, and most traditional journalists are no doubt aware that there are other journalisms besides "the discipline of assembling and verifying facts." I do not believe they meant to exclude interpretation and comment entirely from the realm of quality journalism. Keller's *New York Times* did after all devote two pages each day specifically to opinion. (Before and after Keller was the paper's executive editor, his own essays appeared on one of those pages.) And the prominence of "news analysis" pieces on other pages in the paper increased on Keller's watch. After Abramson replaced Keller, she seems to have begun going further: deemphasizing somewhat the *Times*'s efforts to present its readers with all the important details on yesterday's most important events.*

In fact, interpretation and comment are popping up all over journalism today. (Chapter 4 chronicles their recent resurgence.) Yes, commentary can often be shrill and predictable—on talk radio, on cable television, on many websites. (Chapter 6 includes a critique, based on standards introduced in chapter 1, of the variety of opinionated journalism that often appears on outlets such as Fox News Channel and MSNBC.) But some of this interpretation and comment is original and enlightening—particularly in our better magazines, particularly on our smarter blogs and websites, sometimes in the *New York Times*. The loud and the shrill get the attention of journalism critics, but original and enlightening forms of analytic journalism are pointing the way to the future.

This book is not calling for the invention of something new. It is calling for us to aspire, with more awareness and understanding, to a journalism that *regularly* does much more than simply recount who said or did what yesterday. It is calling for a broader, more ambitious journalism. And it is arguing that such a journalism will not fully arrive without a change in mindset.[45]

---

* Because the *New York Times* is the best and most influential of our traditional news organs, any criticism of current thinking on journalism must take it on. Its efforts, in print and online, are often discussed in these pages. The *Times* has been changing with the times. My argument is that, despite its many strengths, it needs to change more.

Journalism has undergone enormous changes at other times. (Chapter 2 focuses on journalism's transformation in the nineteenth century.) The inventions that spur such periods of change have been hard to miss, as have the methodological improvements, particularly greater speed, those exciting new machines bring. The upheavals such technological advances impose upon the business of journalism have also been seen and grasped without much delay: old enterprises begin to stumble and fall; new enterprises, led by unorthodox innovators, soon call attention to themselves. However, the realization that *understandings* of journalism must also change spreads more slowly—particularly among those who achieved success with the old understandings, particularly among the orthodox. New mindsets are needed to best employ the new technologies and save some of the old businesses. But mindsets inevitably lag behind.

Consider for another example of a mainstream twenty-first-century journalist's mind that of Martin Baron, who took over as the top editor of the *Washington Post* in January 2013. Months earlier Baron had delivered an inspiring speech to newspaper editors in which he had advocated openness to "innovation" and all sorts of change—innovation and change *except* in the newspaper's "traditional purpose and . . . core values."[46]

And what is that "traditional purpose"? Baron's answer, a good summary of a kind of journalistic orthodoxy, began: "Stories that are well reported. Stories that are well told. Stories that offer a window on the communities we serve." He mentioned "insights," but only the sort that arrive, according to the familiar journalistic trope, "from looking beneath the surface"—from digging, from reporting, in other words. "Interpretation" or "analysis" did not appear among the 127 words Baron used to describe what he believes ought to be preserved in journalism.

Baron emphasized in this speech the importance of "doing all of this work—all of this journalism—honestly, honorably, accurately, and fairly." He did not mention, among these "core values," the importance of doing journalism knowledgeably, intelligently, or insightfully. Indeed,

Baron's more than 3,000-word speech did not consider at any point the notion that journalists today might have to offer understandings, not just facts.

Marty Baron, like the other journalists I have been quoting, is smart, accomplished, and public spirited. Neither he nor they are unaware of the value of analytic journalism. In 2005, while Baron was editor of the *Boston Globe*, a series in that newspaper exploring the science and ethics of stem-cell research won the Pulitzer Prize for "explanatory journalism." But when Baron, upon leaving the *Globe*, was asked what he was proud of at that newspaper, he mentioned, in a *Globe* reporter's paraphrase, "its investigative reporting, arts coverage, narrative journalism, and war reporting in Iraq and Afghanistan, as well as its push into digital and multimedia formats."[47] Baron apparently neglected, once again, to mention interpretation or analysis. Mainstream journalists often neglect to mention them.

Indeed, the number of journalists today who continue to overlook the importance of interpretation is evidence that the rethinking of journalism—the transformation of the traditional journalist's mindset—has just begun. It is therefore not surprising that the remaking of journalism has a long way to go, too.

This book argues that quality in twenty-first-century journalism lies not so much in "experienced reporters going places, . . . developing sources, checking and double-checking," as Keller put it—though all those activities are certainly useful. It argues that quality in journalism lies instead in what I am calling "wisdom journalism"—journalism that strengthens our understanding of the world.

Wisdom journalism is an amalgam. It includes, to begin with, the more rarified forms of reporting—exclusive, enterprising, investigative. Though such original forms of reporting remain in short supply, there is no controversy about their worth. Much of what Marty Baron is proud of at the *Boston Globe* would qualify. But wisdom journalism also includes and even emphasizes informed, interpretive, explanatory, even opinionated takes on current events.[48]

Much more of this kind of writing, audio, video, or Web work is needed. It must continue to expand well beyond a few serious magazines, a bunch of thoughtful blogs, and those two pages, a Sunday section, or some "news analysis" pieces in newspapers such as the *New York Times*. It needs to become mainstream. (Chapter 4 includes a detailed account of where such analysis has and has not shown up in coverage of a few specific stories in recent years.) We need to develop standards to help distinguish such wisdom journalism from the shrill and predictable. (Chapter 1 has this task.) And we need to get better at it.

That will require not only a change in mindset, but further and substantial changes in the way journalism is currently practiced: If providing insight rather than gathering facts is to become journalism's main mission—not an auxiliary mission—traditional methods of hiring and promoting might no longer apply. The assignment structure will have to be transformed. (Chapter 7 outlines these changes.) Evenhandedness and dispassion might no longer be dominant values. (Chapter 5 discusses some of the limitations of journalistic objectivity.) Original perspectives will push widely available information from whatever passes for a front page. And we will need to apply as much thought to standards for journalistic argumentation as we have applied to how to cover an event.

This sounds like a new approach to journalism; actually, it is in some ways an old one—from the days before American journalism's enthrallment with realism. The book's first chapter examines journalism as Ben Franklin and Thomas Jefferson knew it and uses pieces of writing from their day to introduce some standards for distinguishing between successful and unsuccessful wisdom journalism.

BEYOND NEWS

1

"PRINCIPLES, OPINIONS, SENTIMENTS, AND AFFECTIONS"

The Journalism Out of Which the United States Was Born

Perhaps because journalists are so focused on the here and now, they tend to avail themselves less of the lessons of their forbearers than do presidents, say, or painters. But if in their current crisis they were disposed to consult history, our journalists might discover that "experienced reporters going places" was not always considered to be at the heart of American journalism.

Bill Keller insists that this kind of "quality journalism" provides "the information you need to be an engaged citizen."[1] The founders of this country certainly did agree that the citizenry requires a free press. "Were it left to me to decide whether we should have a government without newspapers or newspapers without a government," wrote Thomas Jefferson in an oft-quoted but still grand line from a 1787 letter, "I should not hesitate a moment to prefer the latter."[2]

Jefferson spoke in that letter of the importance of giving the people "full information of their affairs thro' the channel of the public papers." But it is hard to see how, for Jefferson as for Keller, supplying that information might have involved reporters "bearing witness, digging into records, developing sources, checking and double-checking."[3] For in Jefferson's America, in James Madison's America, in Benjamin Franklin's America, there weren't any reporters.[4]

All the world's newspapers today can trace their ancestry, if you look back far enough, to Europe. And the earliest printed newspapers in Europe, which appeared in the first decades of the seventeenth century, were mostly collections of short, paragraph-length news items.[5] The oldest surviving weekly newssheet written in English and distributed in London was printed (in freer and more precocious Amsterdam) on December 2, 1620. Its first item concerned Bethlen Gábor, who led a revolt against Habsburg rule in Hungary—an early battle in the Thirty Years War. The style of this item is typical of the genre:

Out of Weenen, the 6 November

The French Ambassadour hath caused the Earle of Dampier to be buried stately at Presburg. In the meane vvile hath Bethlem Gabor cited all the Hungerish States, to com together at Presburg the 5. of this present, to discourse aboute the Crovvning & other causes concerning the fame Kingdom.[6]

According to Carlota Smith's linguistic analysis of "modes of discourse," this article qualifies, as would most such early newspaper items, as a "report." It doesn't—to oversimplify her multifaceted analysis—advance in temporal sequence as a "narrative" might. Time is not "static," as in a "description." The item's account is not general and atemporal, as is an "information." Instead, specific "situations are related to the time of the report"—"this present," "the 6 November." And, of most significance for our purposes, this item is not making a "claim" or "comment," as an "argument" might. It is not composed of "propositions" as an argument would be.[7]

I don't want to lean too heavily on these categories—or on the others it will prove interesting to trot out in succeeding pages. Despite the linguists' best efforts at precision, reports, narratives, descriptions, informations, and even arguments do have a way of blending into each other. Human language resists categorization. When Bill Keller or Jill Abramson are talking about journalism, they certainly do not mean to exclude narrative, description, or information. Yet they are usually talking of kinds of discourse that are most comfortably designated "reports." So it is significant to see a report atop the first English-language newspaper.

But it is also important to note that this first English-language newspaper report is not the product of behaviors Keller or Abramson might recognize as *reporting*. Because such newssheets were too slow to keep up with local news and too cautious, given the danger of annoying the authorities, to cover national news, these earliest European printed newspapers discussed almost exclusively events that had taken place in other countries. (Major events in London may have been discussed in letters out of London and therefore may have appeared in newspapers all across Europe, with one copying the other, but they normally did not appear in newspapers in London.)

The short items from afar that filled the columns of these early printed newssheets arrived almost exclusively via the mail or via other newspapers. Indeed, at the very top of page one of that first newspaper published in English—which makes do without a name—is a telling apology: "*The new tydings out of Italie are not yet com.*" There is no evidence that those who produced such newspapers made significant efforts to seek out "*tydings*" on their own. They waited for them to "*com.*" News of that burial and assembly in Pressburg (now Bratislava), which appears right after that apology, must have arrived in a letter or newssheet originally from Vienna, perhaps having passed through some other letters or newssheets along the way.

America gained its first regularly published newspaper, the *Boston News-Letter*, in 1704. Back in England by that time, those short bits of foreign news were being supplemented and even nudged aside by disquisitions—on contemporary manners and mores, on society, on literature, on philosophy, on religion, or on politics, even British politics. The first issue of the *News-Letter*, for example, borrowed from a London paper a summary of a "letter" warning of a "danger" to "the Protestant Religion" because Catholics had begun to "swarm" in Scotland.[8] Most of these longer, more pointed writings Carlota Smith would label "arguments."

This change is a fateful one, according to the German political philosopher Jürgen Habermas. In the eighteenth century, he observes, the newspaper became—in "*bourgeois*" societies, with "liberal" politics—"no longer a mere organ for the spreading of news." Habermas quotes the German economist and early journalism scholar Karl Bücher: "'Newspapers changed from mere institutions for the publication of news into bearers and leaders of public opinion.'" For Habermas, the consequence of this vigorous circulation of opinion—even though it might upon occasion descend to warnings about swarming Catholics—was nothing less than the creation of his treasured "public sphere."[9]

We can watch this sphere expand in 1721 in Boston, where a debate broke out about the merits of smallpox inoculation. That debate— and therefore this nascent public sphere—was very much aided and abetted by the arrival of Boston's third and America's fourth regularly published newspaper. For in its initial issue, James Franklin's *New-England Courant* launched what probably qualifies as America's first anti-authoritarian newspaper crusade on this new strategy for protecting against smallpox.[10]

The unsuccessful prosecution of John Peter Zenger fourteen years later for publishing criticism of the governor of New York would open the door to more such newspaper crusades in Britain's American colonies. Indeed, America in the decades leading up to its revolution is, perhaps, the textbook example of the power of an opinion-wielding press not just in toppling a system of authority, but in creating a space for public discourse and therefore for democracy. Let the record show, however, that James Franklin's *New-England Courant*—among the earliest megaphones in this world-changing effort to allow a public to be heard—was crusading *against* what it called "the dubious, dangerous Practice of Inoculation."[11]

Benjamin Franklin was working as an apprentice on his much older brother's newspaper. Soon he himself began contributing to this still relatively new phenomenon: the public discussion of issues in print. Sixteen-year-old Ben Franklin, writing under the name "Silence Dogood" and in the voice of a rural widow, began sneaking essays into the *New-England*

Courant. Here is "Mrs. Dogood" attacking something young Ben was making do without: higher education (that is, Harvard):

> I reflected in my Mind on the extream Folly of those Parents, who, blind to their Childrens Dulness, and insensible of the Solidity of their Skulls, because they think their Purses can afford it, will needs send them to the Temple of Learning, where, for want of a suitable Genius, they learn little more than how to carry themselves handsomely, and enter a Room genteely, (which might as well be acquir'd at a Dancing-School,) and from whence they return, after Abundance of Trouble and Charge, as great Blockheads as ever, only more proud and self-conceited.[12]

Although the debate over a college education was not a matter of life and death like the debate over smallpox inoculation, it was no doubt a matter of public concern. And this apprentice printer was helping open space for discussion of such concerns. He accomplished this, as aspiring "bearers and leaders of public opinion" usually do, by expressing and defending an opinion—in his case, with characteristic humor. Ben Franklin, to return to Carlota Smith's categories, had composed an "argument"—replete with claims, comments, propositions.

Smith has a formula, too, for determining whether a particular discourse qualifies as "subjective," a different distinction in her view than that between argument and report. She looks for evidence that it presents a "perspective," performs an "evaluation," or shares the "contents of [a] mind." Smith is alert to the fact that such subjectivity can be found in *all* her "modes of discourse"[13]—presumably including upon occasion even those brief reports that more discursive arguments were beginning to overshadow in colonial America's press. A positive perspective on or evaluation of the anti-Catholic Hungarian leader Bethlen Gábor can, for example, be discerned even in that fifty-five word report that led off the first English-language newspaper—sold in Protestant England, printed in Protestant Amsterdam.

Nevertheless, Smith's indicators of subjectivity run thick in Franklin's argument against higher education—"I reflected in my Mind on the extream Folly"—as they run thick in his brother James's paper in general and in arguments in general. The public sphere in eighteenth-century America was being established by unabashedly subjective arguments.

≈

Benjamin Franklin's Silence Dogood letters borrowed some of their style from Joseph Addison and Richard Steele, who had commented on the behavior of their contemporaries with subtle wit and sharp insights earlier in the century in their London daily the *Spectator*.[14]

Collections of the *Spectator* were prized in Britain's American colonies; young Franklin had secured one. And he had begun disassembling Addison and Steele's prose: jotting down the points made by each sentence, putting those sentences aside for a few days, then trying to re-create their wordings. "By comparing my work afterwards with the original," Franklin writes in his *Autobiography*, "I discovered many faults and corrected them; but sometimes had the pleasure of fancying that in certain particulars of small import I had been lucky enough to improve the method or the language."[15]

Franklin, in other words, had not trained himself for newspaper work by showing up at local fires or meetings, notebook in hand, and distilling out the who, what, when, and where. That was not considered newspaper work in America in the eighteenth century. He had learned the printer's trade, but Ben Franklin also trained himself by learning how to write clearly, cleverly, attractively, and insightfully by studying the work of the essayists Addison and Steele.

Newspapers were in those days primarily the products of individual printers such as James Franklin. The transformation Habermas celebrates was hardly total: those eighteenth-century printers still looked for interesting or important bits of news to decorate their pages. Most of those items were culled, as they had been in the previous century, from out-of-town papers or letters. "We shall from time to time have all the noted Publick Prints from Great Britain, New-England, New-York, Maryland and Jamaica, besides what News may be collected from private Letters and Informations," Ben Franklin announced in 1729, shortly after obtaining control of a newspaper of his own, the *Pennsylvania Gazette*.[16] He would, in other words, be borrowing news items—as all other editors did.

Franklin—more enterprising than most of his fellow editors, than most of his fellow humans—would occasionally obtain information about an event himself:

> Sunday last between 7 and 8 in the Evening we had the most terrible Gust of Wind and Rain accompanied with Thunder and Lightning, that can be remembered in these Parts: It blew down several Stacks of Chimneys, uncovered several Houses, some wholly and others in Part; and quite demolished some weak Buildings. The Violence of it did not continue long, but the Storm was of wide Extent, for we have heard of it from *Conestogoe*, from the Mouth of the Bay, and from *New-York:* At *Conestogoe* it was about half an hour before it arrived here, but in the Bay it was near Midnight.[17]

Franklin, of course, could be interesting on almost any subject—including the weather. In fact, one of his numerous contributions to science was an understanding of the path and cause of storms.[18] However, his *Pennsylvania Gazette* was not often devoted to news from "these Parts." It tended to focus more on goings on in far away "Parts"—"Great Britain, New-England, New-York, Maryland and Jamaica"—and on opinions.

Humans, as I have argued elsewhere,[19] do have a basic "thirst" for news. But the news that has traditionally mattered most to most of us—news of our towns—was still monopolized in Franklin's day by the oldest news medium: word of mouth. News was exchanged in taverns and coffeehouses, on front porches, and on the streets. The residents of Philadelphia not only had experienced for themselves all that "Wind and Rain" accompanied by "Thunder and Lightning" "Sunday last" but had also had plenty of opportunity to discuss it among themselves before Franklin's *Gazette* was finally printed. No printer and no weekly could scoop neighborhood busybodies on an intriguing local political development, crime, or storm. The towns were too small, the newspapers still too slow.

"The Business of Printing," Franklin felt called upon to explain in his *Pennsylvania Gazette* in 1731, "has chiefly to do with Mens Opinions, most things that are printed tending to promote some or oppose others."[20] Although its main product was the newspaper, the "business of printing" in the eighteenth century was not primarily the dissemination, let alone the reporting, of news.

Franklin, as publisher of the *Pennsylvania Gazette*, was lucky that one of history's most talented essay writers and most civic-minded individuals was often eager to hold forth in its pages—usually under one or another pseudonym, usually in a manner both witty and wise. In 1751, as "Americanus," for example, Franklin responded to the mother country's penchant—and excuses—for shipping its convicts across the Atlantic: "Our *Mother* knows what is best for us. What is a little *Housebreaking, Shoplifting,* or *Highway Robbing;* what is a *Son* now and then *corrupted* and *hang'd,* a Daughter *debauch'd* and *pox'd,* a Wife *stabb'd,* a Husband's *Throat cut,* or a Child's *Brains beat out* with an Axe, compar'd with this 'IMPROVEMENT and WELL PEOPLING of the Colonies!'" He then suggests that rattlesnakes be shipped in the opposite direction.[21] Of course Franklin, employing what he probably understood to be Swiftian satire, was making an argument here—as Addison, Steele, Daniel Defoe, and Jonathan Swift made arguments in British newspapers. He also was, as they were, producing what this book calls *wisdom journalism.*

Franklin, always interested in cataloging virtues, hazarded at one point a definition of *wisdom*: "The Knowledge of what will be best for us on all Occasions and of the best Ways of attaining it."[22] That definition fits pretty well with Franklin's own attempt to do what Bill Keller would do—explain what counts as quality in newspaper writing: "*No Piece can properly be called good, and well written,*" Franklin asserted, "*which is void of any Tendency to benefit the Reader, either by improving his Virtue or his Knowledge.*"[23] This book is proposing a standard for quality in journalism closer to Franklin's—though less confident in its understanding of

"Virtue"—than to the standards proposed by Keller, Jill Abramson, the Committee of Concerned Journalists, and many journalists today.

Wisdom journalism is a term suggested by "wisdom literature" and "wisdom philosophy," in which it refers to a tradition of thoughtful advice, good judgment, insight, and sagacity. There is a tradition of journalism in the United States, which goes back to Ben Franklin, that displays these qualities. By naming it, I hope to encourage its resurgence.

Wisdom journalism is journalism that is often, to borrow Franklin's words, filled with "Knowledge of what will be best for us" as a society, but it is not restricted to that category of "Knowledge." It can also elucidate what has happened, is happening, or is likely to happen to some of us. And it can help us think out, often less didactically, what might prove "best for us." And wisdom journalism not only produces "Knowledge," it requires knowledge.

When Franklin had obtained control of the *Pennsylvania Gazette* in 1729, he had taken a moment to consider what qualifications, along with the ability to write "cleanly and intelligibly," someone in his new position ought to possess: "The Author of a *Gazette* (in the Opinion of the Learned) ought to be qualified with an extensive Acquaintance with Languages . . . ; he should be able to speak of War both by Land and Sea; be well acquainted with Geography, with the History of the Time, with the several Interests of Princes and States, the Secrets of Courts, and the Manners and Customs of all Nations."[24]

Although his father had decided not to send him to Harvard, Franklin was managing to gain a more than satisfactory acquaintanceship with matters of "History," politics, "Manners and Customs," and science by applying himself with legendary diligence to books, conversation, and observation. He had earned the right to edit "a *Gazette*" and therefore—as his brother James had put it back in Boston—the right to do some "soaring now and then with the grave Wits of the Age."[25] On many, many subjects he was *wise*, as this book uses that term.

The "Knowledge" that wise journalists supply can arrive, as in Franklin's day, via informed, intelligent, penetrating, even controversial journalistic interpretation and argument. Ben Franklin's satirical attack on the British policy of shipping prisoners to its colonies was not based on reporting; it probably did not involve going any place beyond his own desk. Nevertheless, it taught; it offered an original perspective on an important issue; it was thoughtful, revealing, and clever.

I take a broad view of how journalism might "benefit the Reader"—of how it might improve "Knowledge." I see that happening, as Franklin certainly would have, with insight as much as with information, with interpretation as much as with investigation. Wisdom journalism often features, even emphasizes, informed argument—argument based on a journalist's "Acquaintance" with an area of knowledge, argument of the sort that so excites Habermas. Wisdom journalism is not always subjective, but many wisdom journalists—Ben Franklin certainly among them—are not averse to presenting a perspective, performing an evaluation, letting us know what they think.

However, I will stick with Keller and almost all contemporary journalists and also acknowledge the importance of exclusive, enterprising, or investigative reporting—of going places where other reporters are not, of witnessing atrocities or injustices others do not see, of digging into records that reveal corruption. Such exposés—which usually appear as reports—also have the potential to improve the "Knowledge" and perhaps the "Virtue" of a "Reader," even a society. There's wisdom in them, too.

I needed, therefore, a term for what I want to encourage that is broad enough to encompass two kinds of journalism: the highest forms of reporting, which are already much praised today, if not often enough practiced, but also incisive, revelatory commentary, which has begun to appear more frequently again in recent years, particularly on the Web, but ought to be much more highly valued. None of the modifiers for the word *journalism* currently in use would do. *Wisdom*—which dictionaries today define as "good sense," "insight," "wise decisions," and "accumulated learning"—works. Both exclusive reporting and incisive commentary benefit from these qualities and further them in their audiences.[26]

Wisdom is not a word that has often been applied to journalism in recent centuries. Indeed, it may be jarring to some twenty-first-century ears. I don't mind that. I hope that in its unfamiliarity this term will spur us to take a fresh look at journalism and its purposes. *Wisdom* also sounds a bit highfaluting, even pretentious, for the discussions journalists often produce of sometimes forgettable occurrences. That's okay, too, for I believe our best journalism needs to aim higher, needs to be more ambitious for itself and its audiences.

Simply being somewhere routinely frequented by cameras and other reporters, simply transcribing what some figure in the news has said, simply recording easily available facts—no matter how faithfully—is not wisdom journalism. There was little that might earn this designation in the European newssheets of the seventeenth century. There was a great deal of it in American journalism in the eighteenth century. Ben Franklin's report on the damage caused by a "terrible" thunder storm that hit Philadelphia would not qualify as wisdom journalism without his effort—his brief but original effort—to consider the track and size of that storm.

Wisdom journalism is a term for journalism that is more than workmanlike, for journalism that aspires to do more than just tell the news, more than just report what has happened. I am proposing it as a new standard—a different and, in my view, higher standard—for quality in journalism. It is a standard that can help guide journalists as they grapple with the field's current crisis and take on the future.

A journalism of this sort certainly proved useful in America's past, as the arguments in American newspapers against British policies grew more pressing, more fateful.

One of Franklin's fellow Philadelphians produced a grand example of wisdom journalism—among the most persuasive and influential analyses ever to appear in an American newspaper. This series of highly opinionated pieces was called "Letters from a Farmer in Pennsylvania to the Inhabitants of the British Colonies in America." The "Letters" were written not by a farmer or a printer, but by a Philadelphia lawyer, John Dickinson. The first installment appeared in the *Pennsylvania Chronicle*

on December 2, 1767. The *Pennsylvania Gazette* reprinted that first letter the next day. America had almost thirty newspapers by then; only four of them—two of which were German—failed to reprint the "Letters" in succeeding days or weeks.[27]

Dickinson had set himself a difficult task: the British Parliament had finally repealed the hated Stamp Act, which the colonies had angrily protested. In these letters, the "farmer" was taking on a new series of taxes, the Townshend Acts. The Stamp Act had imposed taxes on *all* paper and other goods, but Parliament had clearly and intentionally imposed the Townshend Acts only on goods imported from Britain. Didn't that fall within Parliament's legitimate authority to regulate trade? Dickinson had to explain why these taxes should be protested, too.

In his "Letters" he conceded that the mother country had the right to regulate its colonies' trade. But he insisted, through an examination of British parliamentary history, that there was no precedent for Parliament's imposing tariffs *only* on colonies and *only* to raise revenues. Dickinson demonstrated, through an examination of the parliamentary debate, that raising revenue from the colonies was indeed the purpose of the Townshend Acts. And he noted that British policy made it difficult for the colonists to obtain the goods in question except through Britain:

> Upon the whole, the single question is, whether the parliament can legally impose duties to be paid *by the people of these colonies only,* FOR THE SOLE PURPOSE OF RAISING A REVENUE, *on commodities which she obliges us to take from her alone,* or, in other words, whether the parliament can legally take money out of our pockets, without our consent. If they can, our boasted liberty is but
> Vox et praeterea nihil [A sound and nothing else].[28]

Unlike many of their twentieth-century counterparts, eighteenth-century journalists generally did not fear appearing bookish—even indulging in a little Latin. Latin is now less often taught, but the twenty-first-century wisdom journalist should be honored to appear bookish. Indeed, a familiarity with history and a propensity toward research—

both of which John Dickinson displayed—are almost de rigueur for the wisdom journalist. Considerable skill in making an argument—interpretation usually being involved, opinion often being involved—is also important. And it helps quite a bit if those arguments, like those of John Dickinson, prove persuasive.

The "Letters from a Farmer in Pennsylvania" played a major role in turning the colonists from being mostly blasé about the Townshend Acts to openly opposing them.[29] The first shots of the revolution were less than eight years away.

Critics of interpretive, opinionated journalism today often use Fox News Channel, MSNBC, or talk radio to demonstrate how narrow, nasty, and close-minded overtly partisan journalism can sometimes be. Clearly, some lines have to be drawn around wisdom journalism—lines that exclude strident, uninformed, unreasonable rants. We have developed reasonably clear standards for what makes for quality in journalistic *reports*. What standards might we use to distinguish good and bad journalistic *arguments*—besides whether we happen to share their point of view?

Most of the rest of this chapter is devoted to considering some such standards for argumentative journalism. All the examples here come from the decades leading up to the American Revolution. Then chapter 6 applies these standards to Chris Matthews, Bill O'Reilly, Rush Limbaugh, and other contemporary journalists.

One possible approach would be to insist that to be of high quality, any form of journalism—no matter how argumentative—should be based on *reporting*. My colleague at New York University, Jay Rosen, was leaning toward this standard when in 2012 he quoted, with approval, a line from the guidelines for new reporters of a respected online news organization, the *Voice of San Diego*: "Write with authority. You earn the right to write with authority by reporting and working hard." Rosen himself then asserted, "The original source . . . for all forms of authority in journalism is to be found in the phrase: 'I'm there, you're not, let me tell you about it.'"[30]

Were the secret of good journalism so simple—just a matter of going somewhere and reporting—then standards for journalistic arguments would conveniently be similar to standards for journalistic reports, and wisdom journalists might then be judged as reporters are now judged: by the accuracy, enterprise, thoroughness, fairness, and perspicuity of their reporting. But it is not that simple.

Eighteenth-century journalism accomplished quite a bit without much in the way of reporting. For there are other ways for a journalist to establish authority besides embarking—with notepad, if not fedora—upon a fact-gathering expedition. One might instead do as Ben Franklin did: read, talk, and observe. Or one might do as Ben Franklin did not: obtain an academic degree. And, of course, enterprising reporting does not always lead to distinguished interpretation.

If Isaiah Thomas, the publisher of the *Massachusetts Spy*, was not "there" on the first day of the Revolutionary War, he was close. The story Thomas produced on May 3, 1775, was—and this was unusual for the time—full of facts, details. It presented a chronology of events. Thomas had even conducted interviews, collecting detailed accounts "from those," he insisted, "whose veracity is unquestioned." Yet the interpretation his story presented was thoroughly jingoistic and unreliable:

> Americans! forever bear in mind the BATTLE of LEXINGTON! where British Troops, unmolested and unprovoked wantonly, and in a most inhuman manner fired upon and killed a number of our country-men, then robbed them of their provisions, ransacked, plundered and burnt their houses! nor could the tears of defenseless women, some of whom were in the pains of childbirth, the cries of helpless babes, nor the prayers of old age, confined to beds of sickness, appease their thirst for blood!—or divert them from the DESIGN of MURDER and ROBBERY![31]

Just being there (or close), just talking to people "whose veracity" may appear "unquestioned," just collecting facts and details—just "reporting and working hard," in other words—do not guarantee that a piece of journalism will present a reliable interpretation or argument on an event. Fortunately, we have the benefit of a whole discipline dedicated to the analysis of argument, albeit mostly oral argument. Ben Franklin would have been familiar with the study of rhetoric; it dates back at least as far as Aristotle.[32]

What follows here is an attempt to apply standards from rhetoric and related fields to argumentative journalism. Such efforts have been relatively rare, and the undertaking remains too difficult for it to be possible to enunciate anything remotely resembling a last word.[33] But my goal here—relying on Aristotle and some much later philosophers, linguists, and scholars of rhetoric—is to explore some considerations that might help us judge the quality of interpretive, argumentative journalism and thereby help explain what does *not* qualify as wisdom journalism.

Character. In the *Rhetoric*, Aristotle notes that the character of the speaker—"ethos," he calls it—can affect the persuasiveness of the argument.[34] The same holds true for the character of the journalist.

James Franklin's tenure as editor of the *New-England Courant* was stormy; he was under attack. So in a later issue even he felt the need to convince his readers that he was fair-minded on what had become the issue of the day: "Both Inoculators and Anti-Inoculators are welcome to speak their Minds" in his paper, Franklin asserted, although it was the "Anti's" that brought him all his notoriety.[35] (If there were any "Inoculators" in the *Courant*, they were quite lonely.)[36] Fair-mindedness (*epieikeia*) is high on the list of qualities Aristotle recognizes as indicating a good character, because, he writes, "we believe fair-minded people to a greater extent and more quickly."[37]

We want to see "virtue" and "goodwill" in our speakers, Aristotle notes.[38] Fair-mindedness is a virtue, a token of goodwill. John Dickinson showed particular skill at signaling that he had given the other side its due. In his "Letters," he made sure to acknowledge, for example, areas in which Britain might legitimately impose laws upon the colonies, and he made sure to air arguments that ran counter to his own: "it may perhaps be objected."[39]

Fair-mindedness enters wisdom journalism initially, therefore, as just this: a "virtue" and therefore an aid to persuasiveness, one of many.[40] Dickinson's concessions to the other side made him seem, as he undoubtedly realized, more virtuous and therefore more trustworthy.

Dickinson also let his readers know that he was temperate—another meaning of the Greek word *epieikeia*.[41] "I am by no means fond of inflammatory measures," Dickinson said in his first letter, "I detest them." But not everyone was aiming at these gentler virtues. In that article on the first shots of the revolution, Isaiah Thomas was anything but temperate and fair-minded. He never even feigned understanding of the difficult situation faced by the British troops. We never get their point of view. The character test that Thomas wanted to pass in this story is surely a different one: he wanted his anti-British readers to be confident that he was sufficiently committed to their cause, that he could be trusted because he was with them. This is another way of looking at the character question in journalism. In partisan times—or, at least, partisan circles—commitment becomes a virtue; ill will toward some is necessary to display goodwill toward others.

Journalists today continue to divide on which of these two possible characters they want to be seen as possessing: reassuringly fair-minded or inspiringly committed. In the United States in the early twenty-first century, CNN and the *New York Times* still try to signal—much more intently than John Dickinson ever did—that they can be trusted to be nonpartisan. As discussed in chapter 5, many contemporary news organs such as Fox News Channel, MSNBC, Rush Limbaugh, the *Huffington Post*, and the *Drudge Report* have taken the other of these well-worn paths: they have settled upon the "character" that will prove most effective in engaging the already mostly persuaded.

This latter approach was long out of fashion in American journalism and American journalism schools. The return of the partisan approach with the rise of talk radio, cable-television news, and the Internet has brought loud complaints that divides are being deepened, choirs being preached to, and the like-minded being segregated into narrow, airless "silos." And, to be sure, fair-mindedness and temperance remain virtues. But there is something to be said for journalists making a point of view a major part of their "character" and announcing, in effect, that they can help sort out recent events and clarify the events' significance for those who share that point of view.[42]

Discourse. Fair-mindedness is everything to most American journalists reporting for newspapers or newscasts today. (They try to display temperance, too, though they can't help but note that their more intemperate competitors on cable or the Internet often gain better ratings or more followers on Twitter.) The strengths and limitations of fairness in contemporary journalism are discussed more fully—along with those of its first cousin, objectivity—in chapter 5, but something else about fairness needs to be mentioned here in this effort to come up with standards for evaluating argumentative journalism—something that goes beyond the perception of the journalist's character: fairness upgrades public conversation.

Improving the quality of serious discourse was, of course, serious business for Aristotle. And for a series of contemporary thinkers, including Habermas, the degree to which standards of discourse or debate are honored has become one way of judging the quality of argument.[43] These thinkers maintain that arguments are often stronger when they acknowledge the other side, even concede some points to the other side; that events are often clearer when looked at from more than one direction; that understandings are often deeper after exposure to a variety of points of view. Honest engagement with opposing positions, these thinkers note, also tests arguments: it strips away their weaker elements; it hones them and strengthens them; it demonstrates that they can withstand challenge. As a rule, arguments that have passed such tests are more valid.

So when John Dickinson displayed openness—when he aired the arguments of his opponents, when he even made concessions to those arguments—he was doing more than *appearing* fair and temperate: he was making a better argument and making for a better conversation. And although Isaiah Thomas may or may not have been establishing a persuasive character when he failed to air or even acknowledge any British points of view in his reporting of the start of the Revolutionary War, he may have been furthering a glorious cause, but he was making a worse argument and debasing the discourse.

Method. The twentieth-century British philosopher Stephen Edelston Toulmin offers three "conditions" necessary for someone's "claim to know" something to be "proper" or "trustworthy." The first condition that must be met is having "enough experience," or expertise, on the subject. The second is having made "all the observations and performed all the tests which can reasonably be demanded" on the subject. The third is having applied "considered" judgment to the subject.[44] Toulmin's attempt to come up with standards for evaluating claims to knowledge is no more perfect than the other frameworks introduced in this chapter, but, like them, it might further my effort to cobble together some loose standards for evaluating attempts at wisdom journalism.

In fact, these three conditions might easily be converted into three behaviors that lead to effectiveness in making a journalistic argument— actions a journalist might take on a particular story in order to *be* "trustworthy" or, to return to Jay Rosen's term, to earn "authority." In these conditions, we might see the outlines of a journalistic method.[45]

Journalists must begin, of course, by making sure they have sufficient "experience" on a subject—that they are well informed. John Dickinson in the eighteenth century presumably gained his understanding of the history of British tax law in part by having studied law (in a law office in Philadelphia and then at the Inns of Court in London)[46] and practiced law.

We are beginning to demand a greater level of "experience" or expertise in this century than was demanded of the twentieth-century reporter.

That demand is still not quite for the "extensive Acquaintance with Languages," "with Geography," "with the History of the Time," with "the Manners and Customs of all Nation," and so on that Ben Franklin called for in the eighteenth century; nonetheless, an "extensive Acquaintance" with the subject at hand—perhaps acquired at a university—is more and more required. Indeed, such a demand is at the heart of wisdom journalism, as discussed in chapter 7.

Armed with such expertise, journalists—to continue applying Toulmin's conditions—must conduct the necessary "observations." This is, of course, the heading under which to fit the reporting so prized by Jay Rosen and most newspaper journalists today. Although physical proximity has obvious advantages, observing does not always require Bill Keller's "going places" or Jay Rosen's being "there." We can also engage in "observations" of a sort through our readings or conversations. And these days we can observe more and more of the world electronically through our various online digital devices.

Toulmin adds an additional requirement to his "condition" that we conduct observations. He also wants us to perform "tests"—to behave as scientists might behave. Some early-twenty-first-century journalists can be accused of underemphasizing this. Upon occasion, they report upon what they have been shown or been told without testing the validity of what they have been shown or told. (This failing is bemoaned at greater length in chapter 5.) These journalists have also not developed, many of them, the social scientist's facility with statistical analysis. And they have, some of them, upon occasion been lazy even in applying less sophisticated tests, such as checking competing claims against the record. The wisdom journalist must do better.

The final element in this outline of a journalistic method—as derived from Toulmin's conditions—is the application of "considered" judgment: thinking something through, evaluating the evidence, reaching a conclusion. This analytic or interpretative skill, too, has been underemphasized in much of our newspaper and newscast reporting. It is at the heart of what I mean by wisdom journalism. John Dickinson thought the Townshend Acts through.

Satisfying Toulmin's conditions is important for someone preparing a journalistic report. Journalists out covering a story must have sufficient experience and expertise to know what they are talking about. These reporters certainly must make the requisite observations, and their reports on the world might improve if they more often tested their understandings of what has taken place. These reporters also must apply some sort of considered judgment at various stages of assembling a version of events.

But satisfying Toulmin's conditions—applying this journalistic method—is particularly important when journalists are making a "claim." When they are crafting an argument, authority and persuasiveness are most at issue. Whether their "claim to know" is "proper" or "trustworthy" will prove crucial.

≈

Style. Aristotle is uncomfortable with recourse to emotion—commonplace in the political and judicial speeches he was analyzing: "It is wrong to warp the jury," he states at one point, "by leading them into anger or envy or pity." Yet even this great logician has to admit to the effectiveness of pathos: it is undoubtedly easier to persuade, he writes, when "the hearers . . . are led to feel emotion by the speech."[47]

Many of our best journalists and our most serious journalism critics are also suspicious of the recourse to emotion.[48] Nevertheless, it is difficult to find journalists who do not upon occasion fortify a piece by "leading" their audiences "into anger or envy or pity"—not least when making an argument.

Yes, John Dickinson detested the "inflammatory"; indeed, he warned his readers to be on "guard against those who may at any time endeavor to stir you up." Nonetheless, in using phrases such as "pernicious to freedom," in warning that "the tragedy of *American* liberty" could be "finished," in instructing his countrymen to "rouse yourselves, and behold the ruin hanging over your heads,"[49] Dickinson, too, was guilty of stirring up, of allowing his readers "to feel emotion."

The test for pathos that Aristotle settles upon is whether it is "proportional to the subject matter."[50] This test seems—and I suspect this compliment has been paid before to Aristotle—intelligent. Appeals to emotion—to say something else obvious—can be overdone.

Ben Franklin was saved from having gone too far in his piece about shipping convicts to America—"a Daughter *debauch'd* and *pox'd*, a Wife *stabb'd*, a Husband's *Throat cut*, or a Child's *Brains beat out* with an Axe"— by the assumption of exaggeration inherent in satire. But even though Isaiah Thomas's subject matter was nothing less than the first shots in a revolution, he may have gone too far: "The cries of helpless babes"? "The prayers of old age"? An enemy possessing a "thirst for blood"? That's a large dose of anger and pity—even for a war. *Sensationalism*—an oft used but problematic pejorative in journalism—is sometimes applied to such recourses to pathos.[51]

Force—a word Toulmin employs in his inquiry into argument—offers another way of looking at the question of style in journalistic argument.[52] Isaiah Thomas wrote with great *force* when he announced that "British Troops, unmolested and unprovoked wantonly, and in a most inhuman manner fired upon and killed a number of our countrymen." His "evaluation" is harsh, his "subjectivity" intense. Thomas wrote, to modern eyes, with too much force.

It is a force unconstrained by qualification, uncertainty, or attribution. Nowhere in his more than fifteen-hundred word article does Thomas make use of words such as *possibly*, *probably*, or *reportedly* or of the phrase "according to American witnesses." There is one "seemed to be"— connected with the question of whether the shots from the British soldiers came from the "whole body" or from just a handful of officers and men. Otherwise, Thomas allowed almost no room for error or doubt until his last sentence—which includes an uncharacteristically humble qualifying phrase: "We have pleasure to say, that notwithstanding the highest provocations given by the enemy, not one influence of cruelty, *that we have heard of*, was committed by our Militia" (my italics).[53]

In contrast, John Dickinson, although staunch in his commitment to his cause, did allow himself seven uses of the word *probably* in his twelve letters. He places a "that it may be said" before a "to be impossible."[54] Similarly, that anti-inoculation statement in the first issue of the *New-England Courant* actually manages to avoid the excessive use of force even in what may be its most derisive phrase: "the dubious, dangerous Practice of Inoculation." Smallpox inoculation in those days involved purposeful infection with the disease itself, not with the gentler cowpox used today.[55] No doubt it was "dangerous," even if (probably) prudent. And *dubious* is an appropriately inconclusive word.

This does not mean that force is always a detriment to good style in journalism. It does mean that for the style of an argument to be appropriate, its force must be, to borrow the word Aristotle applied to appeals to emotion, "proportional"—proportional, in Isaiah Thomas's case, to the degree of certainty displayed by the subject matter. The fog of the first battle of a war is not a good time to be withholding the "probably's."

Evidence. Here's another scheme for analyzing language, this one from the philosopher John Searle. He outlines five categories of "illocutionary points" language might make. What's interesting is that all forms of journalism, even all of Carlota Smith's five "modes of discourse," tend to fit just one of Searle's categories. They are generally *not* "directive"— orders or commands; "commissive"—pledges or vows; "declarations"— pronouncements, which often have legal force; or, though this is slightly less rare, "expressive"—apologies, congratulations, thanks, or welcomes. Instead, almost all of journalism qualifies as what Searle labels "assertive."

Journalism—whether report or argument, whether narrative, information, or description—*asserts* something about "a state of affairs in the world," to stick with Searle's terminology. It asks belief of the audience. It "can be true or false."[56] This is obvious, but it is also important, for journalism relies on this kind of *truth*—meaning "not false."*

---

*   A second important journalistic understanding of truth—truth as something hidden, as something that might be *revealed*—is discussed in chapters 6 and 7.

We want to see evidence that what is being asserted is, in this sense, true. Assertions have, as Searle puts it, "conditions of satisfaction": When they fired their weapons in Lexington on April 19, 1775, were British troops indeed "unmolested and unprovoked"? Doesn't the mustering of a "company of militia" by the colonists qualify as a provocation for the colonial power?[57] Assertions have, to utilize another term from Searle and other philosophers who analyze language, "truth conditions."[58] Clear evidence to fulfill these "conditions" is not always available. But evidence clearly matters.

Aristotle includes at least one piece of advice that would be at home even in a twentieth-century journalism textbook: "It is necessary to have the facts belonging to that subject."[59] It is necessary, too, to display them—to present the audience for an argument, in Toulmin's terms, with the "grounds" or "backing for claims." Jurisprudence is an obvious place to turn when trying to come up with standards to evaluate the "grounds" or "backing"—the evidence. And there, too, the first requirement is simply that you provide some.

"They disregarded the cries of the wounded," Isaiah Thomas asserted about British soldiers in his account of the Battle of Lexington, "killing them without mercy, and mangling their bodies in the most shocking manner."[60] And what evidence did he give for this assertion, aside from his initial, overarching attribution ("We have collected from those whose veracity is unquestioned the following account")? Thomas gave *no* evidence for such disregard and brutality toward the wounded. Might we have been offered if not names, then at least a place and some specific incidents—enough, one would hope, to support use of a plural pronoun? In law, certainly, it is customary to demand specifics. As one legal decision puts it, "General allegations, merely conclusory and unsupported by competent evidence, are insufficient."[61]

Sometimes, in other words, we can judge a piece of evidence on its own terms: Is it too general, too vague? Thomas's account occasionally becomes quite specific: "they were stopped by about fourteen officers on horseback, who came out of Boston in the afternoon of that day." But when it comes to "killing . . . without mercy" and other inflammatory allegations, the specifics disappear. And Thomas's sources—"those whose veracity is unquestioned"—had one thing in common: they were anti-British Americans—outraged partisans, it seems safe to assume. That may be understandable, but it also makes their testimony—and, yes, their "veracity"—questionable.

Thomas also brought to bear "hearsay" evidence. In jurisprudence, "'hearsay' means a statement that . . . the declarant does not make while testifying at the current trial or hearing." The *Federal Rules of Evidence* states that "hearsay," with few exceptions, "is not admissible."[62] Accusations are obviously more believable when we hear them directly, not through someone's testimony about what someone else said. Journalists, though lacking subpoena power, should feel obliged to get as close as possible to original sources of information—the closer the more believable.

They should also whenever possible name those they have called to "testify." That way their audiences can at least judge the source of the evidence and perhaps even hold accountable those who are supplying it. In a colony still under British rule, there undoubtedly was good reason for Thomas not to name his sources. But the quality of his evidence and therefore the quality of his argument against the British certainly suffered significantly as a result.

Evidence also needs to be judged in context.[63] Does it indeed support the point it has been called upon to support? In his account of the Battle of Lexington, Isaiah Thomas described British troops as having a "DESIGN of MURDER and ROBBERY!" There are incidents, if they are to be believed, that qualify as robbery in his account of the British troops' behavior: "They pillaged almost every house they passed by, breaking and destroying doors, window[s], glasses, etc. and carrying off cloathing [*sic*] and other valuable effects."[64] But "MURDER"?

Thomas did say that eight Americans were killed in the fighting. But he provided no *direct* evidence that the killing was undertaken by "DESIGN." His evidence that the British intended all this to happen is instead *circumstantial,* and it is weak: British troops massed, marched, and confronted a "company of militia." They ordered the company to "disperse." Someone—Thomas said "one or two" British "officers," but historians aren't sure—

then fired a fateful shot.[65] It is hard to see how this circumstantial evidence makes it significantly more "probable," a term used in the *Federal Rules of Evidence*, that the British murdered by "DESIGN."[66]

John Dickinson, in his argument for opposition to the Townshend Acts, did a much more effective job of marshalling the evidence. One important step in his argument is the claim that the tariffs these acts imposed were designed not to regulate trade, but to raise money from the colonies. Dickinson's evidence for this is explicit, direct, and based on a written statement justifying the tariffs by the British prime minister, George Grenville, in which he said it is "necessary that A REVENUE BE RAISED IN YOUR MAJESTY'S SAID DOMINIONS IN AMERICA."[67] Dickinson did not stint on his "grounds" and "backing for claims."

≈

Logic. Aristotle's most significant contribution to understanding arguments—and much, much more—is his analysis of logic. The Greek philosopher presents twenty-eight *topoi* or enthymemes—possible forms for logical arguments in rhetoric.[68] They are also possible forms for arguments in journalism.

Number 11 on Aristotle's list, for example, is arguing from "a [previous] judgment."[69] In one of his "Letters," Dickinson did this by relying on the "judgment" that the hated Stamp Act was an unprecedented and unjust effort to raise revenues, not to regulate trade. He then asked, rhetorically, about the new and not-yet-hated Townshend Acts: "What is the difference in *substance* and *right*, whether the same sum is raised upon us by the rates mentioned in the *Stamp Act*, on the *use* of paper, or by these duties, on the *importation* of it?"[70] If, in other words, the Stamp Act, as an effort to raise revenues from the colonies, was wrong, and if the Townshend Acts also represented such an effort to raise revenues from the colonies, then . . . . *If, if, then*—premise, premise, conclusion. Dickinson's argument here, like all good enthymemes, is an effort at deduction, a less formal version of Aristotle's beloved *syllogism*—for him, the most exalted form of logical argument.[71]

Induction—deriving a general conclusion from specific examples—is a somewhat less impressive form of reasoning than deduction, according to this Greek philosopher. In rhetoric, where the standards are looser than in pure logic, the conclusion might just be another specific and might rest on only one or two examples. Aristotle calls this form of reasoning a *paradigm*. He likes it less than the enthymeme, and he has a point.[72] Because in resting an argument on a supposedly paradigmatic example, it is too easy to do what the author of that attack on smallpox inoculation in the *New-England Courant* did: provide an example of inoculation making someone very sick—"*Old Mr. W—b in a few Hours underwent the hot Service of bleeding Vomiting, Blistering, Poultices, &c. and narrowly escaped with his Life*"—and then based on that skimpy, potentially unrepresentative example proclaim, *induce*, the "dismal Consequences" of inoculation.[73]

In an even more egregious example, it was too easy to *induce* that Boston's chief practitioner of smallpox inoculation was suspect because the practice had previously been employed by "Greek old Women." This also seems an example of what Aristotle calls giving "attention to matters external to the subject":[74] How did the fact that this technique was once employed by "Greek old Women" negate whatever efficacy it had while being employed by physicians? We might also label this technique, following a later rhetorical tradition, an ad hominem argument: trying, in this case, to transfer presumed lack of respect for former practitioners of a technique into lack of respect for the technique itself.

Aristotle groups "fallacious" forms of argument into nine categories. Most of them are logical missteps to which journalists are prone. The third "fallacious" form, for example, is "exaggeration" (a close relative of the excessive use of "force," discussed in the earlier section on style).[75] Isaiah Thomas's furious condemnation against British troops at Lexington and Concord is not short on examples of exaggeration: "wantonly," "inhuman." Aristotle talks here of the "accuser" going "into a rage."[76] That appears to be what happened, perhaps understandably, to Thomas. But Aristotle also notes the somewhat more subtle logical fallacy of exaggerating your opponent's claims in order to more easily refute them—creating a "straw man," in other words. That sustained assault on smallpox inoculation in James Franklin's newspaper fell victim to this fallacy: an article in a later issue took great satisfaction in noting that "this Operation" was not "*Infallible*."[77] Who said that it or any medical procedure was?

Aristotle makes a more difficult point when, in presenting the ninth of his fallacious forms of argument, he criticizes a tendency to confuse "what is general and what is not general." That same issue of the *New-England Courant* stated: "Surely it must be needless to the last Degree for any Man to have himself made sick in order to prevent that, which for anything he knows, he is in no Danger of."[78] But the problem is that, as Aristotle might point out, although this rule about not making people sick on purpose sounds reasonable, it is not a "general" rule. It is "not absolute." There may be circumstances in which making someone a little sick in order to protect them against a potentially fatal illness is a good idea.[79]

An analysis of logic has or wants to have an air of clarity about it. We hope to be able to say, "this is good" or "this is bad" more easily about the logic of an argument than we can about its style, say, or about the character of its author. It is not often that cut and dried, however—with Aristotle as our arbitrator or even with a couple of millennia's worth of efforts to improve upon his work.[80] The argument against smallpox inoculation in Boston in 1721 was at points well argued. John Dickinson's argument against the Townshend Acts succumbed, at points, to less than noble reasoning. Valid argument forms are sometimes applied to bad arguments, and fallacious forms sometimes support good arguments. The search for valid or fallacious logic is not going to provide a foolproof method of distinguishing good journalistic argument from bad.

But it can help. And along with considerations of character, discourse, method, style, and evidence, such an analysis of logic might offer some guidelines for beginning to evaluate what journalism ought to accomplish and does accomplish when it presumes not just to give a report, but to make an argument—as it often did in the journalism with which the United States was founded, as it often will do in the wisdom journalism this book is championing.

≈

Argumentative, opinionated journalism helped create the United States of America—nowhere more eloquently than from the pen of Thomas Paine in his plea for independence, *Common Sense*: "O ye that love mankind! Ye that dare oppose, not only the tyranny, but the tyrant, stand forth! Every spot of the old world is overrun with oppression. Freedom hath been hunted round the globe. Asia, and Africa, have long expelled her.—Europe regards her like a stranger, and England hath given her warning to depart. O! receive the fugitive, and prepare in time an asylum for mankind."[81]

Yet argumentative, opinionated journalism, like Tom Paine himself, was hardly always beloved in America—during or after the revolution. Loud opinion usually finds someone to offend—often for good reason given its tendency to oversimplify, if not distort. And the arguments were loud indeed in these decades. Historians refer to American newspapers after the revolution as the "partisan press." Pathos ran high; "force" was often unleavened, as one anti-Federalist editor—Benjamin Franklin Bache, Ben Franklin's grandson—demonstrated weeks after the first president's "Farewell Address": "If ever a nation was debauched by a man, the American nation has been debauched by Washington."[82]

The Federalist John Adams at one point referred to the work of anti-Federalist editors as "terrorism." And in 1798, President Adams signed into law the Sedition Act, under which many of those anti-Federalist editors were indicted and some were thrown in jail. (The old British common-law prohibition against seditious libel was dredged up to indict Bache.)[83]

Although the anti-Federalist Thomas Jefferson let the Sedition Act lapse when he became president in 1800, he was hardly an unabashed fan of the partisan newspapers of his time. Jefferson's complaint, of course, was more with the Federalist press: "I really look with commiseration over the great body of my fellow citizens," he wrote in a letter toward the end of his presidency, "who, reading newspapers, live & die in the belief, that they have known something of what has been passing in the world in their time."[84]

But it was also clear, too, that the considerable triumphs of the American press had been achieved by partisan arguments. In a later letter and in a more magnanimous mood, Jefferson returned to extolling the importance of the press: "The only security of all is in a free press," he wrote. And it is clear in this letter what Jefferson believed must be "permitted freely to be expressed": "public opinion."[85]

Writing in the *National Gazette* a couple of years after he helped draft the First Amendment, James Madison also emphasized how important "a circulation of newspapers through the entire body of the people" is "to liberty." Why? Because it "facilitates a general intercourse of sentiments"[86]—i.e., opinions; i.e., arguments.

Bill Keller's and Jill Abramson's press, the press of the Committee of Concerned Journalists, in other words, is not our Founding Fathers' press. Newspapers then instead had more in common with some cable-news shows today—in their heated partisanship—than with Keller's or Abramson's *New York Times*; they had more in common with many equally partisan blogs—with their emphasis upon interpretation, not fact collection—than with "the professional discipline of assembling and verifying facts" that the Project for Excellence in Journalism now considers a good part of excellence in journalism.[87]

Nonetheless, an innovative and influential democracy was born. Nonetheless, an innovative and influential concept of press freedom was instituted. In fact, the world-shaking triumphs of America's revolutionary generation may have owed as much to printed opinions as it did to arms.

In the end, John Adams, too, saw this, indeed best expressed it: "What do we mean by the American Revolution?" he famously asked in 1818, after that the revolution was long finished. "Do we mean the American war? The Revolution was effected before the war commenced. The Revolution was in the minds and hearts of the people. . . . This radical change in the principles, opinions, sentiments and affections of the people, was the real American Revolution." And, Adams suggested, it was "pamphlets, newspapers, and even handbills" that "contributed to change the temper and views of the people, and compose them into an independent nation."[88] Those printed works changed "principles, opinions, sentiments and affections" in large part by publishing "principles, opinions, sentiments and affections"—such as those of Ben Franklin, John Dickinson, and Thomas Paine.

Arguments—in newspapers and pamphlets—rallied the American colonies against the British. Arguments then helped shape the new democracy. It is hard to imagine anyone at the time having anything as glorious to say about mere news reports.

2

"YESTERDAY'S DOINGS IN ALL CONTINENTS"

The Business of Selling News

It is almost impossible to speak of journalism today without using the word *news*. Our journalists work in "newsrooms" for "newspapers," "newscasts," "news sites," or other "news organizations." We lack alternative terms for these locales or enterprises. But journalism needs to be disentangled from the mere reporting of news.

The word *news* in its current usage is very old. That is appropriate because the type of information it describes is very old.[1] However, the word *journalism* was not in use in English in Jefferson and Adams's day. The activity of collecting, presenting, interpreting, or commenting upon the news had not yet earned a name in large part because it was not clearly seen as a specialized activity. Printing existed as a trade. Politics—making the case for a point of view or candidate, often in print—was expanding as a field as the possibilities of such campaigns and the audiences for such campaigns expanded with democracy, with the public sphere. The eighteenth and early nineteenth centuries had their share of writers and newspaper proprietors (Ben Franklin never uses the word *editor* in his autobiography). But there was as yet no clear job category that included Franklin and Tom Paine but excluded Thomas Jefferson.

According to the *Oxford English Dictionary*, the term *journalism* was first applied to work on newspapers in English in an 1833 article in the *Westminster Review*.[2] The word's meaning had morphed from "journal keeping" to "periodical work" earlier in France. Indeed, that *Westminster* article was a translation from the French. Journalism was defined in this

English translation of a French article as "the intercommunication of opinion and intelligence."[3] From the perspective of a twentieth-century American journalist, this earliest definition of journalism in English might be seen as odd because it gives so much emphasis to opinion. But what was actually most revolutionary about it was the weight it gave—in a field that had been dominated by sentiments, opinions, arguments—to "intelligence." *Intelligence* is an interesting synonym for *news* here, but a synonym nonetheless.

There's pleasure in telling as well as hearing news, which is a sign that there is survival value in the urge to tell as well as to hear news. Humans, by nature, are inclined to give away what news they have come upon. "When you know something that no one else knows and you get to be the first person to share it, that's a really thrilling thing," notes Ana Marie Cox.[4] She is speaking, presumably, of online journalism, to which she came early. But this was also true of newsmongering in eighteenth-century taverns and coffeehouses. Early newspapers stuck to opinion pieces and news from afar in part because trying to sell local news would have put them into competition with just about every seeker of that thrill—being the first to tell—in town, which meant just about everyone in town. And the competition was distributing the product, this most valued of all varieties of news, for free.

The first appearance in English of a word for the activity of filling the columns of periodicals arrived, however, with a definition that implies that the content of those columns was beginning to change. Newspapers in London (more than in Paris or anywhere else) had begun to traffic more often in *intelligence* as well as in opinion. They were increasingly establishing themselves as organs for the dissemination of news. And not just little, borrowed, seventeenth-century-like bits of news, but significant reports. Even newspapers on the outskirts of the English-speaking world, in North America, were beginning to follow suit.

Why? For one thing, cities—London, but eventually also Boston, Philadelphia, and especially New York—were growing larger. They were more difficult for word of mouth to traverse. Meanwhile, newspapers were getting quicker: the first daily had appeared in the United States in 1783 in Philadelphia.[5] By the nineteenth century, most newspapers could therefore carry local news from the day before—relatively timely local news. Then, in the first half of the nineteenth century, many American newspapers—again following their older cousins in London—began hiring individuals to go out after news.

Reporter is another word that was making a transition. It had been applied to individuals assigned to keep someone informed: in a letter in 1796, the British vice admiral Lord Viscount Nelson explained, "I am in great fear my reporter is taken."[6] The term had encompassed tellers or recorders of events: "The reporters of *this* one appear to be peculiarly imaginative," the author of an 1837 book complained about individuals describing a religious mission.[7] And a legal definition lingered and still lingers: "one who draws up official statements of law proceedings and decisions or of legislative debates."[8] In a congressional debate in 1798, the word seems to have been applied to employees of newspapers, but it was used interchangeably there with *stenographer* and *note-takers*.[9]

Nonetheless, the "journalistic" use of the term *reporter*—gatherer of news for publication, with or without the ability to take shorthand—was winning out in the nineteenth century. And newspapers in the larger American cities began employing a few of them—at first, by the 1830s, mostly to cover the police courts. Stationed where interesting things were likely to happen, these paid specialists—if that is not too lofty a word for them—gave newspapers a significant leg up on amateur newsmongers.[10]

It was at about this time that two inventions arrived that would further increase newspapers' growing advantage in the distribution of news. Steam was first used to power a printing press in London in 1814. But the Hoe "double-cylinder" steam press, which debuted in New York in the 1830s, was much faster and more efficient. Looking back, Whitelaw Reid, who became editor of the *New York Tribune* after the Civil War, put it grandly: "When Richard M. Hoe showed how types could be placed on a revolving cylinder instead of a flat bed, he did as much for the profession that now rules the world as the inventor of gunpowder did for the one that ruled it last. From that moment came the possibility of addressing millions, at the instant of their readiest attention, from a single desk, within a single hour, on the events of the hour."[11]

The second of these inventions was displayed in 1844, when Samuel Morse got the first city-to-city telegraph line up and running. He thereby presented the world with the first of many devices that could move news not only faster than a person could run, a horse could gallop, a pigeon could fly, not only faster even than a steamship could sail or a train could chug along, but almost as fast as the speed of light.

So, along with those reports on local news, something else new began appearing in mid-nineteenth-century newspapers—a word almost never before seen in reports from far away cities and states: *yesterday*. And by 1866, when the first successful telegraph cable under the Atlantic became available, accounts of what happened "yesterday" also began appearing in reports from other continents. Here's Whitelaw Reid again: "The journalist, at one leap, took the whole world for his province every morning."[12]

The telegraph moved only information, and it moved it at a stiff price. Individuals sent telegrams, if they sent them at all, only when it became necessary to inform relatives and friends of pressing personal news: "GRANDMA PASSED STOP." But buying time on telegraph lines made great sense for newspapers, for they could sell the story one reporter transmitted over those lines to each of their swelling numbers of readers. Newspapers quickly became the telegraph companies' largest customers.[13] And they reduced costs further by joining together in cost-sharing telegraph cooperatives, such as the Associated Press or by making use of telegraph news wholesalers, such as Reuters. Newspapers had, in essence, exclusive access to telegraphed news.

Meanwhile, reporters, or "correspondents," were increasingly being deployed on "beats"—sometimes down the street, sometimes at the end of one of those telegraph lines. They were given, in other words, a specific area to cover: police court, city hall, the White House, Paris. Beats made newspapers and their fact-collection systems more reliable. The contacts and physical presence of that city-hall reporter ensured that just about any event deemed newsworthy that took place at city hall would become news. News reporting became less hit and miss. This was an outpouring of intelligence that one might regularly expect and about which one might have confidence.

Newspapers thus found themselves with a new product to sell: now for a penny—many of these nineteenth-century newspapers managed to reduce their price—readers could get news that was skillfully reported, reliably fast, and from near and far. Newsmongers and scuttlebutt had no chance against these daily, reported, steam-powered, wired news behemoths.

Then in the United States the normal, nagging human thirst for news was intensified by the largest news story in the history of the country: an unbelievably bloody, fratricidal war. "We must have something to eat and the newspapers to read," Oliver Wendell Holmes wrote in 1861. "Everything else we can give up."[14] Forgetting for a moment that freedom was at stake, forgetting for a moment the horrific number of lives lost, and looking at the Civil War only from the point of view of newspaper economics, it was as if fledgling widget makers found themselves in a country suddenly experiencing a great desperation for widgets. The country was desperate for news.

So the balance in "journalism"—this "intercommunication of opinion and intelligence"—began to tip further toward the latter—toward news. The two still communicated: Opinions, of course, referred to news. Opinions still occasionally made news—Horace Greeley's open letter to President Abraham Lincoln in 1862 calling for him to free the slaves is an example of that.[15] Opinions still appeared on street corners, in saloons, and, often enough, in newspapers. But news in the United States in the second half of the nineteenth century was doing more and more of the talking.

Reporters—especially during wartime—were there to collect intelligence more than to form opinions. Newspapers had become a place to look not for letters, arguments, and clippings from other papers, but for the original information reporters gathered, the reports they produced. In the South, the Civil War induced privations, including shortages of paper; in the North, it dramatically increased the size of reporting staffs, telegraph usage, and the output of those cylindrical steam presses.

James Gordon Bennett Sr., who immigrated to the United States from Scotland, had been in the 1820s among the first to report on the new government in Washington. He had been in 1830 among the first in America to cover a trial. In 1835, Bennett founded his own newspaper, the *New York Herald*, in which he expanded crime coverage and pioneered Wall Street coverage and sports coverage—new beats. Bennett sent sixty-three reporters to cover the Civil War for the *Herald*.[16]

By the middle decades of the nineteenth century—and for the first time in human history—the dissemination of news was becoming a big business. If you could obtain it quickly and efficiently enough, if you could distribute it fast enough (the new railroads also helped here), if you could flood the town with papers filled with it, you could make not just a craft, but a mammoth enterprise out of peddling what humans had always exchanged for free.

≈

Peddling news wasn't necessarily the most distinguished of businesses. An 1869 magazine article on journalism by the American essayist Richard Grant White gives an idea of the status at the time of the mere reporter of news: "Of the two branches of journalism, which are the gathering and the publication of news and the discussion and explanation of the events thus made public, the former is the more essential, the latter the more important."[17]

Technologies, as noted in the introduction, can change quickly—as the technologies upon which newspapers relied changed in the first two-thirds of the nineteenth century. Methodologies can also progress rapidly—as they were then progressing in journalism. Business often races ahead—as the news business was racing ahead in nineteenth-century America. Creative individuals, such as James Gordon Bennett Sr., regularly dash off in search of the future. But—and the contemporary ramifications of this point will continue to be a major theme of this book—mindsets take quite a while to catch up.

John Adams, speaking of a revolution that involved troops and fighting, noted that it was preceded by a change in "minds and hearts."[18] It is usually the other way around, however, when a field undergoes a technology-driven "revolution." In these cases, changes in technology precede, by decades or even centuries, changes in "minds and hearts." Indeed, the new—even as it is being employed and enjoyed—is more likely to be disparaged than welcomed, especially by individuals of culture and distinction.[19] Almost all of what was new in newspapers in the nineteenth century had to do with what White called "the gathering and the publication of news" branch of journalism. It is not surprising—mindsets not having yet adjusted—to find that this new branch was disparaged.

Such attacks are often, at root, moral or at least matters of etiquette. Charles Dickens complained in *American Notes*, an account of his visit to the United States in 1842, that the "Press" in America "has its evil eye in every house."[20] *Harper's Magazine* almost half a century later harrumphed "that our reporterized press is often truculently reckless of privacy and decency."[21]

Richard Grant White was a journalist—a music critic and editor—as well as a Shakespeare scholar. His attack on "the gathering . . . of news" branch of journalism was not really moral: White did, after all, acknowledge that "gathering . . . news" is "essential." But he was making some intellectual judgments, even some class judgments. "If" a journalist "has any other purpose in life than to make money," he wrote, "he is not content with being a news-collector; that is a reporter." In fact, despite his talk on how "essential" this branch of journalism was, White ended up dismissing it as "almost purely mercantile and clerical."[22]

White was arguing instead in favor of a journalism "practiced by men who are wise and well informed" and who "aspire" to the role of "teacher and guide."[23] He got quite respectful, as one often does about the old when it is succumbing to the new, about the importance of "the discussion and explanation" branch of journalism. White honored this more argumentative journalism as "a constant guide, a daily counselor; it at once informs and educates; it expands the horizon of men's thoughts and sympathies."[24]

His essay does not mention the names of any of these "wise" and "well-informed" individuals, but we might think of Joseph Addison, Benjamin Franklin, and John Dickinson. We might conclude that White was celebrating here the construction and maintenance of something very much like Jürgen Habermas's "public sphere."[25] I am certainly willing to accept White's essay, too, as a paean, somewhat overstated and a century and a half before the fact, to what I am dubbing "wisdom journalism." Indeed, all these kind words said on behalf of "discussion and explanation" also, no doubt, had another purpose: belittling the mere "collector and vendor of news"—who presumably did not "expand the horizon of men's thoughts and sympathies," yet who was conquering journalism in nineteenth-century America.

And White was hardly alone in belittling this new form of journalism. In 1881, for example, the English essayist and thinker Leslie Stephen (Virginia Woolf's father) characterized the "reporter of ordinary events and speeches" as "a bit of mechanism instead of a man."[26]

Whitelaw Reid was an early achiever of the new mindset. Reid was a renowned reporter who became a top New York editor and also managed a political career, which led to his nomination as the (unsuccessful) Republican candidate for vice president of the United States in 1892. As an editor, Reid not only understood but, three years after White's disparaging essay, championed the "revolutions" that had left newspapers "crowded with yesterday's doings in all continents"—newspapers that "you skimmed at the breakfast-table, gave your spare half-hours to throughout the day, and can hardly finish till tonight."[27]

Reid expressed little patience with journalists who peddled opinions—"propagandists," he called them.[28] In an 1875 interview, he put his view of the modern newspaper succinctly: "The essence, the life-blood of the daily paper of to-day, is the news."[29]

According to Habermas's reading of journalism history, however, this is precisely where the press went wrong. Given their new devotion to news, newspapers, which had been "'bearers and leaders of public opinion,'" bore, in Habermas's view, less of it and led it less frequently. "The intellectual press" was "relieved," he writes, "of the pressure of its convictions."[30]

Whitelaw Reid obviously did not share Habermas's nostalgia for opinionated eighteenth-century newspapers: a whole year's worth of them, Reid scoffed, contained "scarcely so much news as in this morning's 'Herald.'" He had no nostalgia even for Ben Franklin's newspaper: "It has been common, though rather absurd, to speak of Benjamin Franklin as the father of American journalism. Well, here is his paper, 'The Pennsylvania Gazette,' after he had been at work enlarging and improving it for twelve years. Its entire weekly printed surface is somewhat less than one-eighth of an ordinary daily issue of 'The New York World.'. . . . Its news is only three months old from London, only eleven days old from Boston, and from New York only three."[31]

For Reid, news, fast news, was all. In Habermas's view, making money was becoming all. The press, he writes, "has been able to abandon its polemical position and take advantage of the earning possibilities of a commercial undertaking." And the opinions and news that these newspapers did print tended to reflect, Habermas argues, the concerns of these burgeoning "commercial undertakings." "The public sphere," he adds, "was transformed by the influx of private interests."[32]

Newspapers were certainly proving to be remarkably successful and fortunate "commercial undertakings." Whitelaw Reid had no problems with that. His enthusiasm for the nineteenth-century newspaper "revolutions," which had left Ben Franklin and eighteenth-century journalism behind, extended also to their "mercantile" consequences: "The conduct of newspapers," he explained, "ceased to be the work of journeymen printers, of propagandists, needy politicians, starveling lawyers, or adventurers. Its new developments compelled the use of large capital, and thus the modern metropolitan daily journal became a great business enterprise, as legitimate as a railroad or a line of steamships, and as rigidly demanding the best business management."[33]

Yes, capital had indeed entered the equation. The *New York Sun*, the first of the country's successful penny papers, had been started in 1833 by a printer in his twenties who had earned a little money at his trade. James Gordon Bennett Sr. had had a net worth of $500 when he founded the *New York Herald* in 1835. Horace Greeley, a throwback to the days of influential opinion writing, but also a master at deploying reporters, had started the *New York Tribune* in 1841 with about $2,000 in cash (half borrowed) and another $1,000 worth of printing equipment.

The *Sun* was sold for $250,000 in 1849. And two years later Greeley's former assistant, Henry J. Raymond, needed to raise $70,000 to launch the *New York Times*. Raymond had two partners—both bankers.[34] By 1860, Bennett's *Herald* had the largest circulation of any daily newspaper in United States, if not the world. Then in 1875, the *Tribune*, now edited and published by Whitelaw Reid, built the tallest office building in New York.[35]

News—raw, inflammatory, often anarchic—had become a commodity, the quarry of capitalists. The cylindrical steam press and the mass-circulation newspaper had more or less invented mass production. There was money to be made selling—even for a penny—each "crowded" copy. There was money to be made, too, selling advertising in those copies—another new kind of business being invented by newspapers. That ancient human activity—keeping track of dangers and possibilities—was controlled by capitalists.

Newspapers would still crusade for this and that—war with Spain over Cuba, for example. Opinionated journalism did not disappear quickly, and it never disappeared entirely, but news reports increasingly filled or clogged, depending on your point of view, "the public sphere." And Habermas's dreaded "private interests" operated the pumps.

With the help in the last quarter of the century of much cheaper paper, the telephone, the typewriter, the linotype machine, and even better presses, the news business continued to grow. In 1890, the *New York World* built the tallest office building in the world; the office of the paper's publisher, Joseph Pulitzer, was just beneath its giant gold dome. By the mid-1890s, the *World* spent $2 million a year and had thirteen hundred full-time employees.[36]

Literacy was expanding. Immigrants were pouring into cities in the United States. In those cities, audiences for news—customers for this commodity—seemed almost unlimited. "No printing-press ever devised," Whitelaw Reid had gushed, "could print in the required time as many newspapers as there were eager buyers."[37] By the end of the nineteenth century—and with the help of the partly newspaper-made Spanish-American War—newspapers in New York achieved circulations of one million.

Not everybody got rich, of course. This high-profile, high-influence business was always attracting new affluent proprietors—more than the market, even this expanding market, could support. The competition to get news the fastest and proclaim news the loudest was brutal and unrelenting. Many would-be Bennetts and Pulitzers found owning a newspaper to be a good way to trim a fortune. Even after efforts at consolidation in the first half of the twentieth century—papers closed, papers combined—markets proved difficult to monopolize.

But markets could be dominated. And some newspaper publishers—Pulitzer, William Randolph Hearst, E. W. Scripps—accumulated great fortunes by beating word of mouth every morning, then every afternoon, and in extras as needed to hot, juicy, late-breaking, occasionally even society-nudging news.

And mindsets were catching up. A new understanding of journalism was beginning to take hold. Journalists were fashioning a new self-image. The mere gatherer of news, who could still be dismissed near the end of the nineteenth century as "a bit of mechanism instead of a man," was rebranded.

Back in the nineteenth century, Whitelaw Reid had emphasized freedom from staunch political partisanship: "Independent journalism!—that is the watchword of the future in the profession. An end of concealments because the truth would hurt the party; an end of one-sided expositions, because damaging things must only be allowed against our antagonists; an end of assaults that are not believed fully just, but must be made because the exigency of party warfare demands them."[38]

This was unarguable (though with Fox News Channel and MSNBC it perhaps needs to be argued again today). And it was a start: the "news-collector" was now an "independent" journalist—independent of party if not of "private interests."[39]

But how to justify the absence of the "horizon"-expanding teaching and guiding? This was a harder task for those attempting to upgrade the reputation of the gatherer of facts. The key was proclaiming an independence not only from party, but from any semblance of point of view. "Discussion and explanation" inevitably were tainted by point of view.

"The ambition of the director of every great political journal," Whitelaw Reid suggested in that 1875 interview quoted earlier, "should be to make his reports, his election returns, every article and item of *news*, so impartial and truthful that his political opponents will accept them as unquestioningly as his political friends."[40] "Impartial and truthful" as a standard might serve to eliminate much of what passed for teaching and guiding, but Reid's formulation still assumed that a journalist had political opponents and friends. What was wanted was a more sweeping political impartiality—based on a fervent commitment to something else.

Journalists found that "something else," in part, in what was perhaps the nineteenth century's most powerful intellectual movement in art, literature, and science: the commitment to detail, to facts, to showing the world as it is, to a sometimes revelatory, sometimes disturbing realism. At one point in that interview, as Reid was waxing poetic on the virtues of impartiality and truth, his interlocutor observed, "This seems to hint at journalism as a science."[41] Reid must have been pleased. Many fields in those years were gaining a desire to be a science and deal in facts.

Facts had been increasing their hold on journalism throughout the nineteenth century. "The people of England at large have not so much taste for discussion as for information," wrote one observer of the British press in 1851. "They care more for the facts, or what they suppose to be the facts, than for the most luminous reasoning in the world upon those facts."[42] By 1894, a correspondent for the *Times* of London was instructed that "telegrams are for facts: appreciation and political comment can come by post."[43]

American journalists were, if anything, even more fact crazed, even more eager to deemphasize "appreciation and political comment." The first paragraph of their stories had once been used to intrigue or merely to set up. Now it increasingly was stuffed with facts. According to what would become the twentieth-century journalist's most relied upon and most reductive formula, a news story must begin with the most "important" facts, the five W's—"who," "what," "when," "where," and "why"—or at least four of them, as the last of those required a little "reasoning." (Sometimes "why" would be replaced by an H: "how.")[44]

David Mindich's perceptive and engaging book *Just the Facts* provides the best analysis of the American journalist's discovery of realism and the consequent rise of this formula. Mindich includes the following example, chilling in its refusal to comment, of a four W's lead from the *New York Herald* in 1898: "Charleston, S.C., Tuesday. In Lake City, a town of five hundred inhabitants, sixty miles north of here, an angry mob of from three to five hundred men lynched Frazer B. Baker, the negro Postmaster, his three-year-old daughter Dora, early this morning, and wounded Baker's wife, two grown daughters and a ten-year-old son."[45]

Instead of building to a conclusion or being organized chronologically, the comment-free stories that proceeded from those comment-free leads increasingly arrayed the remaining facts in order of decreasing newsworthiness—an *inverted pyramid*. Fact-hungry, time-pressed readers thus could leave the story at any point confident—to the extent that they trusted these calculations—that the information they had already imbibed was more important than what they might consequently miss. When this new formula for news writing was followed, copy editors could also speedily and safely cut from the bottom.

Reporters of news, gatherers of fact, were now proponents of realism in their writing as well as in their reporting. They found themselves marching—for some happy decades—with artists, novelists, scientists, and other devotees of realism. Reporters of news, gatherers of fact, wanted to be or at least to seem *positive* and *empirical*—as the scientists were or at least seemed to be, as philosophers for a time wanted to be. They subscribed to a low-wattage, true–false positivism of the sort philosophers would come to dismiss as "naive empiricism"—of the sort that might encourage them to treat a mob's murder of members of a family as just another collection of facts.[46]

Edifying printed placards hung in the newsroom of Joseph Pulitzer's *World* in New York in the first decade of the twentieth century. One called for an emphasis on facts, enlivened by intriguing (a critic might say sensational) details: "The Facts—The Color—The Facts!" it read. Another demanded to know, in the incompletely alliterative version of that formula, "Who? What? When? Where? How?" A third contained just three words of instruction: "Accuracy, Accuracy, Accuracy!"[47]

The *World* in those days was by reputation the top newspaper in the United States, with one of the largest circulations. Its reporters were not being asked for "The Meaning—The Insight—The Meaning!" The list of questions they were being told to answer did not include "Why?" or "Of what significance?" or "What next?" or "For good or ill?" The *World*'s journalists were not being instructed to be "Wise, Wise, Wise!" And minus the uncomfortably unabashed, perhaps uncomfortably honest words "The Color," these placards would not have been out of place in most newspaper, radio, and television newsrooms in the United States in any decade of the twentieth century.

Facts came easily to journalism once journalists conquered the impulse to tell their readers what they really thought, once they devoted themselves, heart and soul, to news. And facts were a great philosophical discovery for journalism. Journalists had been Tories and Whigs, Federalists and Anti-Federalists, Democrats and Republicans. Now they shared something of a common ideology: as fact venerators. And the ethic this devotion enforced—thou shall not trammel with the facts—was perfect for the "news-collector." "Discussion and explanation" were out because they debased facts by relegating them to contexts or squeezing them into arguments.

A profound transformation in self-conception was under way. Forget the eighteenth-century pamphleteer and rabble-rouser! Forget the harried printer—willing to set in type whatever crossed the threshold! Forget the bemused spectator! Forget the raconteurs, the satirists, and those who toed a party line! Yes, some could still be found holed up on some pages or in some publications. But more and more journalists now asked to be viewed as responsible *professionals*—a word Whitelaw Reid had begun insisting upon back in the 1870s. Their work—like that of doctors and lawyers—was now seen as a proper subject for university instruction, as Reid had also suggested.[48] The world's first school of journalism opened at the University of Missouri in 1908. Then in 1922 journalists gained a professional association: the American Society of Newspaper Editors. And at its first convention, the ASNE adopted a code of ethics: the Canons of Journalism. Its headings include the words *independence*, *accuracy*, and *impartiality*.

Whitelaw Reid had predicted, back in the 1870s, that journalism would "ascend" from "partisan struggles" to a "passionless ether."[49] It almost happened. In the twentieth century, reporters did their best to become, like all good scientists, *objective*.

This attempt had practical value: as newspaper staffs grew larger and larger, getting everyone politically aligned had been proving more difficult. Now they all could align or try to align to the position of having no position. And the still relatively new wire services, which served newspapers arrayed across the political spectrum, furthered this new just-the-facts style.

Newspapers' worship of facts[50] presented them with one additional and considerable benefit—an economic one. Opinions are fine in a heavily segmented news market, where your best chance of grabbing an audience is to speak directly and loudly to and for a particular segment: Democrats, Republicans, Progressives, the pro-business, isolationalists. But consolidation and competition from other media in the twentieth century began reducing the number of newspapers. Those that were left gravitated toward the middle. And newspapers had set about building huge circulations. That couldn't be done if they regularly alienated large segments of the potential audience. A less offensive, more moderate approach began to make sense—business sense. It would make sense, too, for broadcast stations and networks, which were even fewer in number and were in the ticklish position of occupying government-owned frequencies. Facts were less likely to offend than opinion. Being evenhanded offered some protection against cancelled subscriptions or angry politicians. Objectivity worked.[51]

So it lasted. Novelists and painters were chasing smaller, more rarified audiences. Fact collector was never a hugely inspiring role for such artistes. They moved on. Journalists, trying to attract huge audiences to support large businesses, did not.

This role was quite comfortable for scientists—indeed, they helped originate it. But with the arrival of the twentieth century, the facts they were collecting began displaying some disturbingly nonobjective traits: clocks, they determined, would report different times if they traveled at hugely different speeds; subatomic particles could be both here and there; much depended upon the observer. Physicists in the twentieth century had to become less naive.

The facts journalists were chasing also demonstrated a tendency to be influenced by observers. Lincoln Steffens performed a nice, if unintentional, experiment to demonstrate this influence simply by covering a burglary in New York that would otherwise have been overlooked. Pretty soon—reporters being a competitive lot—many previously ignored burglaries were being covered in the city. The number of burglaries hadn't changed, but for readers of the city's newspapers it looked as if that number had skyrocketed. Steffens had, as he put it, *created* what was understood to be a crime wave.[52]

But most journalists, less playful and self-aware than Lincoln Steffens, managed not to notice that views of the world were being created through their decisions on what to report or not report. That sort of influence didn't fit their self-image. It didn't fit the business model. It didn't fit realism, their ideology. For these former Grub Street sensation mongers were now—having consecrated themselves to facts—scientists, or at least nineteenth-century-model scientists. They were professionals. They had ascended.

To sum up, in the nineteenth century journalists in the United States had come upon an extremely lucrative activity—dispensing news. A professional creed justifying this activity—insisting that it was the noblest activity in which they might engage—followed in the early decades of the twentieth century, and it lasted.

Newspaper writers were once known for their passion, their playfulness, their humor, their fancies, their hoaxes. But journalists had begun to view themselves not as wry observers, but as the most severe and hardheaded of realists. Reporters could now style themselves, with justice, watchdogs in the halls of government; unblinking crime reporters; witnesses to war; incorruptible muckrakers; hard-bitten, seen-it-all chroniclers of one or another demimonde; dogged, democracy-saving investigators. And when even these roles began to seem too romantic, when even that self-image began to seem a bias, an intrusion into the life they were supposed to be merely examining, twentieth-century American journalists eventually would congratulate themselves—falling back upon the most aloof, innocuous, inoffensive of metaphors—for being "mirrors" merely reflecting reality.[53] They had become all eyes—and no voice. The facts, instead, would speak for themselves.

As the twentieth-century began spewing its horrors, the facts, though hardly unassisted, often did speak—eloquently, powerfully. They spoke in coverage of war and atrocities. They spoke in exposés of political and business corruption. They spoke, too, in coverage of the liberation movements of colonial peoples, of African Americans, of women, of gays that graced the second half of that century. Plenty of stories fell through the holes in journalism's fact-collection net, which now stretched around the world: stories, for example, that did not take place on one beat or another—accounts of events on the other side of town from city hall, accounts of events that were never adjudicated in police court. But many stories were captured, and unvarnished facts were often enough to change minds and, upon occasion, even alleviate injustices.

John Hersey's reportage in the *New Yorker* (and later in a book) on the atomic bomb the United States dropped on Hiroshima in 1945 can serve as an example of this variety of journalism—fact-based twentieth-century American journalism—at its very best.[54] It is a tour de force of voicelessness: Hersey and his experiences in getting the story are completely absent from his text. He himself does not opine or otherwise comment on the bomb or the decision to drop it. Yet his account of the bomb's devastation—told from the perspective of those who experienced it on the ground—was revelatory. And the anger, sadness, and horror that Hersey fails to express explicitly are felt, as they are supposed to be felt in this form of journalism, in the voices of the victims and ultimately in the mind of the reader. All the power of interviewing, of reporting, of simply stated facts, of authorial restraint can be found here.

By the second half of the twentieth century in the United States, reporting news—not just "the discussion and explanation" of it—had gained cachet.[55] Ivy leaguers (enamored by the excitement and Hemingway) replaced high school graduates (enamored by the excitement and the regular paycheck) on the White House beat, at city hall, and soon even on the police beat. By "bearing witness, digging into records, developing sources"—to return once again to Bill Keller's formulation—they brought down a president, exposed a massacre in Vietnam, and shined a light on a wide variety of miseries and corruptions. Fact-obsessed reporters became heroes in a fact-obsessed age. Journalism had *become* the painstaking gathering of information on current events.

Journalists in Europe often maintained a more pointed perspective on events—the *Telegraph* and *Le Figaro* from the right, for instance, the *Guardian* and *Le Monde* from the left. These were national newspapers. So there were more of them in direct competition, and they could still spread themselves out on the political spectrum. But in the United States, where news organs increasingly clumped in the middle, "intelligence," as quarry, was generally revered to the point where it was considered sinful to sully it by any "intercommunication" with opinion. The standard of "quality journalism" before which many journalists still genuflect at the beginning of the twenty-first century had been raised. All hailed the reporter.

But there is another way of looking at journalism's twentieth-century triumphs in the United States. Journalism is too large and too variegated to slide completely into one category or another. When we talk of an age of opinionated journalism or an age of fact-based journalism, we are talking of times when one or the other of these approaches, one or the other of these mindsets, predominated. But American journalists in the eighteenth century certainly did not entirely ignore facts. And journalists in the United States in the twentieth century certainly did not entirely ignore interpretation and opinion.

Indeed, in the 1930s there was a flurry of interest in interpretation—evidenced in particular by the rise of news summaries and columnists.[56] And as merely arraying facts is not a hugely effective way to produce distinguished journalism, much of the best journalism of the twentieth century not surprisingly managed to escape the confines of who, what, when, and where. (This escape is noted in chapter 4 and celebrated in chapter 6.) Indeed, there is something that is not characteristic of just-the-facts journalism in Hersey's *Hiroshima.*

John Hersey was already a renowned writer when he took on this assignment for the literary and well-heeled *New Yorker.* He was not chained to anything as limiting as a beat. He could wander the globe. He could hole up in Hiroshima for months. And Hersey ignored that upon which most American journalists would have focused: the larger strategic and political issues. There is something that might instead be welcomed as wisdom journalism in *Hiroshima:* the intensity of Hersey's focus, the experimental form (borrowed from a novel, Thornton Wilder's *Bridge of San Luis Rey*),[57] the willingness to ignore almost entirely death counts and official statements, and, perhaps of most significance, the desire to make, in his remarkably understated way, a point: that the atomic bomb the United States had dropped on this Japanese city caused horrific, unimaginable suffering.

Hersey made use of some aspects of the style of just-the-facts journalism, but he also went well beyond most of the journalism of his time.

His work therefore points to some of the strengths of the predominant style of twentieth-century American journalism, but also to some of its characteristic weaknesses.

Theodore Roosevelt, who became president as that century began, had recognized that by emphasizing nonpartisanship and deemphasizing interpretation, the press had left an opening for others to suggest the meaning of events. Roosevelt aggressively moved into that opening, using the press to get across his messages.[58] Subsequent presidents—eventually all major politicians—would do so as well. And practitioners of the new field of public relations also proved happy to supply the missing interpretations of events. They learned to exploit, in other words, the weaknesses of what was increasingly being thought of as "traditional"* American journalism.

A fact-hungry press could investigate and help bring down a president, as Richard Nixon would learn. But a fact-hungry press could also be used. The press wrote down what officials said, so Senator Joseph McCarthy said that Communists had infiltrated the government. This story appeared in the *New York Times* on April 22, 1952: "Senator Joseph R. McCarthy, Republican of Wisconsin, charged on the floor of the Senate today that Mrs. Leon Keyserling, wife of the chairman of President Truman's Council of Economic Advisers, has been a member of the Communist party and of 'an unlimited number' of Communist-front organizations." Only after six more paragraphs detailing Senator McCarthy's charges against the Keyserlings did the *Times* article note that they categorically denied them.[59]

The Johnson administration similarly fed the press both accounts of the presumably external threat to South Vietnam and trumped up accounts of success in defeating it. This is the first paragraph of a two-

---

* I continue to use the term *traditional* as it came to be used in American journalism in the twentieth century: to apply to the just-the-facts style of journalism. However, it is important to remember, as discussed in chapter 1, that this style was in the nineteenth century an innovation and that journalism in the United States had an older tradition of interpretation and argumentation.

paragraph Associated Press story out of Washington printed in the *New York Times* on June 10, 1966: "North Vietnam infiltrated 19,000 men into South Vietnam in the first four months of this year, but American and other allied troops killed about that many North Vietnamese and Vietcong, officials said today."[60] These official statements are not questioned at all in this tiny article.

And while reporters were standing, notebook in hand, before officials, jotting down such assertions as if they were facts, larger stories went unreported. The problem was not just that much of the American press was late in exposing Senator McCarthy's fabrications or the false claims of success in Vietnam by the Johnson administration, but that mid-twentieth-century American journalism—hypnotized by yesterday's facts or alleged facts—also mostly missed such momentous but protracted stories as the migration of blacks out of the South after 1940.

Many of the failures of American journalism in these decades were failures of perspective. Fact-chasing reporters failed to see forests.

As with all good ideologies, the creed of twentieth-century American journalists was based on a kind of faith: They believed that statements made by officials were facts in themselves. And, more generally and equally dangerously, they believed that facts could exist without opinion, independent of observers, without contexts, without perspective, without—to state the problem most bluntly—understanding. Dostoevsky mocks a version of this last belief in *The Brothers Karamazov*, published in 1880: "I made up my mind long ago not to understand. If I try to understand anything, I shall be false to the fact and I have determined to stick to the fact."[61]

As the business of journalism became selling news, the ideology of twentieth-century American journalism—Whitelaw Reid's ideology, the ideology that still lurks behind many contemporary efforts to grapple with the field's current crisis—threatened to place facts even ahead of understanding.

It was a fact that Senator McCarthy had charged that some numbers of Communists were ensconced in one or another government department. It was a fact that the American military was saying that some number of Viet Cong had been killed in one battle or another. These statements were considered to be news, even if what was being charged or said was not true. But blacks migrated without official announcement and too slowly to produce simple, clear, officially sanctioned facts for the mainstream press. That was not considered news.

What was needed to get these stories right was expertise, "discussion and explanation," understanding. What was needed in the United States in the twentieth century too often was not there.

〜

Back in the 1870s, when Whitelaw Reid was first articulating the view of journalism that would become so influential in the next century, he received a letter suggesting a new Paris correspondent for the paper he edited, the *New York Tribune*. The candidate: Henry James, who had recently moved to Paris. That letter reported that James, already the author of one novel and numerous short stories, had proposed the idea himself.

Despite Reid's commitment to a quick, "crowded," news-oriented journalism, he considered himself a literary man, and the *Tribune*, Horace Greeley's old paper, was still thought of as something of a literary paper. That's why James thought it would provide an appropriate home for his letters from Paris. That's why Reid accepted his proposal. And in the next year or so, nineteen letters from Henry James on France ran in the *Tribune*.

In 1876, he wrote, for instance, on the "cheap and pleasant" resort town of Etretat—a town free, James found, of the "menace of the invasion of luxury." I'll quote it at some length:

> The French do not treat their beaches as we do ours—as places for a glance, a dip, or a trot, places animated simply during the balneary hours, and wrapped in natural desolation for the rest of the twenty four. They love them, they adore them, they take possession of them, they live upon them. . . . Like everything in France, the bathing is excellently

managed, and you feel the firm hand of a paternal and overlooking government the moment you issue from your hut. The Government will on no consideration consent to your being rash. There are six or eight worthy old sons of Neptune on the beach—perfect amphibious creatures,—who, if you are a new-comer, immediately accost you and demand pledges that you know how to swim. If you do not, they give you much excellent advice, and keep an eye on you while you are in the water. They are moreover obliged to render you any service you may demand—to pour buckets of water over your head, to fetch your bathing sheet and your slippers, to carry your wife and children into the sea, to dip them, cheer them, sustain them, to teach them how to swim and how to dive, to hover about, in short, like ministering and trickling angels. At a short distance from the shore are two boats, freighted with sundry other marine divinities, who remain there perpetually, taking it as a personal offence if you venture out too far.[62]

James was writing on culture here, not on politics or diplomacy; still, the insight-to-word ratio is high. Reid, however, although aware of the quality of such passages, was not convinced of their value. "He wrote to James," explains Reid's biographer Royal Cortissoz, "asking him to make his letters shorter and to get more news in them." Reid was respectful, and James's response was not impolite, at least on this surface: "If my letters have been 'too good' I am honestly afraid that they are the poorest I can do," he stated. "I know the sort of letter you mean," James acknowledged, "—it is doubtless the proper sort of thing for the *Tribune* to have. But I can't produce it. . . . It would be poor economy for me to try to become 'newsy' and gossipy."[63] Henry James's association with the *Tribune* ended.

An emphasis on news proved spectacularly good "economy" for journalism in the nineteenth and twentieth centuries. However, the economics of journalism have been changing again—the tale the next chapter will tell. News and gossip are still popular, but they are now endlessly available. There was a period in the nineteenth and twentieth centuries—an odd period, I can't resist calling it—when run-of-the-mill news from Paris might have had more value than the observations and perceptions, the understandings, the teaching and guiding of a Henry James. But that period is ending. And journalists sitting in their "newsrooms" have to realize that their pursuit of the "newsy" is now holding them back.

3

"CIRCULATORS OF INTELLIGENCE MERELY"

The Devaluation of News

The era when professional journalists held a monopoly on news lasted a little more than a century and a half. Although the really big money came later, that era can be said to have begun in the middle of the nineteenth century, when reporting was growing strong, presses and the telegraph were moving news fast, and bankers started investing in newspapers. Although there still remains money to be squeezed out of our shrinking news organizations, that era is drawing to a close more or less now.[1]

This was the period in which many in journalism today or writing about journalism today came of age. Yet it was the exception in human history. Its ending feels sudden. It has not been that sudden.

Early in this period, the United States was the most newspaper-hungry country on earth. In 1870, by one estimate, it had one-third of the newspapers in the world.[2] In New York State in 1910, for a dramatic example, the average household received more than three newspapers a day.[3] But competition was on its way.

The form of radio with which young Guglielmo Marconi experimented in 1895 had two major limitations as a news medium—one technical, one conceptual. First, it was limited to dots and dashes, which made it impossible to communicate with a large audience. In the early years of the twentieth century, Reginald Fessenden and Lee De Forest solved that problem: they managed to load radio waves with codes for sounds, including voices.[4] Wireless telegraphy, in the vocabulary of the time, became wireless telephony.

The conceptual problem was that radio was still being looked upon as a form of one-to-one communication—like the telegraph and telephone, but unlike the newspaper. The realization that radio could gather an audience came to Harry P. Davis, a Westinghouse executive in Pittsburgh in 1920. Davis saw the attention that one of the company's engineers, Frank Conrad, was attracting by transmitting recorded music from his home and had Conrad build a transmitter for Westinghouse. That became, by some definitions, the first commercial radio station in the United States: KDKA. It was not to be a form of one-to-one or hobbyist-to-hobbyist communication, as was most radio at the time, but an attempt by one transmitter, one station, to reach many.*

And what did Davis transmit the first evening KDKA took the air? Something that had long proven its ability to draw a crowd: news. On November 2, 1920, KDKA debuted with the results of the Warren G. Harding–James M. Cox presidential election. Those results were borrowed from a newspaper but, for individuals with a radio receiver, managed to arrive much more rapidly. Radio had two great advantages as a news medium: it could be sent through the air, without need of trucks or newsboys, and it could be delivered instantly. Here for the first time was news distribution, not just newsgathering, taking place at something approaching the speed of light. Radio was at the time, as Davis later put it, "the only means of instantaneous collective communication ever devised."[5] Even newspaper extras were laggard in comparison.

It was hard to imagine charging for what drifted through the air and into homes. Once you owned a radio, "programs" (a term borrowed from vaudeville) would be (unlike vaudeville or newspapers) free. But that raised a question similar to the question being raised by the Internet today: How would anyone make any money? Harry P. Davis's solution was to use his transmissions to increase the value of owning radios, which Westinghouse manufactured. But the fledgling AT&T radio network

---

* At the end of the twentieth century, the ability of radio waves to carry one-to-one communication would ironically be rediscovered with cell phones, as radio's power as a form of mass communication began to decline.

later that decade was based on another business model: charge a toll not to listen to, but to transmit a radio program, just as a toll had to be paid by a caller to "transmit" on AT&T's telephone lines. However, because there were a lot of people listening to a radio transmission—it was a "*broad*cast" (a term borrowed from farming)—that toll quickly began being paid not by chatty individuals, but by companies looking to sell something. And radio obtained what many Internet companies are still looking for—its means of support: advertising.

It also needed a source of news. Newspapers, where Harry P. Davis had turned for his 1920 election returns, were the obvious place for radio networks and stations to look. Virtually all the world's professional news gatherers at the time were employed by newspapers or the wire services that supplied newspapers. However, newspapers, alert to the competition, were not of a mind to help radio out.

The Associated Press is owned by its newspaper clients. Nonetheless, in 1932 the AP agreed to sell returns from the Franklin D. Roosevelt–Herbert Hoover presidential election to the radio networks for one compelling reason: otherwise, the networks were going to buy that news from the United Press. The newspapers were not pleased, and their displeasure led to an agreement the next year that newspapers and wire services would not sell news to radio networks. But it is not easy to monopolize news. The Columbia Broadcasting System and the National Broadcasting Company—CBS and NBC—began hiring their own reporters. Other, smaller wire services sprang into existence to sell to radio. The ban was eventually lifted.[6]

But the threat proved real enough.

Newspaper circulations, which had been growing significantly faster than the population in the United States, lagged a bit in about the year 1920—too early for competition from radio to have been a factor: in 1922, only one in four hundred households in the United States had a radio. But 60 percent of U.S. households purchased a radio between 1923 and 1930. So when newspaper circulations began to wobble in the 1930s, radio's ability to air this evening what newspapers wouldn't be able to publish until tomorrow morning might have been a factor—along with, of course, the Great Depression.[7]

The percentage of U.S. households receiving a daily newspaper rose to 130 percent (many homes purchased more than one paper) in the 1940s—with war, once again, doing its part. Then it began a steady decline. A new and even more beguiling form of "instantaneous collective communication" was rolled out in the United States near the end of that decade. By the middle of the next decade, television had penetrated half of U.S. households. Television does not explain the initial years of that inexorable decline in newspaper circulation per household. Radio was probably still more of a factor. But television does explain about four decades of that decline; it explains why daily newspaper circulation as a percentage of U.S. households had dropped by almost half by the early 1990s.[8]

It wasn't just television news that was stealing the newspaper's audience. Situation comedies, dramas, and sporting events also turned people's eyes from the various *Post*s, *Journal*s, *Tribune*s, *Sun*s, *Mirror*s, *Chronicle*s, *Herald*s, and their cousins. Most newspapers, after all, were selling entertainment along with the latest from Washington: they featured comic strips, "Dear Abby," and crossword puzzles, not to mention sensational crimes and gossip. But the *Huntley–Brinkley Report* on NBC, the *CBS Evening News* with Walter Cronkite, the *Today* show on NBC, and all the other morning, evening, and late evening newscasts on the networks and local stations provided direct competition for newspapers. They, too, were in the business of updating audiences on what was happening at home and abroad. And television newscasts, like radio newscasts, provided those updates at a then unbeatable speed and price: being instant and, unless you counted those short commercials, free. With cable news—CNN debuted in 1980—television news became available around the clock.

By 1980, a wave of newspaper extinctions was already under way. Extras were no longer being hawked on the streets; instead, when news broke, programs were interrupted. Afternoon papers disappeared: Who needed a newspaper to take home when there was a television at home? And where two or more daily newspapers had competed in one city, one or more, with rare exceptions, found a way to bow out, either by merging or dying.

Despite the newspaper closings, the last third of the twentieth century is still recalled fondly by many journalists in the twenty-first. And it was, indeed, a pretty good time for radio and television journalism, with government conveniently limiting the number of broadcast stations. It was a good time, too, for the newspaper or two that survived in every city. Most newspaper proprietors—large corporations increasingly—finally had what they had dreamed of: a monopoly on a city's classified ads, along with its supermarket, department store, automotive, and movie ads. New sections were spawned—lifestyle, arts, sports—producing new, more targeted advertising opportunities.

And with profits plump and reasonably professional corporate managers in charge, this also proved to be a period of journalistic accomplishment: stories became stronger overall;[9] investigations proliferated; a president was toppled. Indeed, those newspapers that had survived may have achieved their greatest respectability even as—And isn't this the way it goes?—they continued to lose their audiences.[10]

That steady decline newspapers had been experiencing throughout the postwar decades meant that the total circulation of daily and Sunday newspapers in the United States failed to keep up with gains in population—not to mention the country's dramatic gains in secondary and college education. Nonetheless, total newspaper circulation in the United States did increase: from more than 88 million in 1945 to almost 125 million in 1990.[11]

Then something rather sudden did happen. From nowhere, with hardly any advance warning, humankind stumbled upon probably the greatest information-distribution machines in history, greater even than the printing press. In 1991, Tim Berners-Lee invented the World Wide Web at the European Organization for Nuclear Research in Switzerland. In 1993, Marc Andreessen developed the graphically oriented Mosaic browser. Widespread use of the Internet became possible.

This led to a dramatic change in the fortunes of printed newspapers. Since 1994, total daily and Sunday newspapers circulation in the United

States—not just per household circulation—has declined every year. Even though there are more and more people in the United States, in other words, the number of newspapers being sold is dropping.

And thanks to the computer-Internet-cell-Web devices that currently rest on our desks, on our laps, or in our palms, that decline has been accelerating.[12] Within a decade and a half, it seemed that sites or apps on these devices, many of them produced by newspapers, could do anything newspapers could do with news cheaper, faster, more capaciously, and with links. In the twenty-first century, even a monopoly newspaper has become a bad business proposition.

Those computer-Internet-cell-Web devices are the greatest newspaper killers we have seen because when it comes to the distribution of news, they are so much more capable than the newspaper. They would soon wreak havoc upon radio and television news, too.

～

Which brings us to today.

And to you: sitting at whatever passes for a breakfast table with a muffin and, if you are old enough to have caught the habit, a newspaper. The muffin, we hope, given that you are a person of discernment, is fresh. However, the news in that newspaper—and this is surprising given the aforementioned discernment—is not.

What is the paper's lead story? Has the president said something important? Has the crisis of the moment led to something distressing? Has something happened to someone, perhaps a celebrity, that is shocking or tragic? All these things would qualify as news. And almost all these things you would have learned if had you watched a news program after work yesterday. You would likely have learned of them—unless they had occurred at night—had you turned on the radio in the car on the way home yesterday. And if you had wandered to a news site or if you had opened your "new tweets," you would likely have gotten word of such occurrences much earlier than that. When? Probably by about 11:30

yesterday if it was a talk by the president or a formal announcement about a crisis; crimes and disasters, of course, are not so carefully scheduled.

I have held a stopwatch to the twenty-first-century race for news on a few occasions since 2006.[13] The events I've tracked through the news cycle have by now almost faded from memory, as old news does. The first was Venezuelan president Hugo Chavez at the United Nations calling then U.S. president George W. Bush "the devil" early on Wednesday, September 20, 2006. That radical eruption of incivility—a moment, therefore, of raw news—was the lead story in the print edition of the *Miami Herald* on Thursday morning, September 21, 2006.

But already by noon on Wednesday, give or take about a half-hour, Yahoo, AOL (of more importance then), and just about every major news site in the country had been trumpeting Chavez's affront—with that combination of amazement and revulsion news organs typically bring to reports of transgressions. The *Drudge Report* had a transcript of the entire speech up before 4:00 that afternoon. The comment was discussed on at least two NPR shows that afternoon or early evening. And by the time the *CBS Evening News* got around to mentioning it, sound-bites from Chavez's talk had, of course, been played over and over on CNN and (with gleeful indignation) on Fox News Channel. By 6:30 Wednesday evening—half a day before Chavez's insult appeared on newsprint in Miami—his entry on *Wikipedia* had even been updated to include an account of his United Nations speech.[14]

And as once slow forms of communication, such as encyclopedias, continue to go digital and speed up, new, even faster forms of communication continue to debut. I next studied a story as it made its way through the news cycle almost three years later. The big global news that day, April 2, 2009, was an agreement reached by the leaders of the world's largest economies, the G-20, meeting in London.[15] This came at one of the (many) frightening moments in the global financial crisis. Then British prime minister Gordon Brown began announcing the agreement at 11:00 A.M., New York time. CNN was among those broadcasting much of that announcement live.

The *Guardian* newspaper in Britain, certainly not alone, was "live blogging" the event—then a relatively new and exciting form of news coverage. Within three minutes of the *beginning* of Brown's talk, the *Guardian*'s live blog had posted a quote from Brown that included the most newsworthy element of the agreement: a commitment by G-20 members of about one trillion dollars mostly to the International Monetary Fund (IMF). The *Guardian* unfortunately made that figure one trillion *pounds*. By 11:10 A.M. New York time, the paper's live blogger published a brief list of all six of the group's pledges—but with the space in front of "1 trillion" now properly occupied by a dollar sign.

At just about the same time—to pick a purposely obscure example— a live blogger, who may have been peeking at the *Guardian*'s efforts, weighed in on a site called *Entangled Alliances*. *Entangled Alliances*—the world's 938,076th ranked blog at the time, according to Technorati— characterizes itself as emanating "from the keyboards of four young leftwing Brits."[16] It published a similar, though not identical, summary of the G-20 pledges ten minutes into Brown's statement—with the currency denomination spot on.

And so it went. *USA Today*, in a web feature called "On Deadline," reprinted an Associated Press alert on the announcement by 11:16. The AP, Reuters, and other news services quickly began reporting and updating the story. Fuller accounts, wire-service accounts, were up on the websites of—and this is just a tiny sample—MSNBC, the *Huffington Post*, the *Drudge Report*, and Yahoo by 11:50. Google News was tracking the G-20 agreement by 12:03. Six minutes later *Politico* joined those linking to the full communiqué. And, of course, within the next couple of hours, details of the agreement rapidly spread over the rest of news-inclined radio, television, and, in particular, websites. Video clips of Brown's statements could even be found on YouTube.

Printed newspapers in this environment are, of course, ridiculously slow. Being a slow news medium is not merely annoying, like being a slow accountant or a slow supermarket checkout person. The first report you encounter of some intriguing piece of news will almost inevitably be compelling, the fourth not so much. When it comes to disseminating news, the race really does belong to the swift. Also-rans risk becoming bores.

Wait a second, you say. Aren't the *New York Times* and the *Washington Post* worth the wait? Can't they produce more comprehensive and smart accounts of the news with the help of their more accomplished reporters and with the benefit of a bit more time? Indeed they can. Don't they help us suss out what was important yesterday? They do. The question is whether the few extra quotes from important sources, a bit of perspective, and that comforting air of reasonableness, trustworthiness, and discrimination will compel the news alert to read or view stories on subjects about which they are already fairly well informed.

Hold on, you say. Not everybody is sitting around checking *Drudge* or *Gawker* a couple of times an hour. Not everybody keeps Twitter open on a smart phone. Not everybody bothers with the news on radio or TV. Some people might be perfectly content to wait until the next morning to get a solid, sober summary of the previous day's news in a familiar, time-tested format.

True, individuals willing to forgo this mad rush for news—perhaps a kind of discernment in itself—can wait for their newspaper to arrive in the morning. The printed version of the *New York Times* can still be the first to update those who have managed to avoid most of the available electronic communication in the previous nineteen or so hours (a talent more commonly displayed by the old than the young). It can still be the first to tell those not really all that interested in the daily parade of news, anyway. (Here the young may have the advantage.)

This group of potential customers for slow news organs would include, in other words, extreme technophobes, those who are stuck in their ways or finally trying to read all of Proust, and people who tend to be indifferent to the news. These are not, however, audiences normally prized by major news organizations. Other more up-to-date and alert readers might have been forgiven a bit of a yawn when they opened their newspapers over breakfast on Friday morning April 3, 2009, only to be told, yet again, that "the leaders of the world's largest economies agreed Thursday to . . . ."[17]

The problem, of course, is that the process of printing and distributing starts newspapers off with about a five-hour disadvantage. The lags built into their editorial processes—some justifiable, some perhaps vestigial— slow things further. And "communication based on moving paper," as Alexander Field terms it, is expensive.[18] You have to cut down all those trees, run those gigantic (and still cylindrical, though no longer steam-powered) presses, dispatch fleets of trucks with bundles of newspapers, then deliver copies to individual doorsteps. The prognosis for the printed newspaper is consequently grim.

This is upsetting not only for those with the newspaper habit or a newspaper job. The history of journalism was essentially the history of newspapers from the beginning of the seventeenth century until radio news began to gain strength in the third decade of the twentieth century. Much of what we know and think about journalism has come from newspapers and is still expressed in terms borrowed from newspapers (*headline, lead, front page, dateline*, etc.). Perhaps of more importance, much of what we know about the world has come to us via newspapers and their extensive reporting systems.

And they are not the only venerable news organizations at risk. Radio, television, and online news organizations are much faster than printed newspapers. Nevertheless, NPR's *All Things Considered* and *Morning Edition* are going to weigh in a little later on most stories than, say, Twitter. The *NBC Nightly News* with Brian Williams, which airs at 6:30 in the evening, is still going to be hours slow on most stories compared to Twitter, Facebook, and many bloggers—even many amateur bloggers.

≈

Despite the sluggishness of their newspapers and newscasts, professional news gatherers do, of course, have useful skills. They are trained for clarity, thoroughness, fairness, and accuracy. (However, if you'll forgive an effort to *induce* from a single example, that pounds-not-dollars error was made by someone at the venerable *Guardian*, not by one of the "four young left-wing Brits.") Professional news gatherers know, too, how to determine what is most newsworthy in a statement or an event and relate it quickly and concisely. The opportunity we now have to watch major news announcements ourselves on cable or the Web would seem to reduce significantly the need for the inverted-pyramid summary journalists have perfected over the past century. Nonetheless, summaries sometimes do have their uses, particularly for those of us unable to watch CNN at eleven on a weekday morning. All things being equal, one ought to want to have a professional gathering one's news.

And many online news sites—*Huffington Post* and Yahoo, for example—do, indeed, depend on such professionals: reporters and writers of their own. Such news sites commonly also link to the pages of other, more established news organizations. They are occasionally, and less nobly, guilty of "scraping"—quoting and posting—content from one of those more established news organizations onto their own pages to support their own advertising. (The *Huffington Post* has been criticized for this.)[19] Online news sites often also feature and pay for wire-service stories.

The Associated Press, Reuters, Bloomberg, and some others clearly have a role in this new digital news world. They employ trained reporters and editors and are thus in a better position to get the facts right than a lonely, harried live blogger—even one employed by the *Guardian*. Wire services—fast, dogged, and reasonably reliable—can get an initial, workmanlike, accurate summary up within an hour of a news event. Moreover, they can—working with audio, video, or written words—take the event, chop it up, and package it, according to the old formulas, as a condensed, clear news story. Yahoo, for example, can then post such an AP story on its site, paying AP for the privilege through a licensing agreement, or, following another model, the *Drudge Report* can simply link to a Reuters story or to someone else featuring a Reuters story, with the eyeballs that follow being compensation enough.[20] Nothing said here is meant to imply that the AP, Reuters, Bloomberg, and whatever cousins of theirs are spawned by the Web should stop gathering and wholesaling news in bulk in return for fees or audiences they can then sell to advertisers.

And, of course, NYTimes.com, WashingtonPost.com, ABCNews. go.com, CNN.com, and other news websites connected to long-established news organization have their own contingents of presumably even more skilled professional journalists to furnish them with content. They have jumped into the crowded competition to get the story up on the Internet and to mobile devices if not first, then at least fast. They are working, in essence, to help scoop their own print editions or news-casts. Their reporters, increasingly outfitted for multimedia, trudge off to the major press conferences and disasters and get some paragraphs or video up not long after the AP does—only at somewhat greater length, with somewhat more thoroughness and sophistication. The assumption is that their professionalism and experience will give them a significant advantage over Yahoo, not to mention all those young or old, left- or right-wing bloggers.

The *New York Times* website was posting and updating its own story on the G-20 agreement in London by 11:32 A.M.—only fifteen minutes after the initial AP alert. The *Washington Post* was just a little tardier. The *Times* story, in a testament to its reporters' skills, did present a par-ticularly solid explanation of the agreement. It highlighted the failure of the Americans and the British to get other countries to agree to further stimulate their own economies. The *Times* and the *Post* then regularly beefed up their stories over the next few hours.

However, it is not clear that these stories, well reported as they may have been, did all that much to distinguish NYTimes.com or WashingtonPost.com from HuffingtonPost.com or any of the other sites carrying the AP story, which did a perfectly reasonable job of summariz-ing the announcement and noting the absence of agreement on further stimulus. Even the quick summary of the G-20 agreement produced by those "four young left-wing Brits" was serviceable.

I discuss investigations and other exclusives later, but for the majority of stories—stories that everyone from the wires to amateurs has a shot at—is this all the *New York Times* is to be: AP plus? Is this all NYTimes. com will have to offer on such stories: the same as everyone else, maybe just accomplished a little more skillfully?

And the *Times* is not just competing with the wire services, some websites, and some amateurs. There was a time—a couple of decades ago—when to see a copy of the *Guardian* or the *Times* of London in the United States required a trip to a special newsstand, and even then it would be a day or two out of date. No more. The limits of geography—how fast a truck can drive or an airplane can fly, how far a broadcast transmitter can reach—have now simply disappeared. So NYTimes.com and WashingtonPost.com are now competing on a big international story such as the G-20 agreement with all the world's other major news organizations, many of whom have some pretty talented reporters of their own hustling to get the news online, too.

Their stories, most of them, will then appear in a list on Google News—differentiated only by an extra fact, quote, or odd angle here or there. Is this all NYTimes.com is to be when it has not uncovered an exclusive: one of the hundreds of websites trying to do a little bit better job with the same story?

Given what is now available online, trying to sell news is like trying to sell food in a town that happens to be served by all the world's supermarkets.

~~~

And the news business has changed in two other crucial ways. First, on most stories none of our major, professional news organizations—not the *New York Times*, not *NBC News*, not NPR—can obtain the news any faster than anyone else, major or not, professional or not. It was easy enough, for example, for *anyone* with access to some electronics to watch Gordon Brown's speech at that G-20 meeting live or to read the actual agreement more or less when the reporters there read it.

Second, *anyone* with a Twitter feed, a Facebook account, or a Word Press address can now post—essentially publish—the news. A printing press or a broadcast tower is no longer required. Tweets or Facebook posts or blog posts are "up" as fast as a story on NYTimes.com is "up," maybe faster. And what a remarkable form of "publication" this is! If we are up to date on our devices, these updates will follow us not only into our homes, but just about anywhere we wander. By 2012, according to a Pew survey, 44 percent of Americans owned a smart phone.[21] The point is that on most stories the major, professional news organizations no longer obtain *or* distribute news faster or farther than can one of those "four young left-wing Brits."

You are unlikely to happen upon an obscure blog run by a handful of young people; you may, in fact, have no interest in happening upon it. We lean toward names we know and trust in news as in most consumer decisions. But if those young people really did come up with something newsworthy that everyone else overlooked, there is a chance their blog would have been linked to, and then that link would have been linked to; there is a chance their tweets, had they tweeted, would have been retweeted and then retweeted again; there is a chance their Facebook posts would have been much "liked" and much shared. Amateur news can occasionally, as we've seen, "go viral."[22]

All of this means that the advantage that reporting, the cylindrical steam press, and the telegraph gave newspapers over amateurs is rapidly fading. Busybodies are back in the news competition as long as they have an Internet connection or a smart phone. Amateurs in general are back in the news competition. Sometimes they get things wrong, as many on social media trying to guess the identities of the Boston Marathon bombers did in April 2013, but often enough—in Mumbai during a terrorist attack, in Cairo's Tahrir Square—they succeed in capturing what professionals are not in a position to see.

In the early morning hours of July 20, 2012, for another example, an eighteen-year-old in Colorado monitored a police scanner as well as social and traditional media as news of the mass shooting in an Aurora, Colorado, movie theater began to break. The result, produced on Reddit, was what *BuzzFeed* described as "an exhaustive, minute-by-minute account of the development of the story, from the earliest indications that something horrible had happened to the emergence of a cohesive narrative."[23]

The Web has been reminding us that there are a lot of talented people out there willing to pitch in on moving news. Some of them are reasonably clear, thorough, fair, and accurate. And they often find themselves—there being so many of them, their being so widely scattered—closer to news events than the professionals. They occasionally bring to such events engaging passions and revealing perspectives not always available to the professionals, with their much-cultivated detachment.

Jill Abramson, the executive editor of the *New York Times*, is right to warn us that "when millions of voices boom on the Web, there is also space for rumor, incorrect facts, and just plain nonsense." But there is space, too, here and there on this million-voiced Web, for original and important reports. Abramson is also right to note that "amateur citizen-journalists sometimes do not have the skills and background to produce the most accurate journalism."[24] But an increasing number of them, I think it is safe to say, do.

Anyone familiar with the wilder corners of the world of print—pamphlets, cheap books and magazines, supermarket tabloids, publications distributed on street corners—knows that this now revered medium in its heyday was not lacking in the amateurish, the paranoid, the slanderous, the outlandish, the frivolous, even the fallacious. All of the above can now be found on the Web. Undoubtedly more of all the above can be found on the Web because it is so easy for just about anyone to publish just about anything.

But those of us lacking an interest in invective, conspiracy theories, and all the rest haven't had all that much difficulty filtering out the foolishness: Most of us are pretty good at learning what not to click on—just as previous generations learned what books, newspapers, magazines, and pamphlets not to buy. Moreover, if our Web wanderings do take us somewhere we ought not to be, closing a browser window is as easy as opening one. All the craziness is not going to disappear: some may enjoy it; some may even be fooled by it. But it is not likely to pose a threat to our democracy. The real question is not whether there will be lots that is useless or worse on the Web; it is whether there will be enough that is good.

The denizens of the Web in the initial decades of its existence may not yet have come up with a way to uncover much of what is now uncovered by the accomplished fact chasers of the *New York Times*, but that doesn't mean they won't. It took the purveyors of newspapers a couple of centuries to develop reporting systems. Bloggers are already pretty skilled at noting, kibitzing, questioning, dissecting, deconstructing, and kvetching. True, many mostly limit themselves to reporting what's on the Web—often from the privacy of their bedrooms. But we can allow them a few more years before we conclude that it will never occur to these bloggers to put on a pair of pants and also report streets and hallways.

And many of these twenty-first-century layperson newsmongers snap their cell phone images, record their fuzzy audio and video, tweet their clever tweets, blog their witness, and post their indignation without remuneration. Telling a wide variety of news online seems no less fun than telling local news on the streets of Philadelphia was in Ben Franklin's day. Lots of people once again seem to want to get into the act.

With journalism perpetrated by amateurs, we will have to remain alert for lapses in accuracy, accountability, fairness, and ethical standards. (To be fair, however, the Internet's hair-trigger feedback mechanisms have made it extraordinarily responsive to criticism and correction.[25]) And if some of those journalistic "amateurs" reporting on events are actually public-relations professionals working for the sponsors of those events, we will have to work hard to correct for lacunae, tilts, and excesses of cheeriness. Reading sponsored news requires skills that may not have been well developed in the newspaper–newscast era. But if the solution is an application of cynicism, I don't think we have to worry about that being in short supply in the early twenty-first century.

Meanwhile, something pleasingly democratic, we must keep in mind, is occurring with this great outpouring of amateur news—at least the nonsponsored kind. For decades, journalism's critics lamented the narrowness of the "gates" through which news had to pass and the limitations and capriciousness of the keepers of those "gates." Journalism's critics are not wont to declare victory, but surely they need lament no longer.

We now have access to news from a shockingly (sometimes unpleasantly) broad range of points of view.

Many of these amateur bloggers or tweeters may sometimes seem too reliably left wing or right wing, Democratic or Republican. They may be guilty, upon occasion, of what Whitelaw Reid decried as "concealments because the truth would hurt the party."[26] But, with the exception of the occasional corporate social media specialist, most are certainly not guilty of being directly controlled by Habermas's "private interests."[27] Those private interests are more likely to be felt behind large, corporate media—the Rupert Murdoch–owned *Wall Street Journal* or Fox, say— than behind bloggers. Bloggers are certainly prone to infection by the same ideologies the rest of us are prone to catching, but making little or no money does offer one privilege: relative freedom from the dictates of capital.

And something else that is pleasingly egalitarian is occurring on the blogs, Facebook, and Twitter: humans no longer are required to surrender the pleasure of finding and telling news to those blessed with a press card. The huge news corporations fed us each day our daily news. Now we are often left to forage for news ourselves on the wide, wild Web. The exchange of news had become a spectator sport. Now once again anyone can play. Multitudes can satisfy the itch to uncover news on their own online. And through email, on blogs, via tweets, in text messages, on Facebook pages, multitudes can then hold forth on whatever they deem to be news—with widely varying degrees of perspicuity and polish, to audiences of widely varying sophistication and size. Amateurs are back in the game.[28] "One thing . . . can't be undone," insists seminal Washington blogger turned *Guardian* columnist Ana Marie Cox, "we will never go back to a period where only a privileged few get to put their voices out. I think journalists are finally coming to terms with that."[29]

There is much indeed for journalists to come to terms with. All these changes in the direction of openness, participation, and democracy are mostly good news for news, but undeniably bad news for news professionals. Journalism's century-and-a-half-old business model is slowly or not so slowly collapsing. And there isn't much evidence of a new online business model that will sustain most of these large news-collecting organizations.

We can consult on the subject no less an authority than the investor Warren Buffett, who has been buying up newspapers in a burst of nostalgia or bargain hunting or both. In a 2007 report to shareholders, Buffett conceded that the newspaper industry's "underlying economics are crumbling." And he dismissed the idea that the Internet would be the solution: "The economic potential of a newspaper Internet site—given the many alternative sources of information and entertainment that are free and only a click away—is at best a small fraction of that existing in the past for a print newspaper facing no competition."[30]

With the benefit of hindsight, the failure of the news-collection business seems obvious: new forms of electronic communication would get and spread news less expensively, thus eliminating the monopoly that newspaper publishers had established. But none of this seemed obvious when colossi such as Joseph Pulitzer, William Randolph Hearst, E. W. Scripps, Adolph Ochs, Otis Chandler, Arthur Ochs Sulzberger, and Katharine Graham were pumping profits out of their indefatigable fact-processing machines. None of this seemed obvious when ace finders of fact such as Lincoln Steffens, Ida Tarbell, Bob Woodward, Carl Bernstein, and Seymour Hersh were upon occasion "afflicting," as that old adage would have journalists do, some among the "comfortable."[31]

Nonetheless, the great century-and-a-half-long anomaly has ended: news is once again being given away, much to the detriment of those who for that century and a half had been selling it. The whole world has now become one big village, tavern, or coffeehouse through which news races almost without impediment. The supply of news has exploded. And here is what is truly new: this plentiful and free news is now as fast and far reaching as anything the nineteenth- and twentieth-century news barons had been selling.

Trying to peddle their wares in this environment is for major news organizations like trying to sell food in a town served not only by all the world's supermarkets, but also by all the world's mom-and-pop groceries

and farm stands. And, if that weren't challenge enough, just about everyone is giving away just about everything for free.

Some of these amateur, mom-and-pop, farm-stand journalists also
have a rather significant advantage over the professionals: a deep expertise on the subjects upon which they are reporting.

≈

On June 29, 2012, the U.S. Supreme Court announced its decision on
whether the Obama administration's health-care law (the Patient Protection and Affordable Care Act of 2010, otherwise known as "Obamacare") was constitutional—another story whose journey through the
news cycle I examined.

No reporters knew in advance what the decision would be: the
Supreme Court is that rare institution whose decisions do not leak
beforehand.[32] But everyone knew by then that the decision would be
announced shortly after ten that Thursday morning in the courtroom
of the Supreme Court Building in Washington. Most journalists also
understood who was most likely to have the news first—and it wasn't
one of the top traditional news organizations, although most of them
in the United States and quite a few from other countries were covering
the story.

Tom Goldstein and Amy Howe are lawyers, married to each other,
who handle cases before the Supreme Court. In 2002, they founded
SCOTUSblog (named after the acronym for "Supreme Court of the
United States") to better report and discuss news of that court. Goldstein
and Howe's blog was not entirely run by individuals without a background in journalism: they employed a reporter, Lyle Denniston, who
had covered the Supreme Court since 1953 for, among other newspapers,
the *Wall Street Journal* and the *Boston Globe*. Denniston was eighty-one
when he and these two lawyers and part-time bloggers entered a competition with most of the country's best-known news organizations on the
Court's health-care decision. "It's our number one ambition to be first
and beat everybody," Denniston acknowledged to the *Washington Post*.[33]

The first reports that morning on the Supreme Court's health-care decision did not appear on *SCOTUSblog*, however. CNN reported on the decision at 10:07 A.M., Fox News Channel just eight seconds later. Both, however, got the decision wrong: "I want to bring you the breaking news that, according to producer Bill Mears, the individual mandate is . . . not a valid exercise of the Commerce Clause," announced reporter Kate Bolduan on CNN. That, in fairness, was correct. What Bolduan said next was not: "So it appears as if the justices have struck down the individual mandate—the centerpiece of the health-care legislation" (Chief Justice John Roberts had, in fact, found another way of justifying the mandate). Bolduan's "it appears as if" then disappeared in the headline that, within the next minute, was displayed on the bottom of CNN's screen, "SUPREME CT. KILLS INDIVIDUAL MANDATE." Three minutes later that qualifying phrase was also gone in the headline featured on the network's website: "Mandate Struck Down." On FOX at 10:07, anchor Bill Hemmer was direct and clear: "We have breaking news on the Fox News Channel: the individual mandate has been ruled unconstitutional."[34]

At 10:08 A.M. (a few seconds earlier on Twitter), *SCOTUSblog* was, to no one's surprise, the first to report what the Supreme Court had in fact decided. When the decision was announced, Lyle Denniston, as planned, had not been in the courtroom, where no electronic devices are allowed. Instead, he was in the pressroom, where, at the moment it was being announced, he was handed a printed copy of the decision. Denniston then hustled to his desk in the building, where he met Tom Goldstein. They looked over the decision—more carefully and perceptively than the folks at CNN and FOX, though it took them only a minute or so. Goldstein then instructed Amy Howe to type these portentous words onto *SCOTUSblog*: "The individual mandate survives as a tax." Two minutes later Goldstein wrote: "So the mandate is constitutional. Chief Justice Roberts joins the left of the court."[35]

At just about the moment when *SCOTUSblog* was correctly reporting the decision, David Leonhardt, the Washington bureau chief of the *New York Times*, posted the following statement on that paper's blog devoted to the subject: "The Supreme Court has ruled on President Obama's health-care overhaul, and *Times* reporters and editors are analyzing the decision. Once we are comfortable with its basic meaning, you can expect a torrent of coverage."[36] There would eventually be a torrent of coverage in the *Times*, but it began as a trickle.

The first substantial story in the *Times* on the decision, by my reading, appeared on that blog eighteen minutes later, at 10:26 A.M.—after *SCOTUSblog* had already noted the major aspects of the decision. This 480-word *Times* news story began: "The Supreme Court on Thursday largely let stand President Obama's health care overhaul, in a mixed ruling that Court observers were rushing to analyze." However, many of those 480 words in this *Times* blog were devoted to background and general information. And when it came to the key question, which *SCOTUSblog* had already answered, the *Times* wrote: "It remained unclear whether the court officially upheld the mandate or chose a more technical path that effectively allowed it to stand."[37] Six minutes after that incomplete, still hazy effort by the *Times*, Amy Howe posted a solid, 155-word, "plain English" summary of the main points of the Court's decision on *SCOTUSblog*.

So this little, specialized blog—then supported by money from a media company, Bloomberg, but not run by any media company—had broken the biggest news story in the United States in quite some time and beaten most of the major news organizations in the United States. Moreover, this little, specialized blog—unlike two of those major news organizations—got the story exactly right. The blog's reputation for doing this sort of thing was such that more than half a million people clicked on SCOTUSblog.com that morning. Included among them were individuals at most of those major news organizations. Indeed, Fox News Channel began correcting itself—once it saw *SCOTUSblog* contradicting its story—by quoting the blog on air.[38]

This was not a journalistic triumph scored entirely by amateurs. Denniston does not qualify, but Goldstein and Howe were not trained or even full-time journalists. Instead, what they and Denniston had to offer was what Goldstein calls a "focused expertise"—a deep understanding of the subject in question.[39] Unlike most of the professional journalists handling the story on air on CNN and FOX, they were specialists on the Supreme Court and the law.

This situation is becoming common: individuals who may or may not have a professional background in journalism but who are specialists on one or another area of news are continually beating major news organizations to stories. Nate Silver had never worked as a mainstream journalist, but he had an extraordinary facility with and wisdom about statistics, honed while thinking and writing about sports—for a blog of course. And Silver was fascinated by the political horserace in 2008. His blog analyzing polling on elections, *FiveThirtyEight*, so outperformed other news media on this subject that it attracted three million visitors on election day in 2008—and was later licensed to the *New York Times*.[40] Brian Stelter's story is perhaps even more dramatic. He not only began what became the most influential blog about television news without any professional journalism experience, but he began it, in January 2004, while still a freshman at Towson University in Maryland. Stelter initially called his blog *CableNewser*. But by July he had made a deal with MediaBistro, broadened the focus, and changed the name to *TVNewser*.

In 2006, the *New York Times* ran a front-page profile of the "baby-faced" college student whose blog had more than a million page views. It included this quote from a senior vice president of ABC News: "The whole industry pays attention to his blog." Stelter's secret? "Passion is the most important trait I bring to my blog," he explained on a Towson website. Stelter is obsessively passionate about goings on in television news. That helped him become extremely knowledgeable on the subject. He, too, has a "focused expertise." When Stelter graduated from college in 2007, the *Times* hired him as a media reporter.[41]

And coverage of media news in the *New York Times* is quicker and smarter now that Brian Stelter is on board—just as Nate Silver's work upgraded aspects of the *Times*'s election coverage. (Silver agreed to take his blog to ESPN and ABC News in 2013.) But even if the *Times* and other media organizations keep snapping up successful bloggers, they now will always face the threat that some passionate college freshman or astute eighty-one-year-old—without benefit of editors, staff, or maybe even a budget—is going to scoop them on news of one aspect of the culture or another. The playing field in the competition to report the news has been leveled: a specialist or two or three—blogging, posting on Twitter—can easily beat a major news organization.

That great journalistic innovator James Gordon Bennett Sr. had predicted in the nineteenth century that with the telegraph "the mere newspapers—the circulators of intelligence merely—must submit to destiny, and go out of business."[42] They did not. As Bennett soon realized, the telegraph, being too expensive and limited to take news into houses, proved instead a boon for newspapers. Radio and television did finally bring fast, electronic news into houses, and they did severe damage to newspapers. But they had limitations, too: transmitting over the air was expensive, and audiences were not given any choice on what stories to listen to or when to view them. Our new computer-Internet-cell-Web devices, however, have no such limitations. A century and a half later, the perfected telegraph has arrived, and Bennett's prophecy is being fulfilled.

≈

On the morning of June 30, 2012, about twenty hours after *SCOTUSblog* had broken news of the U.S. Supreme Court's decision on health care, the country's newspapers hit the streets with headlines such as "Health-Care Law Upheld" (*Washington Post*), "STILL STANDING" (*USA Today*), "Court Backs Obama on Health Care" (*Wall Street Journal*), and, more cleverly, "CLEAN BILL OF HEALTH" (*Chicago Sun-Times*).[43] Similar headlines could still be found that morning on many news organizations' websites. Did they think their readers hadn't already learned this news? Were they convinced everyone needed yesterday's big news restated for them? Did they feel some obligation to record this momentous event for history—even though history is now being recorded on the Web in general, as currently organized by Google, not on any particular website?

My guess is that many of our journalists are simply stuck in an outdated paradigm. They continue to believe their job is to announce what happened, despite the fact that most people already know what happened. The time of "the news paradigm," writes the German journalism scholar Horst Pöttker, "has come to a close."[44]

For it isn't working. There is less and less money to be made with yesterday's news. It has lost much of its ability to surprise, inform, entertain, and therefore bring eyes to ads. There is not even much money to be made with the previous hour's news—not when hundreds of others are also trying to make money off of the previous hour's news. If, in other words, our news organizations remain in the business of routine news gathering—even if they remain in the business of routine news gathering for dissemination online—the prophecy about their future currently being proclaimed by their circulation charts and demographics will in due time be fulfilled.

Yes, Craig's List made off with the lucrative classified advertisements. Yes, print as a medium is dying. Yes, old news organizations were slow in establishing themselves on the new "platforms" that technology and our intrepid entrepreneurs have been creating. Yes, online pages are too plentiful for ads on them to bring what ads in print used to bring. Yes, online pay walls threaten to chase off audiences as they raise revenues. These are huge problems. But the current crisis in journalism, I am arguing, is also very much a crisis in our understanding of journalism: the day of the *news* organization has ended.

No disrespect for news intended. In one of my books, *A History of News*, I make the case that the importance of news for humankind has, if anything, been underappreciated. But that doesn't mean the dissemination of news will remain what it was for about a century and a half: a big business.

Jill Abramson of the *New York Times* is correct when she writes, "There is a human craving for trustworthy information about the world we live in."[45] *Times* media columnist David Carr is correct when he writes, "News is the killer app."[46] But if Abramson thinks there will always be big money in satisfying that craving, if Carr thinks this app will remain lucrative, they are probably wrong. If either of them still thinks that reporting news is the highest form of journalism, then I believe them to be wrong.

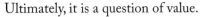

Ultimately, it is a question of value.

The Internet has proven a great and rapid depleter of value. The cost of making available anything that can be transformed into bits—music, video, readings, games, classified ads, university lectures, and most definitely news—has fallen essentially to zero. The supply of everything that can be turned into bits has consequently been exploding. News is everywhere. Journalists must therefore offer something less common, less cheap.

A few of the more traditional and respected ways of adding value to a news publication or newscast still apply in this world of information excess. They have one thing in common: they are exclusives.

One of my theses in this book is that run-of-the-mill news reporting is less demanding and enlightening than many old city editors and some long-tenured journalism professors have led us to believe. However, a reporter does sometimes manage to secure a vantage point that webcams and other reporters do not or cannot occupy—at the scene of some atrocity somewhere, perhaps. In such circumstances, Bill Keller's old-fashioned "going places, bearing witness" certainly can add journalistic value, even moral value. And sometimes a source does pass on something eye-opening to just one trusted reporter. Or an exclusive may, in fact, be the result of "digging into records, developing sources"—other activities Keller celebrates.

Most journalists join in that celebration, but Paul Krugman, an economics professor–*New York Times* columnist hybrid, has a significant hesitation. He notes that "a lot of political journalism, and even reporting on policy issues, is dominated by the search for . . . the insider who knows What's Really Going On. Background interviews with top officials are regarded as gold." But, as Krugman argues, there is reason for a bit of cynicism here. "Such inside scoops are rarely—I won't say never, but rarely—worth a thing," he writes. "My experience has been that careful analysis of publicly available information almost always trumps the insider approach."[47] Krugman buys "digging into records," in other words; he is less impressed by "developing sources."

His point is self-serving, as Krugman himself acknowledges: as an economist, he has great fluency with "publicly available information." But that point cannot be ignored. Sources often allow themselves to be developed and then leak for purposes of their own—purposes that don't always coincide with the public good. And more scoops undoubtedly are hiding in plain sight than reporters realize—obtainable by research and analysis, not by chumminess or stealth. Nonetheless, exclusives and investigations can have significant value.

On the same day that the front page of the *New York Times* featured its day-old account of that G-20 agreement, it also carried an exposé on the death of a Pakistani immigrant being detained in a New Jersey jail.[48] This is an example of a particularly noble variety of exclusive: investigative reporting. It, too, expands our store of knowledge. It should, no doubt, be part of any value-added approach to journalism.[49]

Traditional journalists make much of such exclusives, as well they should, but they exaggerate the amount of news that is observed, exposed, dug up by one reporter exclusively. This is the misunderstanding behind one of the most passionately raised defenses of newspapers.

"Newspapers dig up the news," is how John S. Carroll, a former editor of the *Los Angeles Times*, phrases the point. "Others repackage it."[50] There is some truth here. Just about every day the front page of the *New York Times*, the *Washington Post*, or, perhaps less frequently now, the *Los Angeles Times* contains an investigation or another exclusive that everybody else's website will have to link to, "scrape" (in the current vernacular), or steal. Should newspapers continue to devote reporters to this pursuit? Of course. It is certainly one way to distinguish themselves from the competition.

But the bulk of the news that fills front pages and newscasts each day is not exclusive: it does not require all that much digging, and it is not dependent on newspapers and their veteran reporters for its exposure. Most news, in fact, is announced rather than uncovered.[51] Is great purpose really served by having a reporter from the *Washington Post* standing next to the CNN camera and the AP reporter at each of the day's major press conferences? (Reuters finance blogger Felix Salmon rather tartly dismisses this as "the idiotic syndrome whereby hundreds of journalists from loads of different publications all descend on the same press conference or event, and all file virtually-identical copy."[52]) Are newspapers really contributing significantly to journalism by making sure their reporters are somewhere in the crowd around the sheriff and the fire chief when they are providing the gory details? There are pressrooms at most major news events. Do we care whether there are four or forty or four hundred reporters in them?

Exclusives are rare, too, when the documents upon which they might be based—transcripts, reports, budgets, Supreme Court decisions—are widely available, as they increasingly are nowadays on the Web. *SCOTUSblog*'s well-earned exclusive lasted minutes; its lead on the competition did not survive the hour.

News is mostly not the result of some lonely and intrepid newspaper reporter digging into something. And journalists cannot depend exclusively on such exclusives to give their work value. There aren't enough of them. Even the *New York Times* and the *Washington Post* with their battalions of veteran reporters and their reputations as destinations of choice for leaks usually don't succeed in filling their front pages each day with major scoops.

Fortunately, there is another tack our better journalists might take in the face of this oversupply of rapid, reasonably reported, nonexclusive news. We are not talking fluff. In a world that retains its habit of flirting with disaster, there's plenty of room for journalism on serious topics. We are undoubtedly talking interpretation—thoughtful, incisive attempts to divine the meaning of events. Our major journalism organizations might more often pull back from the race for breaking news and attempt to produce—at daily, not hourly, speed—the most insightful interpretations of that news. They might more often sell something more thoughtful than another account of the day's or the previous day's news.

When James Gordon Bennett Sr. predicted the demise of "mere newspapers" at the hand of the telegraph, he suggested that "magazine literature" might survive.[53] If journalism organizations are to withstand this current assault by the Internet—the ultimate telegraph—they must cease to be what Bennett called "circulators of intelligence merely" and take a cue from our more serious magazines. Journalism must become more insightful. Journalists must once again provide "discussion and explanation"; they must once again "aspire" to the role of "teacher and guide."

After all, interpretative articles, if they're smart and original enough, are also exclusive: wire-service reporters are unlikely to be peddling the same perspective all over the Web. Our best journalists might devote themselves, the point is, not to the dissemination of news, but to the promulgation of wisdom about news.

When a town is crowded with supermarkets, groceries, and farm stands, most distributing food for free, there is no longer a business in selling food. A better strategy is to try—as our best chefs do—to sell unique, high-quality ways of preparing that food.

Our best, most expert journalists should devote themselves to preparing gourmet, if you will, interpretations of news.

4

"BYE-BYE TO THE OLD 'WHO-WHAT-WHEN-WHERE'"

The Return of Interpretation

After big news breaks—a major Supreme Court decision, for instance—we get the traditional, now absurdly overcrowded, race to report it. But these days a second competition then begins for American journalists—one that was not a large part of the twentieth-century tradition: a contest to see who can best help us grasp the meaning of what has happened.

Jonathan Cohn, a blogger for the *New Republic*, had displayed a special interest in President Obama's health-care bill. On June 28, 2012, at 10:26 A.M., eighteen minutes after *SCOTUSblog* first announced the Supreme Court's decision on the constitutionality of the Affordable Care Act, Cohn presented his highly partisan perspective: "In issuing this ruling, the Court has not only validated the Affordable Care Act. It has also validated its own reputation."[1]

Ezra Klein was probably the most widely read health-care act obsessive and supporter. On his *Washington Post* blog, he offered his take twenty-one minutes after Cohn:

This will be covered, in many quarters, as a political story. It means President Obama—and Solicitor General Don Verrilli—are popping the champagne. It means that Mitt Romney and the Republicans who were fighting the health-care law have suffered a setback. It will be covered in other quarters as a legal story: It is likely to be central to [Chief

Justice John] Roberts's legacy, and perhaps even to how we understand
the divisions in the Court going forward.

And, to be sure, it's all those things. But those stories don't capture
the effect this decision will have on ordinary Americans.

The individual mandate, by bringing healthy people into the
insurance market and lowering premiums, means health insurance
for between 12.5 million and 24 million more Americans.[2]

Speed counts in this new competition to interpret the news, as it does
in anything involving news. Some of us will inevitably be clicking around,
hungry for some fast views. But such contests, unlike the traditional race
to report the news, are won in the end not by speed, but by wisdom.

Jonathan Chait, another journalist who had been consumed by the
health-care bill, did not publish his extended analysis for a full hour
and a quarter after *SCOTUSblog* broke the news of the decision. That
relatively laggard—in Internet terms only—analysis rested on two liberal fears. Chait, blogging for *New York* magazine, credited the first
to legal journalist Jeffrey Rosen: the fear that conservatives on the
Court would succeed in imposing what Rosen calls "the Constitution
in Exile"—an alternative view of constitutional law based on the belief
that the Constitution had been desecrated by decades of liberal decisions allowing for expanded federal powers. "A second, darker fear,"
Chait wrote, "was that five Republican-appointed justices would con-
coct a ruling in order to win a huge battle that their party had lost in
Congress—that partisan *Bush v. Gore*-style rulings would now become
regular features of the political scene." Chait then wrote: "The two fears
were, of course, deeply intertwined. What happened, and what hardly
anybody expected was that they diverged. The second fear was deci-
sively refuted: Thankfully, the Court allowed the one reform to our dys-
functional health-care system after decades of paralysis to stand. The
first fear is very much alive."[3]

Chait continued for hundreds of words. Seven minutes later Andrew
Sullivan—live blogging at the *Daily Beast*—managed to be insightful in
only thirty: "To me, the most fascinating part of this is that John Roberts

has revealed himself as an institutional conservative rather than a radical reactionary (as his party has now become)."[4]

Journalists opposed to Obamacare were, dare I say, somewhat underrepresented in this new world of expert, interpretive blogging. But that point of view, too, was certainly expressed. Megan McArdle, who now blogs for the *Daily Beast*, was not heard from for an hour and forty-eight minutes after that initial *SCOTUSblog* report. She began with a touch of philosophy: "As I predicted, my day lilies are still blooming beautifully, I'm still married to the love of my life, and the Commissars do not seem to have started liquidating the kulaks yet." Then McArdle contributed analysis: "Obviously, I would have preferred this decision to go the other way. I also would have preferred a decision [that] made sense. . . . The Court has rewritten the mandate as a tax, even though everyone who passed it said it wasn't one. There's dim hope in the fact that they refused to expand the commerce clause—but only dim, because future expansions of the commerce clause are going to be decided more by the future composition of the court than by this ruling."[5]

This being the Internet age, the clicking public was offered commentary not only by expert journalists, but by experts themselves. Here, too, *SCOTUSblog* excelled. At 3:41 that afternoon, it posted an enthusiastic analysis of the Supreme Court decision by Laurence Tribe, a Harvard law professor: "Today, Chief Justice John Roberts delivered a heroic rebuke to the growing number of Americans who feared the Supreme Court had lost the ability to rise above the narrow-minded partisanship that dominates the country's political discourse."[6]

At 6:10 that evening, *SCOTUSblog* let us hear from an opponent of the health-care act, Jonathan Adler, a professor at Case Western Reserve University School of Law, with a position that seemed the mirror image of Chait's: "While the Court upheld the [Affordable Care Act], it reaffirmed the foundational principles of the nation's constitutional structure and confirmed that the federalism decisions of the Rehnquist Court were not aberrations. In a very real sense," Adler added, "proponents of federalism may have lost the battle, but won the war."[7] Professors Tribe and Adler were among sixteen legal experts of various political stripes whom *SCOTUSblog* asked for their considered interpretations and most intelligible prose that day and the next.[8]

All these interpretations—by journalists, by experts—were instantly available to anyone with an Internet connection. Few if any of these interpretations would have been available to anyone except readers of a few weekly opinion magazines and acquaintances of the individuals who hatched them without the Internet. Most would not exist if American journalism were not in the midst of an often-overlooked interpretation boom.

The twentieth century in the United States, as I have noted, was the high-point of the just-the-facts mode of journalism. Nonetheless, viewers who turned on their television sets to watch *See It Now* on CBS on March 9, 1954, heard the following from one of the country's top journalists:

> The line between investigating and persecuting is a very fine one and the junior Senator from Wisconsin has stepped over it repeatedly. His primary achievement has been in confusing the public mind, as between the internal and the external threats of Communism. We must not confuse dissent with disloyalty. We must remember always that accusation is not proof and that conviction depends upon evidence and due process of law. We will not walk in fear, one of another. We will not be driven by fear into an age of unreason. . . . We are not descended from fearful men—not from men who feared to write, to speak, to associate and to defend causes that were, for the moment, unpopular.[9]

That was Edward R. Murrow, among the best-known broadcast journalists in the United States at the time, helping to bring down Senator Joseph McCarthy. The senator's wild accusations of Communist penetration had cowed many journalists and politicians. Murrow and his producer, Fred Friendly, were not cowed.

In these sentences at the conclusion of their CBS documentary on McCarthy, Murrow was making an "argument"—complete with powerfully stated "propositions" and "claims." And he had no doubt wandered into the "subjective," as Carlota Smith defines it: he was presenting a perspective and performing an evaluation.[10] On this network television news program in the United States in the middle of the twentieth century, Murrow and Friendly found a means of going beyond the facts and saying boldly what they thought of Senator McCarthy's tactics.

The truth is that in a country with a free press, interpretive, opinionated journalism never entirely disappears. Some remarkably insightful commentary managed to find its way into corners of American journalism even in the twentieth century.

Indeed, when it comes time in chapter 6 for me to delineate varieties of what I am calling "wisdom journalism," almost all of my grandest examples will come from the twentieth century: Lincoln Steffens using his investigations of municipal corruption for *McClure's Magazine* at the very beginning of the century to indict, of all people, the American people, for allowing it; the young Walter Lippmann lamenting in the *New Republic* in 1914 humankind's tragic enthrallment with war; Dorothy Thompson in *Cosmopolitan* assessing in 1931 an up-and-coming German politician she had just interviewed, Adolf Hitler; James Baldwin describing in the *Partisan Review* in 1959 his visit to the segregated American South; A. J. Liebling in the *New Yorker* in 1960 summarizing in one sentence the limits of freedom of the press in the United States; Rachel Carson launching the environmental movement in 1962 with a *New Yorker* article and her book *Silent Spring;* I. F. Stone in his own publication in 1965 debunking U.S. government statements on the Vietnam War; Tom Wolfe in *New York* in 1970 analyzing and having some fun with a sudden vogue in upper-class, liberal Manhattan society: supporting the radical Black Panthers; and Joan Didion in the *New York Review of Books* in 1982 conducting a tour of an El Salvador dominated by death squads.

This work belongs to an alternate history of twentieth-century journalism in the United States—one mostly unconstrained by the five W's. However, none of these trenchant perspectives appeared, it is important to note, in a newspaper or newsweekly. Only one, Murrow's, was aired on television, on CBS, and the network's executives refused to advertise it.[11] I. F. Stone started his own tiny, one-man weekly in part because he could find no other place in journalism at the time for his left-leaning, often antigovernment analyses.[12] This was not the journalism being emphasized at most journalism schools in the twentieth century. It was not the journalism being practiced by most journalists. It was not the journalism being experienced by most viewers and readers. These pieces were, in other words, exceptions: glimmerings of interpretive acumen scattered about a mostly fact-obsessed field.

Indeed, the case can be made that the citizens of the United States, most of whom were left to drink from the mainstream, suffered through interpretation privation in the middle of the twentieth century—in the years *before* Edward R. Murrow finally took on Senator Joseph McCarthy; in the decades *before* the press explored, along with James Baldwin, the degradations and injustices of racial segregation; in the years *before* most of the mainstream press joined I. F. Stone in seeing the extent of the U.S. failure in Vietnam.

Mainstream American journalism, to be fair, was not entirely interpretation free even when the veneration of the fact was particularly intense—even, in other words, in the 1950s, 1960s, and 1970s. Newspapers in those decades did have columnists weighing in on the issues of the day—their Walter Lippmanns (the older, less compelling version) and James Restons, their Joseph Alsops and Mary McGrorys. Newspapers did still trumpet their points of view—or their publishers'—in editorials. Walter Cronkite would even surrender the camera for a minute or so on the *CBS Evening News* to Eric Sevareid for his undeniably well-crafted but scrupulously inoffensive "commentaries."

These small appendages to large news organs can be seen, for the most part, as vestigial remnants of a much earlier age in American journalism—Jürgen Habermas's golden age. Pieces bold enough to do more than report the facts had been rounded up and corralled on one or two separate pages—the editorial page, joined later by the op-ed page—or, in their most neutered form, in one or two minutes on television.

Meanwhile, slower news media—weeklies in this age of dailies—survived by occupying more analytical niches in the journalism ecology, as slower media usually do. The cosmopolitan, left-leaning intelligentsia had the ad-rich *New Yorker*—probably the repository of more of what qualifies as wisdom journalism than any other publication or broadcast for much of the twentieth century and so far for the twenty-first. *Time* and *Newsweek* reached larger audiences with for the most part less penetrating analyses and investigations. "Newsmagazines," they were called. Although they presented themselves as news digests, they did regularly step back and function as interpret-the-news magazines. Their articles restricted themselves, however, predominantly to safe, mainstream comments; paths were not frequently broken. The few magazines that hazarded strong points of view—the *Nation* and the *New Republic* on the left, the *National Review* on the right—reached relatively small audiences.

You don't have to share Habermas's nostalgia for the eighteenth century to believe that news alone is not enough, that the public dialogue also benefits from a healthy flow of ideas and insights, points of view, and analyses. For most of the second half of the twentieth century, in the newspapers and newscasts that were the country's major journalistic outlets these more interpretive forms of journalism were in short supply.

Even as late as 2006, mainstream journalism's consumers were still being confronted with situations as odd as this: In an opinion column, David Brooks of the *New York Times* introduced his "War Council"—the "twenty or thirty people" who because of the soundness of their "judgments" and "analysis" he turned to for wisdom about the ongoing Iraq War. One of those people worked at Brooks's own paper, *Times* "übercorrespondent" and Baghdad bureau chief John F. Burns. Brooks featured two quotes from Burns about Iraq in his column, including this assessment of prospects for the U.S. effort there: "I'd have to say the odds are against success, but they are better now than they were three months ago, that's for sure." However, neither of those quotes was from the newspaper that employs Burns, where he ventured beyond the facts only rarely and very cautiously. Instead, they were comments Burns made on the PBS program *Charlie Rose*.[13]

"We would be of little value in our television appearances," Burns later acknowledged in an email interview with me, "if we offered no more than a bare-bones recitation of events, without any attempt to place them in a wider context, and to analyze what they mean."[14] But why shouldn't the same standard of "value" apply to his "appearances" in his own newspaper?

Burns denies that *Times* reporters "are muzzled in conveying the full range of our experience and impressions" under the proper rubrics in the paper. Nonetheless, the "impressions" from this *Times* correspondent that most interested a *Times* columnist did not originally appear in the *Times*.

John Burns is very skilled at traditional reporting, and the factual reporting he and other correspondents produced during the Iraq War certainly contributed to understanding of that war. But recording official statements, getting the body counts right, airing both sides, and exposing the occasional scandal no longer seem sufficient. Non-"bare-bones" interpretations of events of the sort Burns verbalized on *Charlie Rose* were sometimes of more "value" in understanding a major event than news articles in the *New York Times* in the twentieth century and into the twenty-first. Are such interpretations not crucial in helping us think out the merits and consequences of occurrences such as wars?

We are reminded that the traditional emphasis upon news is costing us understandings every time a *Washington Post* staffer publishes a book analyzing the workings of an administration, leaving some *Post* readers wondering why more of those insights did not appear in the newspaper. There was an example of this, too—one that did not involve Bob Woodward—during the Iraq War: Thomas E. Ricks's scathing indictment of the Bush administration's prosecution of that war, *Fiasco: The American Military Adventure in Iraq.*[15] The *Wall Street Journal* also had a hint of this problem during that war when an email from one of its reporters in Iraq that found its way out onto the Web proved not only more controversial, but more interesting than the stories she had been filing: "For those of us on the ground," reporter Farnaz Fassihi wrote about Iraq, "it's hard to imagine what if anything could salvage [this war] from its violent downward spiral."[16]

Interpretation was already spiraling upward by the time the Iraq War had begun spiraling downward. It had begun to escape its corrals, to return to an earlier metaphor. The radio had been among the places this happened first, if often ingloriously. Hosts who commented upon the news, often loudly, had begun drawing larger audiences than newscasters who just read the news every hour. Rush Limbaugh had predecessors. Rush Limbaugh had competitors. And Rush Limbaugh had been attracting many millions of listeners.

And then television fragmented. For decades, American viewers had been limited to three major national networks with three, mostly interchangeable, cheery morning news shows and three, mostly interchangeable, sober evening newscasts, along with some Sunday morning press-conference-like programs. Local newscasts were chattier and, if anything, even more allergic to controversy. CNN debuted in 1980—an alternative source of news twenty-four hours a day. Then in 1996 Fox News Channel and MSNBC joined the competition. And public television had begun weighing in more frequently on public affairs with what became the *NewsHour* and later with shows such as *Charlie Rose.*

Fox was the real game changer: it came from behind in the cable-news ratings race and gained a commanding lead by doing something odd for television, odd for what was then American journalism, but not odd from the perspective of journalism history: Fox News Channel asserted some opinions; it leaned right. After many failed iterations, MSNBC found its niche in the new ecosystem—the ecology metaphor is useful here—by leaning left, or "forward" as one of its slogans would have it. And CNN, the original cable-news network, which still honored the old television and twentieth-century journalism ethic of trying not to lean in any direction, fell behind in the competition for viewers.

The biggest changes, however, came once again with the Internet. Blogs, though mostly unsupported by reporting staffs, certainly have demonstrated an ability to compete in the news race. And if they focus enough on a specialty—as young Brian Stelter did on the subject of television news or *SCOTUSblog* has on the Supreme Court—they can score significant victories in that race: scoops. But blogs—informal, personal, opinionated—mostly offer interpretation.

For "horse race" fanatics, those interpretations of campaign polls by statistics-maven Nate Silver began to seem indispensable during the 2008 and 2012 presidential campaigns. Analyses of the health-care debate of 2009 by policy-wonk wunderkind Ezra Klein began to echo around American journalism and politics. And then there were the evaluations of responses to the financial crash in 2008 by, of all people, economics professors: Brad DeLong of Berkeley and Tyler Cowen of George Mason University, are examples. Opinions, analyses, and perspectives on current events were beginning to roam wild once again with blogs.

Provocative, insightful interpretations were showing up all over this vaster, freer journalistic ecology. Older news media, too, became gradually more interpretive.[17] In the early years of the twenty-first century, however, tradition still dictated that newspaper front pages, newspaper home pages, and network evening newscasts—still the most valuable parcels of journalistic real estate—be devoted primarily not to teaching or guiding, but to retelling what was by now old news.

Let's return to coverage of that G-20 meeting back in London in April 2009. More interesting, more insightful perspectives on the accomplishments of that gathering of world leaders than in all those read-alike news reports did appear in the hours after the announcement. Some writers praised rich countries' willingness to support so much additional IMF aid to developing countries—particularly in hard-hit eastern Europe; others pondered the worthiness of the IMF, with its history of imposing tight strictures, as the dispenser of such large sums. One raised the question of whether all this money being lent out by the IMF wouldn't in fact come from the sort of Keynesian money-printing stimulus the Americans and British supposedly had failed to secure in London. Don't such provocative perspectives provide more of what we "need to be an engaged citizen," to recall Bill Keller's phrasing, than yet another outline of an increasingly familiar agreement, even enlivened by a scorecard on who might have won what at the meeting?

These commentaries appeared on the websites of, for example, the *Economist* and the *Guardian*, in the blog Ezra Klein was then writing for the *American Prospect*, and even in a business column on page A12 of the next day's *Washington Post*.[18] Such provocative perspectives were in short supply, however, on the front pages of the *New York Times* and the *Washington Post* the next morning.

But that, too, was beginning to change. Maybe a correction was unavoidable because traditional journalism had gone too far in the other direction. Perhaps newspapers and newscasts simply stumbled upon interpretation. Maybe newspapers were learning more from blogs than they realized. There isn't much evidence that editors or producers talked it out and decided that adding more interpretation was a way for them to add value in a news-saturated world. But it was.

The front page of the *Washington Post* on March 6, 2009, caused a bit of a stir. A blog sponsored by *Washingtonian* magazine attacked it for supposedly carrying "no news." "Welcome to the new age of daily newspapering," writer Harry Jaffe protested on that blog, "where the actual news of the day has migrated to the Internet or TV or radio or the inside pages of the paper. Bye-bye to the old 'who-what-when-where-why.'"[19]

What Jaffe had spotted was that none of the six stories on page one that day had a traditional five W's lead paragraph. All were important stories: about a sinking economy and plans to improve it (four of them), about Rush Limbaugh and Republican politics, about hunger in North Korea. But instead of just reporting what happened yesterday—though there was a fair amount of that, too—these stories considered; they characterized; they investigated; they measured effects and looked behind the scenes. They were doing quite a bit that day of what they should do a great deal of every day.

This is one sign that my argument isn't as radical as it may seem (or that it isn't as revelatory as I want it to seem). More and more interpretation is already appearing in newspapers and on newscasts. Not just in editorials. Not just in columns, op-ed pieces, and commentaries. Not just segregated on its own pages or segments.

On June 29, 2012, three years after that remarked-upon *Washington Post* front page, the *New York Times* produced a page one of its own that was in large part devoted to interpretation. The subject was the Supreme Court's health-care decision the previous morning. Yes, some of the interpretation in the *Times* that day was confined to the traditional places— the op-ed and editorial pages. And, yes, the paper's front page that day displayed a traditional, appropriately large banner headline, trumpeting what by then just about all *Times* readers already knew: "JUSTICES BY 5–4, UPHOLD HEALTH CARE LAW; ROBERTS IN MAJOR-ITY; VICTORY FOR OBAMA." And, yes, on the top right, there sat a five W's news story on the decision—recapping what, by then, just about all *Times* readers already knew.

However, page one of the *Times* that day was dominated by a large infographic explaining, with pictures, the various alliances the justices had formed on the key issues in the case. And that front page also featured three interpretive articles: the first, labeled "news analysis," focused on the "exquisite delicacy" of Chief Justice John G. Roberts Jr.'s decision; another contemplated the Republican response; and the third assessed the implications of the decision for President Barack Obama.

By 2012, interpretation had established a large beachhead on newspaper front pages. This change in *practice*—a move by some of our best journalists in their most valued spaces away from the mere recording of events—is still hugely, frustratingly incomplete, but it is under way.

Analysis is the journalist's preferred term for such efforts to go beyond mere reportage—probably because it sounds clinical and therefore objective. (The requisite change in mainstream journalism's *mindset* has an even longer way to go.) Some stories in some papers are even anointed with that special designation: "news analysis." On September 9, 2009— in another sign that both the times and the *Times* are changing—a piece so designated was accorded the lead position on the front page of the *New York Times*. It was written by Sheryl Gay Stolberg.

Sometimes these "news analysis" pieces earn that designation—Stolberg's piece on the health-care debate certainly did. It had a real point to make: that a health-care plan along the lines President Obama favored had a better likelihood of passage than "conventional wisdom," as reported in recent news accounts, made it seem.[20] The *Times*'s front-page "news analysis" on the Supreme Court's health-care decision two and a half years later was also more than just another news report; it, too, had something to say.

Sometimes, however, "news analysis" articles don't quite achieve this. These pieces are often limited by the traditional journalists' reluctance to be found guilty of having a point of view. They consequently depend just as heavily as news stories on the comments of mostly official sources.

The *New York Times* did run a "news analysis" on the front page the day after that G-20 summit concluded, but that "news analysis" didn't seem much more analytic than the news story on the summit agreement that ran above it.[21] In fairness, that says something not just about the limitations of that "news analysis" piece, but about what has been happening to news stories. Reporters have been granted increased leeway to characterize—however tepidly—not just transcribe in news stories themselves.

One quick, limited survey may help demonstrate that. In the main *New York Times* story every four or eight years reporting on the first speech given before a joint session of Congress by Presidents Truman through Carter, somewhere between 18 and 37 percent of the words were direct quotes from the speech.[22] In those same stories on Presidents Reagan through Obama, 17 to as few as 8 percent of the words were taken by the *Times* reporter directly from the speech. This rough measure confirms what careful newspaper readers may already have noticed: news stories are less stenographic than they used to be. If you look through news articles from Truman's day to Obama's, wordings that imply some sort of reportorial judgment, such as "thinly veiled swipe," begin to appear more, and direct verbs of attribution—*declared*, for example—are found less.[23]

What is called "analysis" has also burgeoned on television news. On the evening newscasts of the three traditional networks, presumably nonpartisan commentators take a seat beside the anchor and then are asked to step back for larger meanings or to step up with inside dope; the late Tim Russert, who hosted *Meet the Press* but regularly appeared on the *NBC Nightly News*, established the type. The change can even be seen on the proudly, stubbornly nonpartisan CNN. After a major news story has been introduced on one of its news shows, the anchor will turn to "our panel" for some perspective upon it—often partisan perspective, albeit from representatives of what are labeled "both sides." Meanwhile, on FOX and MSNBC, as on talk radio, the anchors are often quite prepared to supply the partisan perspective themselves.

Although I fall back on this word often enough, *analysis* may not, in fact, be the best term for this phenomenon because its primary meaning is "to break down into component parts in search of understanding." Sometimes in that search for understanding journalists synthesize rather than analyze. Sometimes they offer context, background, or a peek behind scenes. Sometimes, unembarrassed by the ad hominem, they connect policy to personal style. Sometimes they explain, predict, or conclude. The most partisan celebrate or more commonly bemoan or even excoriate.

The term *interpretation*—the act of coming up with a meaning, an explanation, or a significance—seems better able to encompass the broad repertoire of tunes such commentators sing. But *interpretation* apparently sounds more subjective. It has made some traditional journalists uncomfortable.[24] The *New York Times* labels some stories on its news pages "news analysis," not "news interpretation."

Indeed, this whole business of moving beyond the mere telling of news has made some traditional journalists uncomfortable even as they have tiptoed in that direction. That explains why the *Post* could be attacked in 2009 for its "newsless" front page and why the paper's then relatively new executive editor, Marcus Brauchli, felt called upon to respond to the charge that he lacked proper devotion to news. The way he phrased that response is instructive.

Brauchli professed a commitment to "tell our readers . . . why it's happening, how it might affect them and what's likely to happen next."[25] He acknowledged—in other words (mine, not his)—that interpretation should be part of the paper's mission, its front-page mission. But before he said that, Brauchli had to establish his bona fides as a "newsman." He had to pay obeisance to the mission that had dominated the old and romanticized "age of daily newspapering." "We tell our readers what's happening," Brauchli insisted, as his predecessors would have insisted. No matter, apparently, that most of those readers—because we have radio and television, because we have the Internet—often already know what happened.

The Global Editors Network was founded at the beginning of the second decade of the twenty-first century by, as its website puts it, "editors-in-chief and senior news executives from around the world . . . working on different platforms." It is refreshingly international, with more than six hundred members from more than fifty countries. Its board includes individuals from the *New York Times*, *El País*, BBC, and *Le Monde* as well as "innovators and media thinkers." Indeed, the Global Editors Network professes to be forward looking: high on the organization's list of goals, in its "manifesto," is the task of defining "a vision for the future of journalism."

That manifesto also proclaims a commitment to "enhance the quality of journalism in its different dimensions." Those dimensions include "newsgathering, news curation, storytelling, fact and data checking, designing, moderating and sharing, regardless of the platform, browser or application used."[26] This sounds like an up-to-the-minute summary of where journalism is heading—with one significant oversight: there is no acknowledgment here that among journalism's "dimensions" might be helping people understand the significance of the news that has been gathered, curated, checked, designed, moderated, and shared.

The point is that, for the most part, our shrinking troop of reporters and editors has entered this perilous new era with an old view of what they are doing. Nothing surprising here: mindsets, as noted, do tend to lag. "When you've finally figured something out and know how to judge it," notes Ana Marie Cox, "having to judge some new thing is tough."[27] Journalists had learned to conceive of themselves and judge themselves as gatherers of news.

Most journalists today realize they must stay up to date. The "global editors" have made an effort to master a new vocabulary: *platforms, curation, sharing*. But "minds and hearts," to return to John Adams's phrase, that have been devoted to one vision of an enterprise usually have great difficulty surrendering it in favor of an alternative vision. Journalism has been witnessing an explosion in interpretation in recent years, but quite a few "editors-in-chief and senior news executives from around the world" either haven't realized that or haven't grasped its significance.

That is one reason why the appearance in newspapers or traditional newscasts of these more interpretive pieces has remained sporadic and unpredictable—even at the *Washington Post* when Brauchli was in charge. (He was replaced as executive editor in 2013.) They have remained sporadic and unpredictable, too, at the *New York Times*.

By 2012, the realization had mostly arrived that after some hours had passed on a major story such as the Supreme Court's health-care-act decision, readers would expect some effort at interpretation. On less momentous events, however, journalists' attention to what to some of them may still feel like "some new" and suspect "thing" is much less diligent. A more analytic piece often illuminates the major news event of the day (or, in print, the major news event of yesterday), but sometimes readers must make do with only the traditional account. And in a newspaper or on a newspaper website, there is no guarantee that a columnist, an op-ed contributor, or an editorial will bother to take up the subject on that day; these personages and pages operate by their own more leisurely schedules—their own whims.

The efforts of mainstream American journalism to explore the territory beyond the straight reporting of news have, in other words, been tentative, spotty, and unreliable.

Indeed, many journalists today remain unable to extricate themselves from the ruins of an old, outdated journalism. The problem is not just that newspapers, still obsessed with keeping some sort of record, give us headlines like the one displayed on the top of the front page of the *New York Times* on August 29, 2012, five months *after* Mitt Romney clinched the 2012 Republican presidential nomination in the primaries: "ROMNEY SECURES G.O.P. NOMINATION AFTER LONG QUEST." (He had just been officially nominated.) It is not just that they still cannot resist telling us what happened "yesterday." The problems run deeper.

Perhaps the traditional American form of journalism has simply been around too long. It seems at times to have grown not just sclerotic, but lackluster, as in the headline atop the lead story in the *New York Times* on the morning of October 4, 2012: "Obama and Romney, in First Debate, Spar Over Fixing the Economy"—as if it is newsworthy that the state of the economy was an issue at a debate in 2012, as if there were nothing more interesting to announce about a debate in which the challenger and underdog seemed, by all accounts, to have outperformed the incumbent and favorite.

The selection of events, yesterday or today, upon which these journalists feel obligated to brief us has also grown overly familiar and often dull. It is constrained by the old beat system.

A civic purpose undeniably is served by having trained reporters stationed, for example, at city hall—as sentries or representatives of the citizenry. Services and taxes are still being determined there. But as we spend more time in communities of interest rather than in our geographical communities, our fascination with city hall—our belief that the parameters of our lives are being determined there—may perhaps lessen. Moreover, the mayor's press conferences and city council meetings can now often be viewed on cable or YouTube. Transcripts, minutes, notices, meeting agendas are often available, if not always easy to access, online. Those local-government obsessives who are left now have, along with the right to declaim at meetings, blogs and Twitter feeds. And similar networks of online civic information are beginning to surround state houses and, to an extent, the criminal justice system.

The newspaper, wire-service beat system sent reporters to civic buildings, courthouses, and war zones. Radio and television networks and stations managed their own scaled-down versions. This was among the great contributions of nineteenth- and twentieth-century just-the-facts journalism: it helped illuminate the world.[28] But the world is beginning to be reasonably well lit by other means—webcams, YouTube videos, Facebook pages, and all sorts of official, unofficial, insider/outsider postings.

And the world's inhabitants have, many of them, discovered interests beyond "Joplin City Council to Hear Comments on Grant Proposals"— a not atypical online newspaper headline, this one from the website of the *Joplin Globe* on August 19, 2012.[29] Editors have been trying to rethink beats for some decades now. Perhaps they should consider sending someone to cover the Joplin City Council who might have something to say about those grant proposals beyond the fact that comments upon them will be heard. Failing that, the agenda for the upcoming meeting might be left to the council's website.

Would we miss the old city-hall reporters were they to disappear entirely? No doubt. It is not at all clear that unpaid, Internet-savvy municipal-government aficionados will reliably be able to duplicate the reporters' tough questions, their eye for conflict, and their nose for scandal. They certainly haven't yet. I was not able to locate any website, besides that of the *Joplin Globe*, that mentioned those grant proposals that were to be discussed, in the wake of a devastating tornado, before the Joplin City Council. But the conversation on our still young online devices is likely to continue to broaden. And the disappearance of the sentries might not seem at all tragic if those beat reporters were to be replaced by journalists imbued with deeper understandings of government or journalists able to use political science or at least a familiarity with the exigencies of public policy to shed light on aspects of local government.

Reporters now covering those old beats lean heavily on quotes from sources. Quotations, or sound-bites in audio or video, serve a number of purposes in traditional journalism, purposes that I have cataloged in a couple of textbooks on traditional journalism. First, they are used to record statements by newsmakers that are "directive," "commissive," "expressive," or "declarations," to borrow John Searle's vocabulary. In news stories—reports—quotations also give eyewitnesses or those affected by an event the opportunity to be heard, to observe, or to opine.[30]

In the interpretive pieces argued for here, quotes may also provide evidence, concurrence, or other support for an argument. For example, the *New York Times* "news analysis" on the G-20 agreement, which was not that analytical, quoted a former IMF China division chief on President Obama's performance at that summit: he "has certainly guided the G-20 leaders to a positive outcome," that source suggested. "All in all, not a bad day's work."[31] This former official was a smart commentator, no doubt, but such quotations have always been a weak point, mostly unacknowledged, in traditional journalism.

Yes, it is crucial that journalists talk to plenty of knowledgeable individuals. It is crucial that they open their ears, as argued in chapter 1, to a wide variety of perspectives and points of view. Their writing, audio, or video is best fortified, tested, honed through chats (of the old-school or digital variety) with intelligent individuals conversant with that issue. Is this a skill some bloggers still need to master? It is. During Ezra Klein's meteoric rise as a blogger, he did a stint at the *Washington Monthly*. Here is what he says he learned from the more "formalized way of journalism" he was introduced to there: "You made calls," Klein told the *New York Times*. "People answered calls. You took down what was said in a respectable account, and that began to influence my blogging. It became a lot less of an 'Ezra affair.'"[32] Yes, the public deserves more than a Clever-but-Isolated-Blogger "affair."

However, traditional journalists sometimes appear to place too much weight on the quotations elicited in phone calls and other exchanges. Sources such as that former IMF China division chief quoted by the *New York Times* are usually being asked to expatiate on complex subjects extemporaneously. And then the reporter slices their comments, often part of extended arguments, into short quotations—with the source in question almost invariably denied a privilege journalists take for granted:

an opportunity to amend or polish their words. (Was Ezra Klein's statement quoted in the preceding paragraph, for example, phrased as felicitously as he would have liked?) This standard and accepted journalistic practice hardly encourages coherent and thorough interpretations—as most whose words have undergone it can attest. That is one reason why many experts have taken to presenting their own thoughts on their own blogs. That is one reason why the journalist the *New York Times* sends to write an analysis of an international economic summit should be as expert an observer as a former IMF China division chief.

Indeed, since traditional journalism discourages its practitioners from expressing their own conclusions, it often compels reporters who *do* know enough to evaluate a situation to put that evaluation into the mouth of a source. These ventriloquists often select as their dummies conveniently unnamed sources: the generic and all too ubiquitous "sources say" or "some observers suggest." In its coverage of that G-20 agreement in April 2009, the *New York Times* trotted out one of those always serviceable locutions—perhaps for this purpose, perhaps not: "The proposed remedies, some critics said, treat some peripheral effects of the crisis rather than its thorniest causes."[33]

When top economics and business reporter Peter S. Goodman left the *New York Times* in 2010 to join the online, more opinionated *Huffington Post*, his explanation included a complaint about this particular requirement of traditional journalism. Goodman explained to Howard Kurtz that at the *Times* he was reduced to "almost a process of laundering my own views, through the tried-and-true technique of dinging someone at some think tank to say what you want to tell the reader."[34] Rem Rieder quoted this statement in the *American Journalism Review*, which he edits, then added interesting evidence of his own: "That comment reminded me of the complaint I've heard over the years from expert reporters at *USA Today* who, because of the paper's strict sourcing rules, often find themselves forced to make points by quoting people who know far less about the subject at hand than they do."[35] "Some observers" think this practice is not only inefficient, but phony.

That is one reason why the "news analysis" that led the September 9, 2009, issue of the *New York Times* was refreshing. Reporter Sheryl Gay Stolberg, well versed on health-care politics, first wrote that "the conventional wisdom, here and around the country" was that the Democrats' health-care plan "is on life support and that only a political miracle could revive it." But then, in paragraph two of this, the lead story in the *New York Times* that day the reporter made an assertion on her own authority: "Here's why the conventional wisdom might be wrong," Stolberg wrote.[36] Even moderated, appropriately, by that "might," this qualifies as an unusually powerful assertion for a *New York Times* reporter. She did not write, "Some observers believe conventional wisdom might be wrong." She did not, to use Goodman's word, launder her views. In fact, Stolberg did not quote a source until the seventh paragraph of her story.

And her analysis—Stolberg's own analysis—proved correct. How long will it be before the *Times* routinely allows its expert reporters this freedom and stops losing journalists such as Peter Goodman? How long will it be before the expertise required for such analyses becomes the leading qualification for a position as a journalist?

Wiser journalists should also be better able to explain and evaluate what sources are telling them. Brad DeLong, now a top economics blogger, teaches economics at Berkeley; the late Susan Rasky taught journalism. Together they prepared a list of advice for reporters covering economics. "Never write 'economists disagree'" is high on that list. "Write WHY economists disagree."[37]

"Why" was always the most demanding of the five W's—and the most suspect. Any such effort to ascribe motives may smell vaguely subjective to the traditional journalist. Editors tended to resist the encroachment of such appraisals onto their "objective," carefully sourced pages. And going beyond a report on what so-and-so said on such-and-such a topic to saying *why* she said it can require much more questioning of so-and-so and others as well as a more comprehensive assessment of such-and-such. "Why," as a consequence, was often replaced in the formula by that non-alliterative but less controversial and easier to get at "how."

However, now that "who," "what," "when," and "where" have been cheapened by overexposure on the Internet, "why" has gained value. It requires thought. It sometimes requires expertise. Yet it provides an element often missing in traditional journalism: an explanation. When applied to sources, disagreeing or otherwise, the "why" enables journalists to get beyond a simple stenographic report of who is asserting what. It enables them to move toward deeper understandings.

This is all by way of arguing that journalists can no longer just fall back on "But that's what they said." Journalists have to think about why they said it, and journalists have to know enough or find out enough to be able to consider whether what they said is valid. This latter point, crucial to the argument for interpretation and against traditional notions of balance, will return in the next chapter.

Many journalists today—unclear about what is happening to their profession—are also having difficulty surrendering the old writing styles. The inverted pyramid, with a gaggle of honking W's forming its apex, can still be spotted with some frequency as traditional journalism heads south. CNN, for example (and examples of this are not difficult to find), used the following headline on its widely perused website in August 2012: "Walmart Shooting Followed Fight at Party, Police Say"; the story then began by essentially repeating that headline: "The four people shot outside a Cedar Park, Texas, Walmart over the weekend had gathered there to fight after an altercation at a party in a nearby city, police said Monday."[38]

Facts are, of course, valuable. Attribution—"police said"—is necessary. But when the facts are vague and unilluminating ("a nearby city") and when they are piled on top of each other like old cars in a junkyard, they contribute little in the way of understanding. It doesn't help when the facts are sheathed in words that only journalists and the thesaurus dependent use (*altercation*) or in locutions only journalists employ (ending a sentence with "police said Monday"). It will be easier to hound writing like this out of journalism when more of its practitioners are disabused of the notion that arraying facts is the be-all and end-all of journalism.

An understanding of the rise of interpretation—and the decline of the fact-dense report—might also help save traditional journalists from some awfully dull reports. My favorite example is a lead that appeared high up on the *New York Times* website in December 2009: "About half of Americans who are unemployed say the recession has been a hardship on them and caused major life changes, and most do not expect relief any time soon, according to a new nationwide poll of unemployed Americans conducted by the *New York Times* and CBS News."[39] One suspects that a reporter looking for an idea, not just a summary, might have found a result a bit more unexpected with which to begin a story on that poll.

Producing more interpretive stories requires journalists to think more—about their reporting, about their use of sources, about their writing, and about their stories. Journalism needs to continue to move in this direction not just to distinguish itself on the Web, but to get smarter, more interesting, better.

As journalists move away from the mere reporting of news, they also become less vulnerable to the distortions inherent in news—one distortion in particular: the fascination news has always had with the screaming anomaly. News reporters yawn when dogs bite men, but let a man show his teeth to a dog, and the notebooks all come out. That's why the world according to traditional journalists is overpopulated with the unlikely and unrepresentative.[40]

Interpretive journalists certainly can participate in perpetuating this view that wildness and weirdness—husbands murdering wives, mothers killing children—are more common than they in fact are. They can mull over the significance of the rare and insignificant. They can lose themselves in ratiocination on the meaning of the meaningless. But any step back from the freak show the news sometimes wants to present can help ease this distortion. And interpretation done well—interpretation informed in particular by social science—can help correct for it.

Gun murders, for example—particularly in mass shootings—receive much more news coverage than gun suicides. The I-News team at

Rocky Mountain PBS did some research and determined that in their state those suicides, nonetheless, take many more lives than those murders. This story appeared, among other places, on the website of a newspaper in Colorado, *Steamboat Today*, in 2013: "During the 12-year span between the mass shootings at Columbine and Aurora, Coloradans used guns to kill themselves about four times more frequently than they used them to kill one another, an I-News analysis of death certificates found."[41]

Analyses like this are beginning to be done more frequently. They add perspective to a field that has not always been well supplied with perspective. Journalism is getting wiser.

Are there individuals in twenty-first-century American journalism who can be said to be playing the role played by Whitelaw Reid in the nineteenth—who see, accept, and try to further understand the change going on in their enterprise? The Young Turks of interpretive journalism, the bloggers themselves, have not surprisingly done a pretty good job of figuring out what journalism is becoming and ought to become.

"It's trite to say it," Ezra Klein has written, "but the news business is biased toward, well, news. There are plenty of outlets that tell you what happened yesterday, but virtually no organizations that simply tell you what's going on."[42] "What's going on" is not a particularly clear wording here, but what Klein is calling for, he quickly explains, is explanation: as in (my example, not his) that *Times* infographic on the health-care decision, as in that sometimes missing "why."

Klein is, in the words of the *New York Times*, a "multiplatform superman of blogging-twittering-column writing"[43] at (as I write) the *Washington Post*, Bloomberg, and occasionally the *New Yorker*; he is also a regular contributor to and guest host at MSNBC. Explanation is a noble component of interpretation and a noble component of Klein's journalism on all these platforms, though it is probably not the largest component of either interpretation or his journalism.

Matthew Yglesias, who currently blogs and tweets for *Slate* on business and economics, can help broaden and sharpen this view of a new journalism—first by noting what he does not regularly do. On that much-clicked-upon *Slate* blog, Yglesias wrote up some comments made by House minority leader Nancy Pelosi at a luncheon he had apparently attended. Then on Twitter he promoted that post with the sly phrase: "rare reporting outbreak."[44] Kinds of reporting are certainly involved in his work: reading and research in particular, at which Yglesias is an ace, and sources do sometimes appear in his stories. But, yes, Yglesias is clear that most of the time he is doing something other than merely transcribing what newsmakers say.

What is he doing, then? Yglesias initially settles upon the same term for his enterprise that Klein, a former colleague, uses: "I always think of myself as an explainer." But then Yglesias takes his explanation of his explaining a step further: "I just try and put sophisticated ideas into the news cycle and connect people with smart ideas that are relevant."[45]

Felix Salmon, who persistently unleashes "smart ideas" on his finance blog for Reuters, labels big-press-conference, big-event, hang-out-with-the-pack stories—of the sort upon which Yglesias rarely reports— "commodity news." Salmon dismisses it as "low-hanging fruit in terms of journalistic effort." The fruit at the top of the tree, in his view, is not a variety of reporting. It is "insight,"[46] that for which Salmon himself, along with Klein and Yglesias, certainly appears to be reaching.

Nate Silver's May 21, 2012, post "Swing Voters and Elastic States" is a fine example of that hard-to-reach insight—and another of this book's illustrations of what wisdom journalism might be. That post, on Silver's blog about polling and campaigns, *FiveThirtyEight*, began with these paradoxes: "North Carolina is a swing state that has relatively few swing voters. Rhode Island is not a swing state, but it has quite a lot of swing voters." This is the sort of minor conundrum that few of us puzzle over. Silver did—in more than two thousand words, two charts, and one graph. In the process, he was able to clarify considerably our understanding of what is meant by a swing state—a much-discussed entity in contemporary American presidential politics.

Indeed, Silver added to our vocabulary here the term *elastic state*: a state such as Rhode Island that has numerous independent voters who are "relatively sensitive or responsive to changes in political conditions" and therefore who might switch their votes. Rhode Island is not, however, much of a swing state: an unusual number of voters would have to switch for it not to vote for a Democratic presidential candidate. In contrast, most voters in North Carolina are committed to one party or the other and are unlikely to switch. However, the number of reliable Democratic voters there is sufficiently close to the number of reliable Republican voters that even a relatively small number moving one way or the other could *swing* the state from one party to the other. Turnout in a nonelastic swing state, Silver noted, can be crucial.[47]

Nate Silver presented his own thoughts on where journalism is heading in a graduation speech at Columbia's Graduate School of Journalism in 2011:

> One of the things that distinguishes . . . "new journalism" from some of its more traditional forms is that the reader is really going to be looking for analysis, meaning, context, argument. Unless you come across some *really* fresh and proprietary information—it's great to get a scoop, but it won't happen very often—it's not enough just to present the information verbatim. . . .
>
> The reader is going to be asking you to develop a hypothesis, weigh the evidence, and come to some conclusion about it. . . . *Good* journalism has always done this—but now it needs to be done more explicitly.[48]

There are a hypothesis, plenty of evidence, and some conclusions in Silver's post "Swing Voters and Elastic States." He was not plumping for any particular policy or candidate, but he was *arguing* for some new ways of looking at how states vote. Silver was also providing an impressive explanation of how states and voters "swing." He added a smart new concept, elasticity, to our understanding of voting patterns. And he offered some original insights into how elections are determined. Not bad for a blog post.

Finally, on the matter of style in this new form of journalism let's consult one other young, mostly online insight purveyor: the entertaining and observant Ana Marie Cox, who has written for a variety of blogs and publications, most recently the *Guardian*. Cox, almost as self-deprecating as she can be politician deprecating, speaks of the "wavery, total-BS, very partisan, barfly stylings of folks like me."[49]

We might want to focus on three words here. The first is *barfly*—which I understand not as someone prone to braggadocio, but someone relaxed, chatty, open, even ironic, and, if you'll allow a paradox, without BS. The second word is *partisan*—unabashedly opinionated, but also upfront and honest about said opinions and a bit *wavery*, the third word (and, yes, it is a word), in holding them—that is, not a rigid ideologue or not, in other words, Whitelaw Reid's one-sided, truth-concealing party journalist.

If you stir together these various attempts at self-definition by leading young bloggers, you get a pretty good summary of where journalism is heading and ought to be heading: toward "analysis, meaning, context, argument," combined with explanation plus large doses of "smart ideas" and "insight," all presented with honesty, openness, flexibility, and, often enough, relaxed good humor. Add some occasionally severe "outbreaks" of reporting, not squandered on over-reported events, and this is a good summary, too, of what I mean by wisdom journalism.

~

But those I have chosen to speak here are members of the vanguard of the revolution, not, as Reid was, distinguished representatives of the ancien régime, not traditional journalists who have changed sides. For that, we have to look farther afield.

The *Independent* is a serious British national daily newspaper in both a rapidly declining market, because we are talking print, and a highly competitive market, because we are talking Britain. There are three other serious British national dailies—all much older and more established, all with higher circulations. So the *Independent*, in its search for a means of survival, began devoting most of its front page (as weeklies often have) to a single story—a story covered (weeklylike) with considerable perspective and depth, a story in which the paper is not shy about exhibiting (weeklylike) a point of view. The best known of those front pages was not conceived by the newspaper's visionary editor, Simon Kelner—something of a rock star in English journalism; it was conceived instead by a real rock star, Bono, to whom Kelner gave control of the *Independent* for one day, May 16, 2006. That front page, done up in red, featured the headline "NO NEWS TODAY" and underneath it, in much smaller type, "Just 6,500 Africans died today as a result of a preventable, treatable disease (HIV/AIDS)."[50]

Simon Kelner served as the paper's top editor on again, off again from 1998 to 2011. In a 2006 interview I did with him, he recalled that his understanding of the situation of the daily newspaper "crystallized" during coverage in England of the American presidential election in 2004. The *Independent* had reported the results along with the other major British papers. "It was a really expensive, exhaustive exercise for us all," Kelner commented. Yet the next morning circulations actually fell. For up-to-the-minute results, people had turned instead to the radio, television, and the Internet. Kelner admitted that when he woke up, he, too, switched on radio and TV. However, he explained, "the next day the *Independent* published twenty-one pages of analysis and interpretation of the election, and we put on 15 percent in sales."[51]

Kelner got the message. Kelner gained the mindset. "The idea that a newspaper is going to be peoples' first port of call to find out of what's going on in the world is simply no longer valid," he explained. "So you have to add another layer: analysis, interpretation, point of view." Kelner began dubbing his daily a "viewspaper."

Compare the *Independent*'s response to one particular story to that of the *Washington Post*. My example comes from October 5, 2006, during the period when Kelner's experiment was perhaps most vibrant. The story was a visit by then U.S. secretary of state Condoleezza Rice to the Middle East as President George W. Bush's administration was pushing its "road map to peace." The *Post* reported on a joint press conference the secretary of state held with Palestinian Authority president

Mahmoud Abbas on page A26 under the unexciting headline "Rice Cites Concern for Palestinians, but Low Expectations Mark Visit." "The old 'who-what-when-where-why'" was well represented. The *Independent*, that same morning emblazoned this headline on its front page: "The Road Map to Nowhere." Using a series of five short items—each divided into "The Promise" (headlined in red) and "What Happened"— the paper then compared on that front page what the Bush administration had claimed for its Mideast policy with the little, nothing, or worse (the Lebanon War was mentioned) it had achieved.

Now that opinionated headline—"Road Map to Nowhere"— probably did not, in fairness, appear quite as radical in Britain as it might in the United States. In Europe, with its tradition of a more ideological journalism, papers are less shy about saying what they think. What was new was the magazine-like boldness and focus—think the weekly *Economist*—with which the *Independent* was presenting its evaluation.[52]

The Economist, which is chockablock with smart evaluations, is not only worth thinking about here; it has done some of this thinking: "In a world where millions of new sources are emerging on the Internet," the magazine wrote in 2011, "consumers are overwhelmed with information and want to be told what it all means."[53] Kelner understood that. But the *Independent's* editor was less than forward looking in another area: he was not a big believer in an online presence. That hurt as readership for print newspapers continued to plummet.

Now Kelner is off again as the *Independent's* editor, and the print newspaper, still losing circulation, has reverted to more traditional front pages—and a more traditional form of journalism: "Coalition Loses EU Budget Vote in Commons." It is hard to imagine that any model, short of having a different rock star edit each day's issue, could save the *Independent* in print in the long term.[54] The Web and its mobile cousins will obviously dominate any potential solutions. But in 2006 Simon Kelner was practicing a more compelling form of journalism than anybody else in the daily newspaper business—with the possible exception of Mike Levine.

Levine edited a very different kind of newspaper—one located in Middletown, New York, not London. A former columnist, he had observed what we might call the "John Burns phenomenon": the analyses that reporters unburdened themselves of in the newsroom were often much more interesting than "the usual ping pong of 'he said, she said'" they ended up presenting in the paper. "Walk into any newsroom in America," Levine explained, "turn the reporters upside down; and a hundred stories will come falling out. They know so much about the communities they cover, but they don't get it in the newspaper."[55]

When he took over as executive editor of the *Times Herald-Record* in 1999, Levine was determined to change that. "We simply asked reporters to give the readers the benefit of their intelligent analysis," he explained. This meant paying less attention to the mere fact that a hospital administrator resigned in Sullivan County. It may have even meant leaving the account of the resignation to the paper's website. It definitely meant giving more attention in the paper to what that resignation might signify.

"We're not the infantry anymore," is how Levine put it. "We don't just go out to board meetings and take dictation. That's not really much of a contribution to the community. What are needed are journalists who can connect the dots." Levine, in other words, was not afraid of letting his reporters—after they had done the reporting, when they knew as much about a subject as most of their sources—find meaning in dots.

Here is an example of what happened when they did do Levine's kind of reporting. It is from a multipart *Times Herald-Record* series on a renaissance in the city of Newburgh by reporters Tim Logan and John Doherty:

> The city is shaking off three decades of inertia. It's an exciting time. The real-estate market is hot. City politics are more harmonious. And there are plans galore. Plans for a community college on lower Broadway, plans for the long-empty stretch of land on Water Street, a master plan under way for the city as a whole.
>
> But there's no plan for the city's poor.
>
> . . . If this city is truly going to rebuild, if it will ever fill the void at its heart, if it can transform itself from a drain on the rest of Orange

County into the thriving hub the county desperately needs, Newburgh can no longer ignore its poverty.[56]

Note that's not, "Some observers suggest Newburgh can no longer ignore its poverty." Nor was this an editorial or a column. This point was being made in news pages, at a small, local newspaper, by journalists based on what they had learned on their beats, based on their own reasoned and informed appraisal of the situation.

The *Times Herald-Record* at the beginning of the twenty-first century is not exactly the journalism behemoth the *New York Tribune* was in the middle of the nineteenth century. But its editor, too, was a traditional journalist whose mindset had changed. When American journalists were first saying hello to "the who-what-when-where-why," *Tribune* editor Whitelaw Reid understood that the "essence, the life-blood of the daily paper of to-day, is the news." Mike Levine understood that the "essence, the life-blood" of journalism in his day could no longer be simply reporting news. Instead, it is connecting dots. It is interpretation—even, as in "Newburgh can no longer ignore its poverty," opinion. (Mike Levine died of a heart attack in 2007 at the age of fifty-four, his experiment incomplete.[57])

5

"MUCH AS ONE MAY TRY TO DISAPPEAR FROM THE WORK"

The Argument Against Objectivity

A commitment to objectivity—with its debt to nineteenth-century realism—lives on in twenty-first-century journalism. It survives as a goal, a standard, and, if truth be told, a fear. To work for a traditional American news organization today is to live not so much in fear that you'll be accused of bias, for of course you will be, but in fear that such an accusation might stick.

Consider this response from John F. Burns of the *New York Times* in 2006. I had just criticized him for being less interesting in his reporting from Iraq in his own paper than he was in an appearance on *Charlie Rose*. (The criticism discussed in the previous chapter.) Burns got, appropriately, defensive, but, inappropriately though understandably, not about that for which he was being criticized. He was concerned, instead, that he might be accused of having let slip on TV some opinions on the war: "Our appearances on television are a challenge because there are no editors to filter what we say and to ensure that tidal breaks between news and opinion are maintained," Burns explained in his email to me.[1]

American journalists have trained their audiences, as they have trained themselves, to treat an opinion as a sign of corruption. Their reward has been that letter writers, journalism reviews, and media websites on the left and the right are now always ready to pounce should a reporter, such as John Burns, express something that appears partisan.

And this is happening even as interpretation is on the rise and belief in traditional forms of journalism is fading. The Objectivity Police have yet to be demobilized. NPR fired Juan Williams in 2010, for instance, after he acknowledged candidly on Fox News Channel that he grew nervous when he saw people in "Muslim garb" on an airplane. "NPR argued," according to the *New York Times*, "that he had violated the organization's belief in impartiality, a core tenet of modern American journalism."[2]

Sportswriter Thomas Bowles was also accused of insufficient fealty to this tenet. Bowles was working on a freelance contract for *Sports Illustrated* online in 2011, reporting on a particularly dramatic—seventy-four lead changes—and inspiring Daytona 500. At the finish, Bowles did something "objective" journalists are not supposed to do: caught up in the moment, he clapped. "That day marked my first and last claps working as a NASCAR reporter for SI.com," he writes. "Many insist 'sacred rule #1' of being a sportswriter is Don't Cheer in the Press Box." *Sports Illustrated*, part of Time Inc., fired Bowles. "Time Inc. policy," a representative of the company told *Inside Line*, "is that the editorial staff is expected to conduct themselves in the manner representative of the journalistic tradition."[3]

No wonder Burns, being accused of being uninteresting in his newspaper reports, was instead paranoid about being accused of being too partisan. Oh, the effort traditional journalists must consequently make, the assistance from tidal breaks and editors they may even require, to repress the urge to say what they think!

The Objectivity Police help keep traditional journalism focused on facts, not interpretations, but this eagerness to pounce on any trace of opinion is also a result of this focus. As long as journalists are seen primarily as collectors of news, as mere witnesses, they will be judged by the evenhandedness with which they collect, by the faithfulness and dispassion of their witness. If they are seen as mere mirrors of reality, they will be criticized for any tint or tilt in the reflection they provide. Opinion will have to be suppressed, and journalists will end up putting considerable energy into disguising whatever point of view they may have achieved. A great deal of what is wrong with American journalism, as it takes on the challenges posed by new media, can be traced to this often misguided effort.

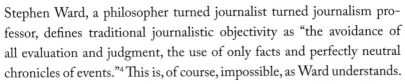

Stephen Ward, a philosopher turned journalist turned journalism professor, defines traditional journalistic objectivity as "the avoidance of all evaluation and judgment, the use of only facts and perfectly neutral chronicles of events."[4] This is, of course, impossible, as Ward understands.

"Much as one may try to disappear from the work," John Hersey acknowledged in 1984, "there is a kind of mediation that takes place in journalism, no matter what. By selecting nine-hundred and ninety-nine out of a thousand so-called facts, you are bringing your own bias to bear."[5] One might go further: By selecting whom to interview on a story— An official, not a gadfly?—"you are bringing your own bias to bear." By selecting which sides of a complex political dispute to air—Democratic or Republican, but not Green Party or Libertarian, not MoveOn.org or Tea Party?—you are bringing to bear a conclusion on what qualifies as a legitimate position. You are, in other words, evaluating; you are judging; you are not being "perfectly neutral."

And such judgments and "evaluations"—evidence of *subjectivity*, to recall Carlota Smith's use of that term[6]—can be detected at every stage in the production of a "story." Even a decision to anoint as newsworthy one out of the thousand occurrences going on in any given place at any given moment requires conclusions on what is and is not interesting and important—conclusions with political and cultural colorings and consequences. Even the effort to squeeze occurrences into narratives—into stories—requires various less than "neutral" elisions and rearrangements.

At times during the twentieth century, philosophy, literature, art, and to some extent science all pondered the inevitability of what Hersey calls "mediation" and therefore the bankruptcy of the concept of objectivity.[7] Their theorists spoke of "discourses" and "paradigms" and fretted about the "uncertain," the "relative," the "fragmented," the "multiperspectival," the "culturally given," and the "socially constructed." They abandoned, to a large extent, the dream of evaluationless, judgmentless neutrality.

The philosopher Thomas Nagel, writing in the 1980s, produced a succinct and comparatively mild version of this critique. He did not question the idea that "the world" exists "independently of how it appears to us or to any particular occupant of it." That is a pretty large concession for a post-Einstein, post-Heisenberg thinker. But Nagel did abandon the idea that this independently existing world "coincides with what can be objectively understood," for, he wrote, "the way the world is includes appearances, and there is not a single point of view from which they all can be fully grasped."[8] There may, in other words, be an objective reality, but there is not any one objective description of this reality. People see things differently. Even at the hands of the least partisan, least opinionated reporter, there is not, consequently, an objective journalism.

By the beginning of the twenty-first century, many journalists were finally ready to concede the point. "'Objective' is not a good term, because nobody's objective," then *Washington Post* executive editor Leonard Downie Jr. told a *Frontline* interviewer in April 2006. Downie insisted, instead, that his reporters try to be "fair."[9] That's one of the terms journalists who have grown suspicious of objectivity but remain uncomfortable with mixing news and opinion substitute for *objectivity*. *Impartial, unbiased*, and *balanced* are others.[10]

These are all, in Aristotle's terms, virtues—of use, as discussed in chapter 1, in establishing the "character" of the journalist and therefore in persuading; often of use, too, in improving the quality of discourse. When writing on his *Washington Post* blog of the acceptance speech given by Republican vice presidential nominee Paul Ryan in 2012, the Democratic-leaning Ezra Klein noted, "I wanted us to bend over backward to be fair, to see it from Ryan's perspective, to highlight its best arguments as well as its worst."[11] Klein wanted—for understandable, maybe even exemplary reasons—to display the virtue of fairness.

But when examined as guides to journalistic practice, these alternatives to objectivity also, not surprisingly, prove problematic. We can't be "fair" to all, anymore than we can see the world as it is seen by all. Given limitations of space and time, how do we select the positions on an issue to which we should accord "fair" treatment? Are we to present "fairly" points of view that may be based on errors or distortions? Ezra Klein, in the end, didn't find much to praise in Paul Ryan's widely criticized speech.

For that matter, can politically aware journalists actually be "impartial"?[12] Here are the steps Leonard Downie Jr. said he took to preserve his impartiality or detachment[13] as editor of the *Washington Post*: "I didn't just stop voting, I stopped having even private opinions about politicians or issues so that I would have a completely open mind in supervising our coverage."[14] For most of us, those seem very large, unmanageable steps.

And would making such an effort even be enough? Perhaps we can guard against an overt tilt toward the Republicans or Democrats. But whether we vote or not, no matter how carefully we filter out our attitudes and conclusions, don't most Americans share, in the second decade of the twenty-first century, a belief in capitalism and representative democracy? Don't most of us share a bias in favor of the brave, charitable, or entrepreneurial and a bias against those who cheat, dissemble, take too many handouts, have sex with minors, or get violent (except when authorized to do so by the state)? How could anyone truly avoid being influenced by the values, mores, and assumptions of a social circle, let alone a time and place?

And, were it possible, do we really want journalists whose minds are *that* open, who are so "impartial" they don't allow themselves a point of view on the issues of the day? Blogger Matthew Yglesias mocks "the odd notion that the ideal reporter would be someone who *actually doesn't have opinions*, as if 'the facts' were purely transparent and could be merely observed, processed, and then regurgitated into inverted-pyramid form without passing through the muck of 'judgment' or 'thoughts about the world.'"[15] Isn't some sort of thinking about politics required to write about politics in any but the most stenographic forms?

More to the point, because few attempt the extreme exercise in mental noninvolvement Downie says he undertook, do we want to obtain our accounts of the world from people struggling not to *reveal* their ideas and their passions? Do we want to hear about the Iraq War from the John Burns who says what he believes on *Charlie Rose* or from the *New York Times* John Burns whose evaluations have been filtered out by editors or by his own fear of saying anything that might be confused with partisanship? Back in 1986, *New York Times* columnist Russell Baker dismissed the practice of such hypercautious, resolutely unassuming journalism—and there weren't many mainstream alternatives to it in the United States at the time—as "the Bland Impartiality Game."[16]

Moreover, do we want to see the world through the eyes of journalists who are, in Yglesias's telling phrase, "pretending to not have opinions"? Journalists often have a chance to evaluate a situation: John Burns in Iraq is a classic example. Why ask them to make believe that they have not? Why ask them to swallow their conclusions? Another accomplished blogger, Andrew Sullivan, suggests that "untruths fester" whenever "people feel required to suppress their real views."[17]

"Balance" may be an even more problematic standard for journalists. It has been the subject of vigorous debate recently, but decades ago Russell Baker had captured the nub of the argument against the attempt to balance liberal and conservative, charge and countercharge, thesis and antithesis, yea and nay: "In the classic example, a refugee from Nazi Germany who appears on television saying monstrous things are happening in his homeland must be followed by a Nazi spokesman saying Adolf Hitler is the greatest boon to humanity since pasteurized milk."[18]

Here, for an actual example, is the headline the *New York Times* printed atop an Associated Press story on July 4, 1952: "M'CARTHY BENTON EXCHANGE CHARGES." Senator William Benton was trying to get Senator Joseph McCarthy ousted from the Senate for destroying careers through wild, unsubstantiated allegations of Communist leanings. Senator McCarthy's characteristic response was to name, similarly wildly, "seven persons—'dangerous to America' . . . who served under Mr. Benton."[19] Yet, according to the *Times* and the rules of balance—which were followed in the article, not just its headline—this was merely an "exchange" of charges.

Economics professor and blogger Brad DeLong calls this compulsion to balance even the legitimate with the ridiculous "opinions-of-shape-of-the-earth-journalism."[20] *Daily Show* satirist Jon Stewart, focusing on CNN, labels it "leave it there" journalism. He notes how "panels" of wildly disagreeing commentators yell at each other on CNN programs for some minutes and then the host—without any effort to check or evaluate their competing claims—simply says, "We're going to have to leave it there."[21]

The name most commonly given this recourse to a "false balance" today is "'he said, she said' journalism."[22] "He," a panelist or a source, says one thing. "She," a panelist or a source with a different opinion, disagrees. The journalist, thus having achieved a "balance," makes no effort to determine whether "he" or "she" is correct.

An Associated Press story picked up by Yahoo! News and numerous other news organizations on July 17, 2012, began with a "he said": "Investigators for an Arizona sheriff's volunteer posse have declared that President Barack Obama's birth certificate is definitely fraudulent." We then get four more paragraphs of such allegations from the office of controversial Sheriff Joe Arpaio. Only in paragraph nine does a strong version of the "she said"—or, in this case, "they said"—appear: "Hawaii officials have repeatedly confirmed Obama's citizenship, and state officials did again Tuesday."[23] A rebuttal to the charge is (eventually) included. The story is therefore "balanced." And because the uncredited AP reporter who transcribed this charge is "objective" or "unbiased" or "impartial," he or she never tells us that such "birther" allegations about President Obama had been widely, consistently, and long previously discredited. We are never reminded that those who make these accusations have slipped into the "earth is flat," "Hitler is a boon to humanity" realm of discourse. Instead, the article makes it sound as if this is just another typical political back and forth in which it is impossible to decide which side is correct. "We're going to have to leave it there." Even if the Associated Press is to limit itself to just news reporting, it can do better and has done better.

There are many problems with the compulsive effort at balance still engaged in by most traditional American see-no-right-or-wrong, believe-in-no-right-or-wrong journalists. First, there inevitably are a limited number of seats on their seesaw. The range of positions that are balanced is limited—usually to two. The range of discussion will thereby be circumscribed.

Second, the assumption will be furthered that the "truth" lies somewhere between those two positions—in this case, between those who think President Obama has a valid birth certificate and those who don't. "The American press has always had a tendency to assume that the truth must lie exactly halfway between any two opposing points of view," the columnist Molly Ivins has written. "Thus, if the press presents the man who says Hitler is an ogre and the man who says Hitler is a prince, it believes it has done the full measure of it's journalistic duty."[24]

Jay Rosen at New York University—one of the leading critics of "'he said, she said' journalism"—believes this traditional split-it-down-the-middle coverage flattens understandings of politics: "No distinctions between the parties are tenable," he writes. "It's fifty–fifty all the way down. Symmetrical. Equal and opposite. Neat and clean. Exquisitely balanced."[25]

But the main problem with a journalism based on such automatic, unthinking balancing may be that, as Jon Stewart puts, it is too willing "to leave it there." It is lazy. It relieves journalists of any responsibility for determining whether "he" or "she" might be in error. Once again, "untruths fester." Oh, the efforts some traditional journalists will *not* make to figure out who in one of these debates might be wrong!

"The genuflection toward 'fairness' is a familiar newsroom piety," wrote Joan Didion in 1996, "the excuse in practice for a good deal of autopilot reporting."[26] Didion's own journalism—she has also written fiction and memoirs—rarely if ever strives to balance the way different sides of an issue are treated. She is "fair"—after extensive reading or reporting—only to the truth as she sees it. Is that not more valuable? Does that not help explain why many dozens of stories produced by traditional newsrooms would likely not contain as many perspective-shifting, understanding-sharpening insights as one story of hers?

Let me add some balance to this discussion of balance by quoting *Washington Post* reporter Paul Kane. Kane was responding to the complaint that reporters fail to note that the Republicans are sometimes more to blame for stalemates in Congress than Democrats: "I think this point is just absurd and ridiculous," Kane declared during an online chat with readers in November 2011. "It's just stupid. If you want someone to tell you that Republicans stink, read opinion pages. Read blogs. If you really don't want to hear anything about the other side of the story, I really do encourage you to stop reading the news section."[27]

Hearing the other side is indeed important, but, after listening carefully, is it really "stupid" to expect "the news section"—to the extent that there should still be a "news section"—to help us figure out which side on the seesaw might have the weightier arguments?

Of course, both sides often have a point. Of course, such debates often just come down to matters of interpretation. Of course, there isn't always just one right answer. But sometimes there is. President Obama's birth certificate had been released and had been sufficiently well investigated. There may be legitimate reasons occasionally to hear out those who claim Obama was not born in Hawaii: fringe allegations with some following should not be totally ignored. But such a claim should not be aired without making clear that the evidence is much, much stronger on the other side. Reporters, the point is, should always be ready at least to question whether the different sides in a dispute are making equally valid arguments: Do they have the evidence? Are their analyses cogent and coherent? Are their arguments logical? Reporters should "test," to return to Stephen Toulmin's term from chapter 1.[28]

Indeed, to broaden the discussion a bit, reporters should be asking such questions, performing such tests, even when they are not covering a debate between sources; they should ask them when they are simply quoting a source. It is not enough merely to report what "she said" if "she" may be demonstrably wrong or contradicting herself.

Two *Washington Post* reporters were accused of this failing by the liberal media watchdog organization Media Matters in 2009. They had quoted Senator Olympia Snowe opposing Democrats' use of the "reconciliation process" to bypass a filibuster during the Obama administration. But these reporters had failed to note that Republicans, including Senator Snowe, had used the same process during the Bush administration.[29] One of the accused reporters was Paul Kane. He was not contrite, as was apparent in another online chat with readers: "We reported what Olympia Snowe said. That's what she said. That's what Republicans are saying. I really don't know what you want of us. We are not opinion writers."[30]

Let Matthew Yglesias answer Kane here: "What we want is that if you're going to quote someone saying something dishonest, you report the fact that [that person is] lying. Or if in this case you're quoting someone who's arguably being hypocritical, you inform readers of the broader context. . . . Otherwise, operating by Kane['s] standards you could do an entire article that consisted of accurately quoting people who are lying, and wind up badly misinforming your readers."[31]

"Ah yes," sneered Alec MacGillis in the *New Republic* in July 2012 after yet another reporter had failed to challenge yet another gross distortion on the part of a political campaign, with the excuse that it was just part of the back and forth of politics, "if only there was someone whose job and *calling* it was to ferret out the truth of such things, to provide some context for voters. Let me think, there must be someone we can think of, a profession of some kind perhaps, sort of like a researcher but also a communicator."[32]

The point is that objectivity, fairness, impartiality, and balance—I'm not sure it matters that much which word you choose—can sometimes be used as excuses for journalists not to do what journalists are supposed to do, as excuses for not doing their jobs. That may be the best argument against continued devotion to those standards.

And some questionable journalistic behaviors often fill the vacuum. The reluctance to appear biased by actually evaluating a statement or policy leaves journalists—taken to seeing themselves as "watchdogs"—with a very limited repertoire of barks: it often seems as if the only aggressive sound they can emit, while maintaining their treasured objectivity, is "gotcha!" They are reduced to pouncing on obvious slipups.

Now "gotcha!" is a journalistic exercise with a long pedigree. It is in a sense what Matthew Yglesias was calling for Paul Kane and that other *Washington Post* reporter to have done when quoting Senator Olympia Snowe's opposition to Democrats' use of the "reconciliation process": point out that she had supported it when Republicans had used it. Indeed, catching errors has an often distinguished pedigree. It is, in a sense, the exercise in which Bob Woodward and Carl Bernstein were engaging during their Watergate investigation. President Richard Nixon and some of those working for him had slipped up in ways that, it now seems clear, threatened the Constitution. There, as in most good investigative journalism, misbehavior of moment and consequence was being exposed. In the case of Senator Snowe, it could certainly be argued that her hypocrisy ought to have been exposed. But the journalist's urge to pounce begins to look mean, even destructive, when the blunders being pounced upon are minor.

This certainly happens often enough in heavily opinionated journalism, but it also seems to be encouraged by the rules of objectivity. The traditional journalist, afraid of questioning the merits of a position, is too often reduced to uncovering some minor contradiction in that position. The late Tim Russert, longtime host of NBC's *Meet the Press*, was a master of this variety of "gotcha": picking out and usually displaying on screen contradictory statements a politician had made, often quite some time apart—as if a rigid consistency were the only true measure of a politician's merit. He caught then senator Barack Obama in October 2006:

MR. RUSSERT: But it's fair to say you're thinking about running for president in 2008?

SEN. OBAMA: It's fair, yes.

MR. RUSSERT: And so when you said to me in January, "I will not," that statement is no longer operative?[33]

Gotcha! And maybe Senator Obama deserved to be caught in the contradiction. But that contradiction seems something less than hypocrisy and much less than malfeasance.

It is not uncommon for a government official or candidate to hold a news conference or participate in a debate in which significant policy ideas are expressed, but for reporters to pay little attention to those ideas. Instead, the reporters focus on some impolitic phrasing the official or candidate had the misfortune of having employed—a gaffe: President

Gerald Ford's saying in 1976 that there was "no Soviet domination of eastern Europe" is an example, as is President Barack Obama saying about the weak economy in 2012, "The private sector is fine."[34] Gotcha!

Yes, it is news when politicians contradict themselves or say something silly. Perhaps their inability to avoid an infelicitous phrase is revealing. But President Ford knew the situation in eastern Europe. President Obama knew the economy—public and private—was underperforming. And such slipups often seem to be given so much attention that there is little space or time left for discussion of actual policy positions.

Traditional journalism not only *filters* what journalists can say but *filters* the view of the world they present: sometimes making political disputes seem more balanced than they are, sometimes reducing complex policy discussions to standoffs between warring parties, sometimes diminishing policy discussions to trivial "gotcha!" games. Objectivity, fairness, impartiality, and balance in journalism can limit our ability to know the world through journalism.

≈

However, reducing devotion to these problematic standards does not—as the next chapter emphasizes—mean abandoning them entirely. Other values that I have recourse to in this book—honesty, truth, reason, understanding—also raise, at least in their most pure and doctrinaire forms, philosophical problems, yet they still have important roles to play in journalism. Objectivity, fairness, impartiality, and balance do, too, but they will have to be seen as virtues rather than commandments. We will have to remain alert to their impurities. They must not be used as excuses to forgo reason and evaluation. And they should not be turned into bludgeons with which to beat down other, sometimes more honest efforts at truth or understanding.

Openness to other points of view remains a good quality. Airing opposing ideas is useful, invigorating. Unfair, unbalanced, truth-denying rants contribute little—as is demonstrated everyday by the enraged radio, cable, and Internet carnivores who roam journalism's increasingly broad, increasingly wild savannas. To be clear, this chapter is not calling for more of the unreflective party-line journalism Whitelaw Reid was trying to overcome.

Here is Jay Rosen arguing that objectivity can be turned from an epistemological limitation of journalism into a source of strength:

> If objectivity means trying to ground truth claims in verifiable facts, I am definitely for that. If it means there's a "hard" reality out there that exists beyond any of our descriptions of it, sign me up. If objectivity is the requirement to acknowledge what is, regardless of whether we want it to be that way, then I want journalists who can be objective in that sense. Don't you? If it means trying to see things [from a] fuller perspective . . . pulling the camera back, revealing our previous position as only one of many—I second the motion. If it means the struggle to get beyond the limited perspective that our experience and upbringing afford us . . . yeah, we need more of that, not less. I think there is value in acts of description that do not attempt to say whether the thing described is good or bad. Is that objectivity? If so, I'm all for it.[35]

If there are so many potential positives in it, can't traditional journalistic objectivity be preserved by simply tweaking it a little? The first adjustment that most of its critics, including Rosen, are now calling for is more checking of allegations: more calling a lie a lie; more applications of reason; more honesty about distortions and hypocrisy.

During the 2012 presidential campaign, there were some impressive and, given the continuing power of the Objectivity Police, surprising examples of that. One appeared in a line from a *New York Times* news story. It was a word—a harsh word—that does not normally appear in the paper's news pages without attribution: "The Romney campaign is airing an advertisement falsely charging that Mr. Obama has 'quietly announced' plans to eliminate work and job training requirements for welfare beneficiaries." That's *not* "which some critics claim falsely charges." Another example turned up in the news pages of the *Los Angeles Times*—in, of all places, a headline: "Rick Santorum Repeats

Inaccurate Welfare Attack on Obama."[36] That's *not* "which Democrats charge was inaccurate."

The fact that both of these examples debunk the same, easily debunked charge makes it more difficult to find in them a trend. Nevertheless, they definitely represents progress away from the habitual "he said, she said" toward the occasional "he said but was wrong." On these occasions, at least, the mummery of "some critics" and the stylized thrust and parry of charge and countercharge have blessedly been abandoned.

But even if it does become more widespread, this improvement on traditional methods, although useful, is not enough.

"I think objectivity is really important and is a goal to strive for," stated Nicholas Lemann, then dean of the Graduate School of Journalism at Columbia University, in 2008. "And the fact that people can't achieve it doesn't mean it should be thrown out as a goal."[37] Yes, objectivity, fairness, impartiality, and balance are not bad qualities to strive for in journalism—as long as their limitations are recognized and addressed. But as a "goal" for journalism, even this improved, more self-aware objectivity seems rather unambitious.

What should journalism be trying to achieve?[38] In chapter 1, I maintained, following Benjamin Franklin, that journalism should improve *knowledge* on current events. Let's see how that understanding of journalism's purpose—at the heart of this call for wisdom journalism—might apply to one of American journalism's proudest accomplishments.

Here is Carl Bernstein commenting in 2010 on what he and Bob Woodward were trying to achieve in the Watergate investigation they conducted as reporters for the *Washington Post* from 1972 to 1974: "Our object was the best obtainable version of the truth."[39] Surely that is— appropriately qualified as it is—a reasonable goal.

Truth has two possible meanings in journalism. The two meanings are connected but worth distinguishing. First, *truth* means not being false. It mean that what is said is in accord with reality, with the facts, or—in a slightly less philosophically presumptuous wording—with what is understood to be the case. When in chapter 1 I say, following John Searle, that the "truth conditions" of the assertions journalism makes must be satisfied,[40] this is the kind of truth to which I am referring. This truth undergirds all journalism, all responsible nonfiction. It means that circumstances, occurrences, and details—unless presented as hypothetical, speculative, fanciful, or figurative—have not been invented, as they might be in fiction, or even fudged or even guessed at. Recall Aristotle's statement: "It is necessary to have the facts belonging to that subject."[41]

This understanding of truth—as the absence of falsehood—is behind the traditional journalist's noble obsession with accuracy. As I have tried to make clear, the wisdom journalist should share that obsession. This view of truth is honored, too, in the first half of Jay Rosen's outline of what might be valuable about objectivity. It is part of what Bernstein means when he tries to explain the "object" of his and Woodward's Watergate investigation.

As Bernstein wisely indicates through the use of the words *best obtainable*, even this type of truth can be slippery—we never get an entirely clear peek at reality; facts are always susceptible to human perceptions; understandings of what is the case can change with the arrival of more information. Journalists struggle to cobble together a more reliable "version" of the truth as they work on a story. Historians make a living correcting those versions. Nonetheless, the process of aiming for truth, in this sense, is crucial for journalism. It demands that the information that can be verified *be* verified—checked and confirmed as thoroughly as possible. It requires that the necessary and appropriate "evidence" be provided. Truth, in this sense, is something journalists—all journalists—have to work to get *right*.

But truth is also something the best journalists struggle to get *at*. This is the second journalistic meaning of *truth*—as something that is often obscured or hidden. This is the truth behind events, the truth beyond what we already know. Journalism, for the most part, is not after the sort of Truth that believers—guided mostly by faith—proclaim. But the best journalists—guided by experience, observation, tests, and considered judgment, making use of evidence—do strive to *reveal* truths with a lowercase *t*.

In "Letters from a Farmer in Pennsylvania," John Dickinson did not just want to get the facts right. He wanted to reveal the truth that the Townshend Acts were no less a violation of the colonists' rights than the Stamp Act. Woodward and Bernstein desperately wanted to get all the facts right. But the main "object" of their investigation was to reveal the truth behind the Watergate break-in and eventually the truth that President Richard Nixon's reelection campaign and administration had violated the law. This truth is not just verified; it is disclosed—sometimes through enterprising investigation, sometimes through perceptive interpretation.

This second variety of truth is even more limited to Bernstein's *versions*: new versions of Nixon's wrongdoings have been revealed over the decades as new evidence is uncovered or new interpretations appear, including one written by Woodward and Bernstein themselves for the *Washington Post* in 2012 under the headline "Nixon Was Far Worse Than We Thought."[42] Historians inevitably spot meanings that journalists missed at the time. But this second variety of truth—even if it is provisional—is among the highest objects of journalism.

Indeed, both these varieties of truth seem inseparable from knowledge. Little, as a rule, is contributed to our knowledge about current events by information that is false. And little is so useful in increasing our knowledge of current events as investigations or interpretations that reveal important hidden aspects of those events.

In their Watergate investigation, Woodward and Bernstein set out after revelatory truths in traditional journalistic fashion—by sticking very close to factual truths. They displayed an aversion to comment and a fidelity to what sources "said."

This is the lead of the first story Woodward and Bernstein wrote together: "One of the five men arrested early Saturday in the attempt to bug the Democratic National Committee headquarters is the salaried security coordinator for President Nixon's reelection committee." The story's next eight paragraphs all feature the verb *said*. (The news pages of the *Washington Post* in 1972 were much more dedicated to transcribing the comments of sources than they are today.) This is the third of those paragraphs: "In a statement issued in Los Angeles, [former attorney general John N.] Mitchell [head of the Committee for the Re-Election of the President] said McCord and the other four men arrested at Democratic headquarters Saturday 'were not operating either in our behalf or with our consent' in the alleged bugging attempt."[43]

Hearing what such well-placed individuals as the "GOP national chairman," "police sources," "sources close to the investigation," "a high Democratic party source," and Mitchell "said" as well as what the White House did not say would prove of great value in furthering this investigation. In conjunction, of course, with congressional and judicial investigations, the press played its role in uncovering the Watergate crimes in part through the slow, painstaking, dramatic reporting of what sources revealed.

With the help of some in-the-know individuals on background or deep background, an impressive and shocking version of the truth was obtained. The president eventually resigned. But there are other ways to obtain revelatory truths—some often more direct. The Watergate investigation was in some senses traditional American journalism's finest hour. But other American journalisms might also have risen to the task—some, perhaps, more efficiently.

The aversion to displaying any overt point of view is strong and conspicuous in those early Woodward and Bernstein reports. Yet a deftly deployed point of view can also lead to "the best obtainable version of the truth"—hidden truth. Might the Watergate investigation have proceeded faster had there been bloggers around then to note and debate—each day, each hour, in their posts, on Twitter—the omissions and contractions in what those various sources were claiming? Might the investigation have proceeded faster if journalists had been freer to explore various possible scenarios for what had really occurred?

Peter S. Goodman, the business and economics reporter quoted in the previous chapter, recently left the *New York Times* for the more opinionated Web pages of the *Huffington Post*. Here is one of the reasons

Goodman gave for this move from the highest reaches of traditional journalism to a relatively new, alternative form: "For me it's a chance to write with a point of view," Goodman told Howard Kurtz. "Old conventional notions of fairness make it hard to tell readers directly what's going on."[44] The best obtainable version of "what's going on" often includes a point of view.

Here is Goodman writing for the *Huffington Post* in August 2012:

> Let us assume that the Justice Department vastly would have preferred to prosecute Goldman Sachs for its shady dealings in peddling toxic mortgages during the real estate boom, rather than put out the statement it issued late Thursday saying in essence, "Never mind, and enjoy the Hamptons."
>
> . . . Had prosecutors at Justice been able to make a good case— a case likely to put some Goldman people behind bars—they would have done so, because the deterrent effect of American law enforcement in the next financial orgy that inevitably lies ahead is looking mighty weak. A prominent win for the prosecutors might have helped.
>
> The same logic explains more broadly why nearly all of the seamy characters who profited while bludgeoning taxpayers, working people, retirees and homeowners have gotten away scot-free: The prosecutors can't muster cases with a good enough chance at winning.
>
> All of which means there is something seriously amiss with the laws and regulations that allowed the financial crisis to build to such proportions.[45]

In the *Huffington Post*, Goodman is allowed to "assume," to discuss what people "would have done," to call some unnamed people "seamy," to use a verb such as *bludgeoning* and a fanciful wording such as "Never mind, and enjoy the Hamptons." He is also able to make clear what "logic explains" and offer his point of view on what it all "means." These are steps away from objectivity as it has been defined in traditional American journalism. Yet they can be, if done intelligently, steps in the direction of revelatory truth—of what's really "going on" or the way things really are.

And Goodman's analysis offers something besides more of that variety of truth: it offers insight. *Insight* (Felix Salmon's term in the previous chapter[46]) measures discernment and the quality of a perspective—its originality, its aptness, its lucidity. In the earlier example, Goodman is trying to help us see a failure to prosecute as something somewhat different: as a failure of regulation. Surely such insights, too, are important kinds of knowledge.

If you'll allow me to load one more weighty word on Goodman's fine but not necessarily exceptional paragraphs, I'll maintain that their explanations, revelations, and insights produce understanding. And of the qualities I've mentioned, *understanding* may be the closest to knowledge itself; it measures the grasp of a situation that a work of journalism and therefore its readers have achieved. Insight and understanding, too, qualify as "goals" for journalism—more important goals, I would suggest, than remaining objective. Why shouldn't journalists consecrate themselves to insight and understanding—along with truth—before they honor such more flawed and more limited standards as impartiality or balance, which may or may not contribute to knowledge?

Some of the efforts at objectivity that Jay Rosen says can have value are certainly useful in achieving understanding: trying to broaden your perspective, for example. But don't insights most frequently spring from a point of view—from a reasonable, well-founded, but pointed point of view? The history of journalism is full of examples of fact-based opinions—from Thomas Paine's "These are the times that try men's souls" to Émile Zola's "J'Accuse . . . !"[47]—that have more than held their own with opinion-free facts as ways of understanding the world.

Readers of Woodward and Bernstein's regular reports for the *Washington Post* gained—over time—insights into what was behind that burglary at the Democratic National Committee headquarters; they gained—over time—an understanding of the corrupt workings of the Committee for the Re-Election of the President and of the Nixon administration. This was a monumental series of reports. But arguments like those made by Peter Goodman in the *Huffington Post*—well thought out, if not monumental—can often impart insights and understandings more efficiently, over less time.

Goodman provided one final explanation for his decision to leave the *Times* for the *Huffington Post*: "This is a chance for me to explore solutions in my economic reporting," he told Kurtz. A June 2012 article by Goodman in the *Huffington Post* provides an example of such "solutions journalism"—a term I have borrowed from David Bornstein:[48]

> Anyone waiting for Washington to fix . . . problems is likely to be waiting for a long time. . . .
>
> But while the center of national power may be a void, creative people in myriad localities are increasingly taking matters into their own hands, forging innovative solutions to vexing problems tearing at their communities. In the Cincinnati area, an entity known as the Strive Partnership—a fusion of about 300 local, non-profit, social service agencies, foundations, school districts, universities and private businesses—has organized to prepare area young people with the skills needed to embark on successful careers.[49]

The great early-twentieth-century muckraker Lincoln Steffens also had "solutions" in mind—though that seems a tepid description of what he was after in his unflinching, unrelenting, muck-disturbing investigations of municipal corruption in the United States. Steffens revealed many truths and collected many facts in those investigations. However, in the introduction to the 1904 book *The Shame of the Cities* in which these facts were collected, Steffens wrote: "I did not gather with indifference all the facts and arrange them patiently for permanent preservation and laboratory analysis. I did not want to preserve, I wanted to destroy the facts."[50]

Destroying facts, demanding reforms, providing solutions, improving the world, changing the world require two specific types of knowledge: revelations of what is wrong (long a specialty of journalism) and insights into how things might be improved (long overlooked by journalism). Knowledge that might lead to solutions is surely another worthy goal of journalism. And achieving this knowledge is often easier beyond the strictures of objectivity—beyond the indifferent arrangement of facts. Lincoln Steffens investigated, but he investigated with a point of view.

Let's switch now to the less delicate term: not *point of view*, but *opinion*. Lincoln Steffens deployed some unvarnished, undisguised opinions in his investigations of municipal corruption. Here is one: "The misgovernment of the American people is misgovernment by the American people."[51]

Steffens presented plenty of evidence to support his argument that in tolerating corruption in their cities, citizens are encouraging that corruption. His argument is based on thorough reporting. His style is firm but not overheated. Yet this is an opinion—involving, to be sure, a considerable degree of overgeneralization. And it is revelatory.

Most American news organizations today are still phobic about opinion. That phobia may be expected of newspapers, but these news organizations often attempt to impose their fears even on twenty-first-century platforms such as Twitter and Facebook, where opinion seems, on the face of it, much more at home. Here is the Associated Press's policy as stated in July 2011: "Social networks, however we may configure our accounts or select our friends, should be considered a public forum. AP staffers should not make postings there that amount to personal opinions on contentious public issues."[52]

Reuters suggested similar guidelines in 2010.[53] And the standards editor of the *New York Times*, Philip B. Corbett, who has tried to keep its social media policy loose, did decree that "newsroom staff members should avoid editorializing or promoting political views."[54] To the extent that such traditional news organizations have managed to maintain their devotion to objectivity online, they have had to ignore what just about everyone else on Twitter and Facebook understands: the fact that smart and clever opinions can help build audiences.

It was possible, of course, to understand this long before Twitter and Facebook: "It occurred to me that nothing is more interesting than opinion when opinion is interesting," wrote Herbert Bayard Swope, who is credited with inventing the modern op-ed page at the *New York World* in 1921.[55] But there weren't that many journalists—or at least journalists in power—to whom this did occur in the twentieth century. And there are plenty today who still haven't figured it out.

New-style journalist turned old-style novelist Tom Wolfe used to sneer about the dullness of so much journalism and how off-putting it was for readers: "When they came upon that pale beige tone, it began to signal to them, unconsciously, that a well-known bore was here again, 'the journalist.'" Wolfe wanted more "personality, energy, drive, bravura." He thought that they might arrive via "style."[56] But opinion also can emit "personality, energy, drive, bravura." And the effort to "filter" out any hint of opinion, of passion, can leave what remains a "pale beige."

This brings to mind the analogy to late-nineteenth-century French painting given in the introduction: part of what the Impressionists understood and the detail-obsessed Ernest Meissonier did not is that "personality, energy, drive, bravura" can be found in some colorful subjectivity—in flaunting an *impression*.

The blandness that traditional, just-the-facts journalism sometimes exudes also can reduce civic involvement in the issues upon which it reports. Minha Kim of Sungkyunkwan University in Korea has actually tested reactions to various configurations of journalism: "News articles that are written through the eyes of a mere observer, without a perspective or slant," Kim writes, "can foster political disaffection among citizens."[57] In other words, there are easier ways to inspire or outrage than merely arraying unvarnished, balanced, nonpartisan facts. Opinions get citizens riled up.

Riled-up citizens aren't always pleasant to watch. And journalism has other roles to play in politics: facilitating communication between leader and led, analyzing public policies, serving as a watchdog. Nonetheless, it is hard to imagine an energetic, smoothly functioning democracy without some riled-up citizens. They certainly were present at the beginnings of this particular democracy.

If journalism is—to recall the first use of this word in English—the "intercommunication of opinion and intelligence," the latter, intelligence or news, dominated in the twentieth century. But because opinion draws audiences, because it adds interest, because it displays personality and bravura, because it is colorful, because it helps keep citizens engaged, the balance is tipping back toward opinion in the twenty-first century. And there is one other good reason for that shift: opinions can also be enlightening. Lincoln Steffens imparted an important lesson not just by detailing municipal corruption, but by expressing the opinion that the American people, through their tolerance of this misgovernment, bear responsibility for that corruption.

Yes, opinions are too often pigheaded, too often oversimplified: *all* Americans can't be blamed for municipal corruption. Opinions also can be profoundly, spectacularly wrong. Ah, but when they are right! Opinions that have ossified into doctrines can obstruct thinking, but an opinion that is lithe and lightly held can open up new perspectives. An opinion that is accepted without reflection can interfere with learning, but an opinion can also provide an impetus and a framework for learning. If we use opinions to sort out to whom we will deign to listen, they can narrow our perspectives, but turning to someone with a like mind can be useful in adapting old principles to new situations.[58] And opinions can serve as convenient, attractive containers for ideas.

In the just-the-facts era, with the Objectivity Police always on patrol, all opinions in news sections or newscasts were hidden—hidden even sometimes from the occasionally ideologically naive journalists promulgating them. If opinions are, as they had to be then, injected into stories only surreptitiously or unconsciously, then opinions can be sinister. But an opinion openly held is easy, as Jay Rosen puts it, for the audience to "factor . . . in":[59] But she would say that, wouldn't she? She's a Democrat. It is possible to disagree and still learn.

And opinions on current events don't have to array themselves on the political spectrum to be stimulating. Indeed, the less they fit traditional notions of partisanship the more thought provoking they often are. All that is required is that they be considered and important or interesting.

Why must most mainstream journalists—reporters such as John Burns of the *New York Times*—work so hard to disguise the fact that they might be blessed with an opinion? Will worthy institutions such as the *Times* still be nobly proclaiming that the "divide" between news and opinion has been "maintained" even as they are overrun by dozens of more entertaining and more enlightening journalism organizations?

This book is not a call for more opinion in journalism. In the next chapter, in fact, I delineate some situations where opinions are unhelpful. This book is, however, a call for more wisdom in journalism—and that wisdom is often enough the product of the making of an argument, of the formulation of a considered opinion.

6

"THE WORLD'S IMMEASURABLE BABBLEMENT"

What Does and Does Not Make Journalism Wise

T
he first issue of the *New Republic* appeared on November 7, 1914, a few months after the European powers had jumped into what was quickly understood to be a world war. That issue featured an attack on the war—and on war itself—by twenty-five-year-old Walter Lippmann. It began with two extraordinary sentences: "Every sane person knows that it is a greater thing to build a city than to bombard it, to plough a field than to trample it, to serve mankind than to conquer it. And yet once the armies get loose, the terrific noise and shock of war make all that was valuable seem pale and dull and sentimental."[1]

Lippmann was clearly making an argument here—with a precocious understanding of humankind and its foibles, with rhythm, with power, with a command of logic. He constructed, Aristotle would be pleased to note, an enthymeme of sorts. The first sentence proposes three premises, the first two of which at least seem unarguable. The second sentence does not deign to state the conclusion that follows from those premises: the foolishness of war. Instead, it assumes that point has been made and explains why—in an unfortunate but familiar irony—it is being ignored.

This is an exalted example of where journalism appears to be heading a century later. It is an example of one type of wisdom journalism. This chapter also discusses and includes examples of other types. But first it undertakes a less uplifting task: outlining what kinds of journalism, however interpretive, do not qualify as wisdom journalism and do not point to a future for journalism.

Some traditional American journalists, partisans of shoe-leather reporting, dismiss interpretive journalism as "thumb sucking"—a lazy alternative to gathering the facts with which they might, to pursue the metaphor, nourish themselves and their audiences. And it is true that our burgeoning number of networks and our billions of web pages are filled with plenty of unimportant, uninteresting, even inane interpretation. Some can be found in our newspapers, too, nowadays. But vacuity is not the only problem. Bullheaded, overheated opinion—dispiriting to listen to, dispiriting to click on—is also hard to avoid on the airwaves and the Web. And although, as Herbert Bayard Swope understood, "nothing is more interesting than opinion when opinion is interesting,"[2] a silly report is rarely as annoying as a shrill, misguided, uninformed, or mushy opinion.

No, it won't be hard to demonstrate that our collective wisdom is not often increased by the failure to honor some of the standards of argument introduced in the context of revolutionary America in chapter 1. So any typology of interpretation will have its louche categories, where diatribes, close-mindedness, unbending partisanship, faulty reasoning, unsupported charges, blathering, evasions, and thumb sucking hang out.

Some of the targets of my criticism here may appear too easy—examples of on-air commentary that most would not consider serious journalism. But a common response to my suggestion that we need more interpretation, even opinionated interpretation, in journalism today is to ask whether that would not mean more of the unedifying rants we sometimes hear on cable news or talk radio. So I thought I should devote a few pages to making clear why such rants represent anything but wisdom journalism.

As is probably apparent by now, my personal politics, like those of the young Lippmann and most in the milieu I inhabit, incline to the left of center. That's why, to demonstrate character and do my part for the quality of discourse, I ought to criticize someone who shares my orientation. So I begin by excluding from my vision of what journalism's future should be these sentences by MSNBC's Chris Matthews from September 2012:

I watched Secretary Clinton with President Obama today out at Andrews Air Force Base honoring Ambassador Chris Stevens and the three others killed in Benghazi. That moving scene is America at our best, honoring our fellow citizens, especially those who serve our country, as individuals and public servants worthy of personal reverence.

What a contrast with the ratty politics being played on the other side: this dirtball attack that never seems to end on the President's birth in this country, this relentless effort to paint him as "the other"— someone who snuck in the country, someone who "pals around with terrorists," who "sympathizes" with the attackers, who gets his politics from "overseas."[3]

Before getting to the vocabulary being employed here, I should say something about the *logic*. Matthews begins with a Democratic president and secretary of state at a particularly solemn occasion—a rather limited example from which to *induce*, in Aristotle's terminology, conclusions about their politics. Then he compares this scene with a few of the wildest charges made by the least respectable Republicans—these examples, too, are extreme and not convincingly *paradigmatic*. It is an unfair comparison. Another way of understanding Matthews's error here is that he is guilty, in Aristotle's words, of "omission of consideration of when and how";[4] he is comparing behavior in quite dissimilar circumstances. He is implying that some Democrats do not also level wild charges, of whatever degree of malice and speciousness, or that Republicans are not also capable of solemnity. This is not a wise argument.

Logic does have a way of retreating on partisan cable television or talk radio. This is due in part to the fact that its practitioners have to do quite a bit of talking—producing many, many more words per week than, say, a newspaper columnist. Nonetheless, they ought, Chris Matthews ought, to do better.

I'm not sure whether we have a right to expect logically correct analyses at this point from conservative radio talk-show host Rush Limbaugh, who has developed a reputation for provocative, even irresponsible comments. But we might note that he employs, with some regularity, the Aristotelian fallacy of exaggerating his opponent's argument—creating, in other words, a "straw man."[5] Speaking after an attack on a U.S. diplomatic compound in Benghazi, Libya, in which four Americans were killed, Limbaugh fumed:

> All we've heard since Obama killed bin Laden is that Al-Qaeda's been destroyed and the War on Terror is essentially over. . . . Yet not only are US embassies and businesses all across the Middle East being attacked and torched, the University of Texas at Austin had to be evacuated. Bomb threat. Somebody claiming to be Al-Qaeda. Don't these people read the *New York Times*? Don't they listen to Obama? Don't they know there is no more War on Terror? Don't they know that with Osama being buried wherever, that that was the end of Al-Qaeda?[6]

Limbaugh in this passage "amplified," as Aristotle puts it,[7] President Obama's claim: the president never said the struggle with terror was over, nor did he say al-Qaeda was finished.[8] Limbaugh was also exaggerating the terror threat to the United States at that time.

Wisdom journalists—unlike Chris Matthews and Rush Limbaugh in these examples—are concerned with the quality of their logic. They are also concerned with their language. Which brings us back to Chris Matthews. "Ratty"? "Dirtball"? The *character* this MSNBC host is establishing through such name-calling does not appear to display the "virtue" of "fair-mindedness." Nor is it temperate. Matthews has, in Aristotle's phrase, gone "into a rage."[9]

Chris Matthews, Rush Limbaugh, and their brethren or antagonists on MSNBC, Fox News Channel, talk radio, and partisan websites have seemed increasingly interested in displaying the alternative variety of character—that exemplified by Isaiah Thomas's reporting on the first battle of the American Revolution, that of a journalist reliably devoted to a cause. But when Republicans are dismissed as "dirtballs," or when Limbaugh speaks, as he regularly does, of Democratic president Obama's "regime,"[10] the chances decline that supporters of these two parties might engage in reasoned *discourse* and display openness to each other's ideas.

I don't mean to imply that all the individuals named here are equally unbending or equally prone to flaws in their logic. But I do want to highlight a sad fact that I believe does apply to many of the Democrats on MSNBC and many of the Republicans on Fox: they can get so consumed by what Whitelaw Reid had called the "exigency of party warfare" that they deny themselves the opportunity to learn from the opposition. Wisdom journalism does not withhold opinion, but it should be opinion that not only is fair to other points of view but has been tested and strengthened by exposure to contrary opinion.

These party-line partisans, in contrast, tend to focus—and in this there is some equality—not on the most interesting or challenging of statements that someone in the other party has made, but on the most absurd of their statements. Indeed, their main entertainment often seems to be lying in wait for someone, anyone, remotely associated with the other tribe to say something, anything, really stupid. Given the numbers of people now having their say on the Internet or on something that qualifies as a network, the wait is never long. Our ideology-driven error hunters are aiming their shotguns into increasingly crowded barrels. And the fish they end up targeting are sometimes sufficiently obscure to be pleased to be receiving any attention. The whole point is to enable these partisans and their audiences to join together in grand and satisfying choruses of "Can you believe what they're saying now?" Somehow this particular brand of politically committed journalist manages to be at once shocked, *shocked*, that anyone could have said such a thing and smug because he or she knew all along that the other side secretly thinks such things.

In my favorite example of this game, the shock and smugness were inspired by a *fourteen-year-old* "talk-show host" in West Virginia—heard, as best I can determine, only on the Internet. According to the outraged liberal website *ThinkProgress*, this young man claimed that "'President Obama, Vice President Biden is [*sic*] making kids gay!'" The *Huffington Post* and Bill Maher's HBO show also picked up the story.[11] What is being illuminated by any of these revelations beyond the fact that any political position will attract its share of loose-talking, loose-thinking, undereducated adherents—adult and teenaged? This becomes a party-line version of the traditional journalist's "gotcha!" game—with the number of individuals who might be gotten now numbering in the tens of thousands.

The journalism I am calling for does not involve traveling the ever-vaster media seas for outrages.

Unwavering, unreflective, support-the-cause journalism also leads to problems with *style*, to continue to recall the guidelines for argumentative journalism introduced in chapter 1. Not only do terms such as *ratty* and *dirtball* stem from anger, but they seem designed, in Aristotle's words, to lead an audience "into anger."[12] They are recourses to emotions. Our louder bloggers and radio and television "hosts" frequently can be accused of using excessive "force," as philosopher Stephen Edelston Toulmin would put it.[13]

Fox News Channel's biggest star, Bill O'Reilly, sometimes manages to constrain his language with qualification, uncertainty, and attribution. In one of his monologues, aired during the 2012 presidential campaign, O'Reilly included an "I'm assuming" twice and a "my analysis is based on" once. But qualifications, expressions of uncertainty, and attribution have not been common in his pronouncements. Here is a short selection from that monologue: "The U.S. government is broke. The feds are borrowing heavily, $3.5 billion every day. And now they're manipulating the dollar in order to pay the bills. That's economically insane. That's Greece."[14] And this sort of overstatement is heard too often on cable news in the United States in the second decade of the twenty-first century—where liberal, if I might use that word, applications of rhetorical force seem to have become accepted. The talking heads our more partisan shows and networks feature can seem a little shrill, unfair, or uncomprehending. Unlike, say, Greece and pace Mr. O'Reilly, the U.S. government in 2012 was having no difficulty selling Treasury bonds at extraordinarily low interest rates and thereby funding its debt.[15] Whether this counted as paying its bills may be debatable, but to say the U.S. government was broke seems a bit much.

Much talk radio shares this weakness for overstatement. Finding an example of excessively forceful rhetoric from Rush Limbaugh is itself a bit like shooting fish in a barrel. But here he is explaining an action by Ben Bernanke and the Federal Reserve in September 2012: "If they didn't do this, it's double-dip recession time, and Bernanke, of course, doesn't want that during a campaign 'cause he is in the tank for Obama."[16] No qualification, uncertainty, or attribution to be found.

I don't mean to imply, however, that the mere presence or absence of qualifying phrases, acknowledgments of uncertainty, or attribution will be enough to sort out what qualifies as wisdom journalism. I. F. Stone—whose work does, I believe, qualify—was certainly capable of a forceful statement. Here's an example from his own publication, *I. F. Stone's Weekly*, in 1965, during the Vietnam War: "The South Vietnamese regime is one we have tried to impose on its people against their will."[17] No qualification, uncertainty, or attribution to be found.

But the case can be made that Stone's *logic* is sounder and his *style* somewhat less emotional than Limbaugh's. Stone probably also holds an edge in the *method* he employs. For Limbaugh's allegation that Ben Bernanke "is in the tank for Obama" does not appear to meet Stephen Toulmin's three conditions for determining when a "claim to know" something is "proper" or "trustworthy."[18]

Limbaugh's expertise on matters economic and on the Fed chair's psychology seems limited. Stone, on the other hand, does appear, to borrow Toulmin's words, to have had "enough experience" to speak on the Vietnam War, not only having followed it as intently as any Washington journalist, but also having written a book on the Korean War and done extensive reporting overseas. Limbaugh also does not seem to have performed a lot of "observations" on Bernanke's behaviors—including his reluctance in previous months to take steps to heat up the economy and thereby help Obama.[19] Nor has Limbaugh conducted a reasonable number of "tests" on his conclusion—running it by some people who know Bernanke, for example. Fact checking has been in vogue in American journalism recently. But the Left often "tests" the claims of the Right, not their own, and conservatives such as Limbaugh mostly scrutinize the assertions of liberals.

Whether Limbaugh has applied "considered" judgment to the subject—the final element in Toulmin's method—depends to some extent on whether you think Rush Limbaugh is a reasonable fellow, which depends to some extent on your politics. But phrases such as "in the tank for," no matter how well they play on the radio, seem more indicative of a snap than a "considered" judgment.

The last of the standards for judging arguments introduced in chapter 1 is *evidence*. It is among the most important of these imperfect determinants of what might qualify as wisdom journalism.

Newsweek magazine was on the verge of death in August 2012—operating jointly with the online *Daily Beast* and under the editorship of veteran magazine resuscitator Tina Brown. In this desperate state, the magazine decided to call attention to itself by doing something very unnewsmagazine-like: putting highly controversial stories on its cover. One such cover story featured the following provocative headline: "Hit the Road, Barack: Why We Need a New President."[20] It provides an example of running afoul of the evidence.

The article was written by Niall Ferguson, a history professor at Harvard, with a specialty in economic history. It was filled with economic statistics and charts. It was highly interpretative and, as is obvious from its title, unabashedly opinionated. Ferguson nonetheless was careful to be honest about his own position on the political spectrum—that he advised John McCain in the 2008 presidential election—so that readers could, in Jay Rosen's words, "factor . . . in"[21] that position. All that prevented this article from standing as a prime example of wisdom journalism was that its claims, as a number of commentators noted at the time, were sometimes incorrect or dangerously misleading.[22]

I will give a couple of examples, both of which come when Ferguson takes on the Obama administration's health-care plan: "The Patient Protection and Affordable Care Act (ACA) of 2010," he wrote, "did nothing to address . . . the 'fee for service' model that drives health-care inflation." But it did. As Sarah Kliff pointed out in the *Washington Post* earlier that same year, the act includes a number of payment "reforms" designed to "move the country's health system away from one that pays for volume and toward one that pays for value."[23] Whether Ferguson believes these reforms will work is another matter, but they *are* in the act. He either did not "have," in Aristotle's words, "the facts belonging to that subject"[24] about which he was writing, or he fudged those facts. "Truth conditions," to switch to philosopher John Searle's terminology, have not been satisfied for this "assertion."[25]

But that was not Ferguson's major critique of what had become known as "Obamacare." He then included this odd pairing of sentences: "The president pledged that health-care reform would not add a cent to the deficit. But the CBO [Congressional Budget Office] and the Joint Committee on Taxation now estimate that the insurance-coverage provisions of the ACA will have a net cost of close to $1.2 trillion over the 2012–22 period."

Here Ferguson clearly pulled a fast one. "Net" implies a final reckoning, but Ferguson conveniently left out of that reckoning anything besides increased health-insurance costs. He cleverly ignored all the revenue-generating provisions included in the Affordable Care Act— measures that both the Congressional Budget Office and the Joint Committee on Taxation said will offset those costs and actually help the act, in total, *reduce* the deficit.

So Ferguson supported his implication that, despite President Obama's pledge, health-care reform will increase the deficit with evidence that is not relevant to that point and seems purposely misleading. He included only half of the balance sheet and seemed to imply that two respected organizations said that the president violated his pledge, when they did no such thing.

Certainly, there is an interpretative, partisan, and wise argument to be made against President Obama's health-care plan. But Ferguson's argument is interpretive, partisan, and wrong. He failed in achieving the first, most basic form of truth. The accurate and aboveboard presentation of the evidence—of the facts, if you will—is a necessary, though not sufficient condition, of wisdom journalism. Once again, arguing that our best journalists ought to do more than just present the facts on widely reported stories certainly does not mean that the interpretations they may craft are relieved of responsibility for getting the facts right. Accuracy is as important in arguments as it is in reports.

Did Rush Limbaugh have the facts when he said Ben Bernanke "is in the tank for Obama"? Bernanke, a registered Republican, was appointed chairman of the board of governors of the Federal Reserve by President George W. Bush in 2006; before that, he had served as chairman of that Republican president's Council of Economic Advisers. Bernanke was reappointed to his position at the Federal Reserve by President Obama in 2010. Although there has been plenty of conservative scuttlebutt on Bernanke, to the best of my knowledge no reputable evidence of his leanings in the 2012 election have surfaced. Indeed, on the day before Limbaugh made his charge, Bernanke had said, at a press conference, "We have tried very, very hard . . . to be nonpartisan and apolitical, to make our decisions entirely based on the economy."[26] I can find examples of Rush Limbaugh restating his charge against Bernanke;[27] I can find none where he provides any *direct* evidence that Bernanke was lying.

One might think that, with the evidence so thin, a bit less force—a "probably" or "seems to be"—might at the very least have been called for on Limbaugh's part.[28] Perhaps qualification or uncertainty or attribution, even when the evidence is flimsy, does not make for good talk radio. In that case, then, talk radio does not make for wisdom journalism.

Journalism that leaps out ahead of the evidence, that is surer than it has reason to be sure, that pontificates, spouts, hazards guesses, or "tells" when it is indeed "too soon to tell" is not the kind of journalism I see leading the way out of the current crisis. One of the early champions of a more interpretive journalism, Mike Levine of the *Times Herald-Record* in Middletown, New York, was clear on the subject: "It's not like talk radio."[29]

However, the tentative efforts our traditional news organizations have been making to engage in a little interpretation often seem to err in the opposite direction. When asked for some insight, reporters trained not to reach conclusions sometimes merely echo the consensus on the beat or at dinner parties. Or, and too often, they come up with mealy-mouthed, "on the one hand this, on the other hand that" news analyses, which demonstrate that it is also possible to weigh in with too little force.

In such tepid analyses, "some" can be counted on to have "voiced concerns" that "developments" may have "profound ramifications," although, "on the other hand," as "some analysts say," the "outcome is still not clear," for "it is still too early to say," according to "some observers." (Such analyses usually add up to less than the sum of their "some's.") We don't get, therefore, much beyond the obvious. The tenor of the genre is well captured by such pithy "news analysis" headlines as "Voices of Peace Muffled by Rising Mideast Strife" in the *New York Times*, "Papal Gaffe Was Setback for Religious Dialogue" in the *San Francisco Chronicle*, and "For Mayor, Opportunity and Daunting Challenges" in the *Los Angeles Times*.[30]

Some percentage of what passes for interpretation in newspapers and traditional newscasts nowadays consequently produces the squishy, methodical sound of toothless rumination. It is too timid, too flat, inescapably anodyne.

As these analysts rephrase conventional wisdom in ragged-right newspaper columns or furrow their brows across from television anchors, their tepid musings, designed to offend no one, often end up as predictable as the overly aggressive opining of the talk-show hosts. The latter at least tackle issues. In their fear of revealing any political leaning, mainstream news analysts too often confine themselves to discussions of political strategy or to speculations on who came out on top—efforts at interpretation that, although less offensive than bluster or rage, still don't add much to understanding of public policy. The word *wisdom* does not often come to mind when considering either excessively forceful or insufficiently forceful efforts to chew over the news: interpretation with fangs or without any bite.

The word *snark*—invented by Lewis Carroll—now designates another questionable characteristic of contemporary journalistic *style*: a droll, derogatory cynicism. The news and gossip website *Gawker* may be our foremost purveyor of snark. The aforementioned Rush Limbaugh in this instance is the victim not the perpetrator: "On Wednesday, Rush Limbaugh once again proved that he's unafraid to ask questions the rest of us avoid because the blood vessels to our brains aren't occluded by hog fat and Macanudos."[31]

Snark can be entertaining. Snark can be useful in deflating pretentions. But one danger here, to return to the earlier discussion of logic, is an overreliance on the ad hominem. Snark often involves using people's personal characteristics—the fact that Limbaugh is stout and has a taste for cigars, in this case—to denigrate their arguments. And to return to the earlier concern with openness to other's points of view, all this nastiness clearly does not help us reason together—another danger.

There is a little snark, too, in Jon Stewart's satire on *The Daily Show* and in Stephen Colbert's on *The Colbert Report*. Humor is certainly one route to knowledge. Controlled doses of irony can allow us to make more nuanced comments about the world. Satire can skewer—deftly, entertainingly—where a skewering is due. In other words, a little meanness—even snark—is sometimes called for. In the many evenings, over many years, that their shows have been broadcast, Stewart and Colbert have often risen to the level of wisdom journalism. They provide insights as well as laughs.

However, satirists such as Stewart and Colbert—useful and talented as they and their writers are—frequently mine the same territory: the distance between what people say and what they do or between what they say and what they said. It is rich terrain, to be sure, but unvaried and in the same neighborhood as that explored in the "gotcha!" game. One wouldn't want a generation's understanding of the world reduced to the revelation that people, in particular powerful people, are often hypocritical. There are other, more interesting routes to wisdom.

Oh, and let's not forget another generally unedifying style of commentary—one with long roots in America: the paranoid.[32] The particular question that snarky *Gawker* caught Limbaugh raising is an example of this style. "What if," Limbaugh wondered, "Ayman al-Zawahiri and other al-Qaeda leaders gave up Osama bin Laden for the express purpose of making Obama look good? Giving Obama stature, political capital?"[33]

A. J. Liebling—to switch to an example of someone who does qualify as a wisdom journalist—helped originate the role of press critic in the mid–twentieth century. He also managed to be among that distinguished group of nonfiction writers who produce sentences so clear and compelling they can stand as maxims. Here, originally hidden away in a parenthesis in a *New Yorker* article about declining competition among newspapers, is Liebling's most famous line: "Freedom of the press is guaranteed only to those who own one."[34]

A maxim, Aristotle explains, is the conclusion of an enthymeme without the premise.[35] (Crafting maxims was among the many arts at which Ben Franklin excelled.) The unstated, unnecessary premise in this example from Liebling, written in 1960, might be: because what a publication says will ultimately be determined by the person who controls that publication. . . .

The stated conclusion—Liebling's maxim—itself qualifies as an example of wisdom journalism. In an era in which journalism's only other route to a significant audience was an even more expensive broadcast transmitter, Liebling brought insight and understanding through his snappy statement of the advantage those wealthy enough to own something like that have over their fellow citizens. And Liebling's maxim even carried the hint of a solution: perhaps a democracy could come up with a system in which the rich had less of a monopoly on the means of opinion.[36]

The previous chapter spoke of insights, understandings, and solutions—along with truth in two varieties—as ambitious but appropriate aspirations for journalism, the best journalism. The remainder of this chapter is devoted to exploring some of the packages in which those happy gifts might arrive. I have tried to use mostly examples as mighty as that sentence by Liebling—examples tested by time. Nonetheless, it is certainly possible to do wisdom journalism—especially while operating under deadline pressure—without writing quite as well as Joan Didion or accomplishing quite as much as Rachel Carson.

≈

Making facts "sensible." A. J. Liebling's maxim—"Freedom of the press is guaranteed only to those who own one"—told its readers, it must be admitted, something they mostly already knew. Or, rather, it enabled them to see more meaning in a situation with which they were already familiar. In 1960, near the height of the period when news was big business, it provided an insight: our cherished free-press system has a serious limitation if it is hard to bring political ideas before a large audience without the backing of someone with large amounts of money. Liebling's clever and concise wording maximized the power of this insight. His maxim didn't offer any new facts, although the article in which it was embedded offered plenty of them. But this sentence helped its readers better understand the extant facts. It *interpreted* them—a crucial purpose of wisdom journalism.

Louis Menand, another *New Yorker* writer as well as a Harvard English professor, has pondered the information/understanding dialectic in another discipline—history: "We read histories for information, but what is it we want the information for? The answer is a little paradoxical: we want the information in order to acquire the ability to understand the information. At some point we want the shell of facts to burst. . . . Information alone doesn't do it . . . for when we are equipped with the intuition, every fact becomes sensible."[37] We might substitute the word *insight* here for Menand's more mystical-sounding *intuition*, but his analysis also applies to journalism.

Lincoln Steffens provided quite a bit of information in the introduction to his investigations of municipal corruption in a series of American cities (when those cities were more ethnically homogeneous):

> When I set out on my travels, an honest New Yorker told me honestly that I would find that the Irish, the Catholic Irish, were at the bottom of it all everywhere. The first city I went to was St. Louis, a German city. The next was Minneapolis, a Scandinavian city, with a leadership of New Englanders. Then came Pittsburgh, Scotch Presbyterian, and that was what my New York friend was. 'Ah, but they are all foreign populations,' I heard. The next city was Philadelphia, the purest American community of all, and the most hopeless.

This is information with a purpose—information in the service of an insight: "The 'foreign element' excuse," Steffens wrote, "is one of the hypocritical lies that save us from the clear sight of ourselves." And what might Americans have seen when they looked at themselves? The following hard-to-hear sentence—used as an example of opinion in the previous chapter—is where Steffens answered that question and burst "the shell of facts": "The misgovernment of the American people is misgovernment by the American people."[38]

A former student and then colleague of mine, Sarah J. Hart, has suggested to me that news is what happened; journalism is what it means. There are also other things journalism can be, as Hart would acknowledge; nevertheless, that view is a noble one. It is certainly a pleasing circumstance when, as in the passage by Lincoln Steffens, journalism succeeds in locating meaning. The news in Steffens's book was that a large number of American cities were very corrupt. The *meaning*, he insisted, was that this was because Americans of all backgrounds accepted that corruption.

A. J. Liebling and Lincoln Steffens, like many wisdom journalists, made facts "sensible." They traveled beyond news.

And this is an increasingly important journey for journalists to undertake. Now that most of humankind's knowledge is being rapidly uploaded to the Internet, information, facts, news pour out of our laptops, our tablets, our smart phones. There was a time when humankind hungered after information, after facts, after news. That era—the age of insufficient information—has ended. Our hunger now is for help in making sense of all the facts we have.

~~

Revealing hidden truths. "It is part of the business of the writer—as I see it," wrote the journalist and novelist James Baldwin in 1955, "to examine attitudes, to go beneath the surface, to tap the source."[39] Certainly, this is part of the business of the wisdom journalist. Here Baldwin is, four years later, writing for the *Partisan Review* about his visit to the American South as an African American man raised in the North. He is discussing two subjects that were kept hidden beneath the surface at the time, as they had been at most times—sex and race:

> What passions cannot be unleashed on a dark road in a Southern night! Everything seems so sensual, so languid, and so private. . . . In the Southern night everything seems possible, the most private, unspeakable longings; but then arrives the Southern day, as hard and brazen as the night was soft and dark. . . . Perhaps the master who had coupled with his slave saw his guilt in his wife's pale eyes in the morning. And the wife saw his children in the slave quarters, saw the way his concubine, the sensual-looking black girl, looked at her—a woman, after all, and scarcely less sensual, but white.[40]

In this section, I am not pointing to the basic and important variety of *truth* that journalists, traditional or nontraditional, must struggle with on a daily basis: getting, in essence, the facts right—truth as in not reporting something that is false. Indeed, that is less of a consideration in this excerpt from Baldwin than in any other passage quoted in this book. Baldwin instead is after the kind of truths that have been buried.

Hidden truths can be revealed by journalistic investigations, as they dredge up damning facts. That's a large part of what Lincoln Steffens was up to. That's what Woodward and Bernstein were up to. Such truths certainly can be revealed by attentive, intensive, empathetic reporting on a place or situation that journalists otherwise tend to ignore, as in the intriguing first two paragraphs of Katherine Boo's extraordinary 2011 book on life in a Mumbai slum:

> Midnight was closing in, the one-legged woman was grievously burned, and the Mumbai police were coming for Abdul and his father. In a slum hut by the international airport, Abdul's parents came to a decision with an uncharacteristic economy of words. The father, a sick man, would wait inside the trash-strewn, tin-roofed shack where the family of eleven resided. He'd go quietly when arrested. Abdul, the household earner, was the one who had to flee.
>
> Abdul's opinion of this plan had not been solicited, typically. Already he was mule-brained with panic. He was sixteen years old, or maybe nineteen—his parents were hopeless with dates. Allah, in his impenetrable wisdom, had cut him small and jumpy. A coward: Abdul said of himself. He knew nothing about eluding policeman. What he knew about mainly was trash. For nearly all the waking hours of nearly all the years he could remember, he'd been buying and selling to recyclers the things that richer people threw away.[41]

An honored wing of the palace of wisdom journalism is occupied by "immersion journalism": accounts such as Boo's based on in-depth reporting and filled with poignant facts about cultures that might otherwise be ignored—in this case an Indian "undercity." But no facts, as traditional journalists or Katherine Boo might understand them, are included in James Baldwin's account of "passions . . . in a Southern night." He knows his history. He has sniffed around. That, rather than evidence, is the source of his authority. Otherwise, Baldwin's musings here are in a sense all insight, all intuition. He is reporting—using all the freedom nonfiction might allow—on what might have been: an imagined wife and an imagined slave woman contemplating each other during an imagined affair. He is reporting on humidity, on scents, on ghosts. Yet Baldwin conducts a kind of investigation: much is revealed—much that is subterranean, hidden; much that is true. It is journalism. And it is wise.

Journalism's claim to honor is based in large part on the ameliorative power of frankness. For those of us optimistic enough about human nature to follow this idea far—even to honesty about desire, even to honesty about humiliation—there is something deeply honorable in James Baldwin's journalism. Yes, it is full of injustice, pain, and anger. But there are also intimations of understanding (among the women, perhaps, in that passage).

Tom Wolfe stripped bare a very different set of racial attitudes for *New York* magazine in 1970—attitudes in the minds of upper-class white people in Manhattan in 1970 as they raised money for the radical Black Panthers. Wolfe dubbed those attitudes "radical chic":

> As in most human endeavors focused upon an ideal, there seemed to be some double-track thinking going on. On the first track—well, one does have a sincere concern for the poor and the underprivileged and an honest outrage against discrimination. . . . One understands why poor blacks like the Panthers might feel driven to drastic solutions, and—well, anyway, one truly *feels* for them. One really does. On the other hand—on the second track in one's mind, that is—one also has a sincere concern for maintaining a proper East Side lifestyle in New York Society. And this concern is just as sincere as the first, and just as deep. It really is.[42]

I would argue that there is also plenty of insight, of a type more familiar in journalism, in I. F. Stone's analyses of the Vietnam War in 1965. In January of that year, for example, Stone did what he did as well as anyone: use publicly available documents to point out official government omissions, if not lies. Here is how he began: "The Senate Foreign Relations Committee last week put out what purported to be an objective volume of 'Background Information' on the war in Vietnam. It is supposed to be a compilation of the important official statements. But the record is tailored." Stone then listed a series of important earlier government statements on that war that were conveniently ignored in that Senate volume because they had painted a rosy picture of America's ally, South Vietnam, and its prospects—a view that subsequent events revealed as foolish. The fact that U.S. officials had repeatedly put forward an unreasonably optimistic picture of what was going on in Vietnam was hidden in the Senate volume by, as Stone puts it, "discreet editorial scissors."[43]

I would acknowledge that Rush Limbaugh's analyses upon occasion also offer insights. He is certainly capable of analyzing news clips or documents and uncovering liberal hypocrisy. But Limbaugh's unsupported allegation that Federal Reserve chairman Ben Bernanke "is in the tank for Obama" seems more fulmination than revelation. In it, I see prejudices confirmed more than truths revealed.

"Journalism is chores," Norman Mailer has written. "Journalism is bondage unless you can see yourself as a private eye inquiring into the mysteries of a new phenomenon."[44] Mailer escaped that bondage with some frequency in his journalism—whether examining the tensions between police and protesters at an antiwar march or the motivations of a murderer.[45] Private eyes reveal. Wisdom journalists often do, too.

Providing perspective. Rachel Carson helped launch the environmental movement in a *New Yorker* article and then in her 1962 book *Silent Spring*:

> The history of life on earth has been a history of interaction between living things and their surroundings. To a large extent, the physical form and the habits of the earth's vegetation and its animal life have been molded by the environment. Considering the whole span of earthly time, the opposite effect, in which life actually modifies its surroundings, has been relatively slight. Only within the moment of time represented by the present century has one species—man—acquired significant power to alter the nature of his world.[46]

Sometimes it pays to get some perspective: if not "the whole span of earthly time," then perhaps a century or a decade. And sometimes the payoff is not just insights and understandings and not just prospective solutions, but actual solutions: in this case, a global, if still woefully incomplete, effort to reduce the damage to the earth's water and atmosphere caused by humankind.

A. J. Liebling's maxim is twelve words long. If insight can be packed into so few words, there is no reason not also to look for it in 140-character tweets. My next example—a series of three tweets, actually—is not snarky or even particularly clever. It is not finely written, and, unlike Rachel Carson's paragraph, it lacks the ambition to change the world. But this series of tweets, like Carson's paragraph, did employ history, and it did provide a perspective that was of use in interpreting current events.

These tweets were sent, within minutes of each other, by master poll interpreter Nate Silver of the *New York Times*'s *FiveThirtyEight* blog at a moment in September 2012 when the presidential election seemed rapidly to be slipping away from Mitt Romney:

Nate Silver @fivethirtyeight Is Romney a "bad" candidate? Depends on what the control group is. A lot of the incumbency advantage is in drawing mediocre opponents.

Nate Silver @fivethirtyeight List of challengers to elected incumbents since WW2: Stevenson, Goldwater, McGovern, Reagan, Mondale, Clinton, Dole, Kerry.

Nate Silver @fivethirtyeight Romney worse than Reagan or Clinton. Better than McGovern, Goldwater. In the same league as Stevenson, Mondale, Dole, Kerry.[47]

In three tweets, Nate Silver helped us look at Mitt Romney's candidacy for the presidency differently.

Evaluation. Critics evaluate. Other journalists—at least those freed from the straightjacket objectivity and balance can become—can evaluate, too.

This is Dorothy Thompson, writing for *Cosmopolitan* after a 1931 interview with Adolf Hitler—whose vacuity she saw, but whose danger she underestimated:

> He is formless, almost faceless; a man whose countenance is a caricature; a man whose framework seems cartilaginous, without bones. He is inconsequent and voluble, ill poised, insecure—the very prototype of the Little Man. . . .
>
> [Hitler's] social and economic theory is a tale told by an idiot. Beside it Lenin's consequent Communism and revolutionary program glitters with intellect. But reason never yet swept a world off its feet, and Hitler, an agitator of genius, knows this. Self-interest, expressed in pathetic terms, does. Hitler is the most golden-tongued of demagogues.[48]

Evaluation—not a mere recounting of circumstances—requires by definition that a journalist have a point of view. Film reviewers, for example, usually must at some point praise or criticize. Critics of society or its leaders certainly do not have to reduce everything to thumbs up or thumbs down, but this mode of journalism is best adopted by those who can come up with something provocative to say.

James Baldwin, again, from his 1959 *Partisan Review* article:

> I was . . . but one generation removed from the South, which was now undergoing a new convulsion over whether black children had the same rights, or capacities, for education as did the children of white people. This is a criminally frivolous dispute, absolutely unworthy of this nation; and it is being carried on, in complete bad faith, by completely uneducated people.[49]

It is not usually necessary to use that much force, but when evaluating, some force does help.

Expanding views of the world. This can be done through reporting. And Joan Didion—another journalist and novelist, as well as a memoirist—certainly could report, as she demonstrated with her account for the *New York Review of Books* of goings on in El Salvador in 1982, when the country was very much in the grip of death squads:

> There is a special kind of practical information that the visitor to El Salvador acquires immediately, the way visitors to other places acquire information about the currency rates, the hours for the museums. In El Salvador one learns that vultures go first for the soft tissue, for the eyes, the exposed genitalia, the open mouth. One learns that an open mouth can be used to make a specific point, can be stuffed with something emblematic; stuffed, say, with a penis, or, if the point has to do with land title, stuffed with some of the dirt in question. One learns that hair deteriorates less rapidly than flesh, and that a skull surrounded by a perfect corona of hair is a not uncommon sight in the body dumps.[50]

But Joan Didion is never just reporting—or if she is just reporting, then reporting can be a much more engaged, opinionated enterprise than it has been in traditional American journalism—for in her nonfiction Didion is not shy about criticizing, explicating, saying what she thinks. And she is always thinking—even when reporting, for example, on a murder for the *Saturday Evening Post*, a popular magazine, in the 1960s. Didion is capable of expanding our view of the world even when, in that murder story, writing about something as close to home as the San Bernardino Valley in Southern California:

> The future always looks good in the golden land, because no one remembers the past. Here is where the hot wind blows and the old ways do not seem relevant, where the divorce rate is double the national average and where one person in every thirty-eight lives in a trailer. Here is the last stop for all those who come from somewhere

else, for all those who drifted away from the cold and the past and the old ways. Here is where they are trying to find a new life style, trying to find it in the only places they know to look: the movies and the newspapers.[51]

≈

Expressing what the public is feeling. This category violates rules laid down in other categories—or, as the expression goes, proves them. For it acknowledges that journalism sometimes has a role to play not in surprising us, enlightening us, challenging us, or expanding our horizons, but in crystallizing and clarifying our own thoughts.

Thomas Carlyle noted this talent and celebrated it (I think) in his quick 1851 sketch of Captain Edward Sterling—an editorial, or "leader," writer for the *Times* of London: "Sterling rushes out into the clubs, into London society, rolls about all day, copiously talking modish nonsense or sense, and listening to the like . . . comes home at night; redacts it into a *Times* Leader,—and is found to have hit the essential purport of the world's immeasurable babblement that day, with an accuracy beyond all other men."[52]

As an example of "hit[ting] the essential purport," I have chosen an editorial cartoon. It appeared in the *Washington Post* very early on November 4, 2008—after a night in which a significant number of Americans and commentators on television surprised themselves by growing teary-eyed at the realization that the United States, with its history of racism and slavery, had just elected an African American man president. In the cartoon, Tom Toles drew the White House, with this phrase from the Declaration of Independence written in the sky above it: "We hold these truths to be self evident, that all men are created equal." Walking toward the White House is a small, big-eared, dark-skinned figure carrying a large briefcase.[53]

In practicing this variety of wisdom journalism, one captures the essence of what a group of people are thinking at any given moment.

One expresses widely held thoughts for those less able to express well. And one provides, perhaps, "a script," as literary historian Dallas Liddle explains, for people's conversations throughout the rest of the day.[54] George Will and Peggy Noonan and William Kristol do this for conservatives today; Paul Krugman and Rachel Maddow and Jon Stewart do it for liberals.

The Internet has given us all access to our own printing presses. To the extent that there is always a chance that what we publish there might reach a significant audience, to the extent that what we choose to share might be something more significant than a joke or a cat video, the promise of a free press has perhaps once again been extended beyond wealthy publishers. But the Internet has also, of course, added immeasurably to "the world's immeasurable babblement." Hitting its "essential purport" is thus quite a trick.

Expressing a public's feelings seems a less glorious service than surprising, enlightening, challenging, or broadening—than standing apart from the "babblement" and saying something kind of, sort of new: "Only within the moment of time represented by the present century has one species—man—acquired significant power to alter the nature of his world." Hitting "purport" can too easily deteriorate into confirming conventional wisdom or even prejudices. Nonetheless—done with sufficient perspicuity—it can provide an important service.

≈

Looking for larger principles. First on John Adams's list of the factors that turned American "minds and hearts" to revolution is "principles." The assertion of principles undergirds John Dickinson's "Letters from a Farmer in Pennsylvania." They hold an honored place in wisdom journalism.

Edward R. Murrow and his producer Fred Friendly helped bring down Senator Joseph McCarthy primarily with principles in their 1954 CBS documentary. Here are some of the basic American principles of justice and freedom they invoked in the selection quoted in chapter 4:

- "We must not confuse dissent with disloyalty."
- "We must remember always that accusation is not proof and that conviction depends upon evidence and due process of law."
- "We will not walk in fear, one of another."
- "We will not be driven by fear into an age of unreason."
- "We are not descended from fearful men—not from men who feared to write, to speak, to associate and to defend causes that were, for the moment, unpopular."[55]

Not all public disputes are this stark. But a wisdom journalist should be able, when the occasion calls for it, to find larger issues, if not moral themes, in contemporary events.

Francis Jeffrey was one of the first editors of what became the *Edinburgh Review*. He wrote this in 1843 in the preface to a collection of his own articles from that publication:

> The *Edinburgh Review*, it is well known, aimed high from the beginning:—And, refusing to confine itself to the humble task of pronouncing on the mere literary merits of the works that came before it, professed to go deeply into *the Principles* on which its judgments were to be rested; as well as to take large and Original views of all the important questions to which those works might relate. . . . I think it must be allowed to have substantially succeeded—in familiarizing the public mind (that is, the minds of very many individuals) with higher speculations, and sounder and larger views of the great objects of human pursuit, than had ever before been brought as effectually home to their apprehensions.[56]

Francis Jeffrey's *Edinburgh Review* focused on books, but I see no reason why the principles, if you will, he articulated should not be applied to journalism in general. Going "into" "principles," taking "large and original views" of "important questions," challenging and expanding "the public mind," tackling "the great objects of human pursuit," aiming high. That is pretty close to the outline of the purposes of wisdom journalism I have put together here. Indeed, that is a pretty good account of what

Walter Lippmann accomplished in the two sentences on war that began this chapter.

Lippmann helped invent a new journal in 1914, the *New Republic*, as a home for his ambitious, original, insightful sentences. The final chapter of this book calls, a hundred years later, for the renovation of journalism so that it might provide a home for many, many more such sentences.

7

"SHIMMERING INTELLECTUAL SCOOPS"

The Wisdom Journalist, the Journalism Organization,
Their Audiences, and Our Politics

"Once spilled, news quickly becomes a commodity," *New York Times* media columnist David Carr noted with his usual verve in 2012, "so ideas—shimmering intellectual scoops—have very high value."[1] That, of course, is one of this book's central points. In borrowing Carr's term *intellectual scoops*, I don't mean—and I believe Carr didn't mean—that we need more reports on literary theory or neuroscience, though they might also be welcome.[2] I mean that journalism ought to be able to exhibit more intellectual heft while discussing the meanderings of politics, society, and culture today. I mean that journalists—while studying what they study, current events—ought to adopt or give birth to more important ideas.

Most news is now spilled more or less as soon as it happens. The journalism business must consequently become an idea business.

However, many traditional reporters, including perhaps some of Carr's colleagues at the *Times*, have spent too long pursuing and writing "just the facts" to easily begin fashioning those facts into ideas. Some of their editors have spent too long resisting the encroachment of anything that is not carefully sourced, that might be perceived as less than objective, to easily welcome such ideas—shimmering or not—into most of their pages now. Indeed, as jobs flee and the lessons of a lifetime in journalism are being devalued, some traditional journalists today are too busy crying over spilled news to do much more than wonder if perhaps they ought to master HTML or learn how to read on camera.

A considerable amount of new thinking, retraining, and new hiring will therefore be required if we are to move from *news* sites to *journalism* sites or, perhaps, even some lingering but recast *journalism*-papers and *journalism*-casts. A considerable amount of new thinking, retraining, and new hiring will definitely be required if we are to achieve more "shimmering intellectual scoops" sites.

Once again let me emphasize that there is still room in this vision of a new, wiser journalism for a few reporters, perhaps from wire services, to show up at tragedies and press conferences and make sure we are not deprived of who, what, when, and where. Let me emphasize, too, that investigative reporting certainly is important, as are efforts to witness what other reporters have failed to see, as Katherine Boo did in a Mumbai slum, or to otherwise obtain exclusives. Reporters trained to chase these more traditional scoops will share *journalism*-rooms, not *news*rooms, with those "shimmering intellectual scoop" chasers.

"Shimmering" is a lofty goal. "Intellectual" is a formidable qualification. There is another, also ambitious, way of saying this. The traditional five W's—four of which are now often readily available online—might be replaced as guidelines for journalists by the five I's: "informed," "intelligent," "interesting," "insightful," and "interpretive." Journalists still produce paeans to the glory of fact collection and transcription. The five I's, however, ask much more of journalists: more study, more intellection, more discernment, and more originality.

It is significant how many of the most respected names in the history of journalism—from Joseph Addison to James Baldwin, Joan Didion, and Tom Wolfe; from Benjamin Franklin to Lincoln Steffens, Walter Lippmann, and Rachel Carson—were, indeed, known for stories that were often reported, usually marvelously written, but also thoroughly informed, unquestionably intelligent, consistently interesting, consistently insightful, and freely interpretive. The disruptions caused by the new news technologies will prove a blessing if they allow journalists to stop romanticizing the gathering and organization of facts and aspire, once again, to that level of accomplishment.

This final chapter focuses on how such a wiser, more ambitious journalism might be accomplished and what the consequences of accomplishing it might be not just for journalism, but for its audiences and our politics.

What if we were constructing from scratch a twenty-first-century *journalism*, not *news*, organization? With whom would we staff it? Certainly, with people obsessed with the contemporary world and its turnings. But at this point, given digital-distribution patterns and our evolving interests, that obsession might want to be as much with the divorce rate in the San Bernardino Valley, the "double-track thinking" of liberal East Siders, or life in the slums of Mumbai as with the machinations of local city councils.

And certainly we would want to staff our new journalism organization with individuals who can write—or record audio or produce video—engagingly. The competition is too intense now for sentences or audio or video sequences that are a chore or a snooze—fact dense, formulaic, awkward, or obvious.

The first paragraph of the *New York Times* story reporting on the first presidential debate in 2012—the paper's lead story that day—provides a not atypical example of how writing standards can get a bit lax in traditional journalism. I criticized the headline atop this story in chapter 4 for taking a timid, humdrum approach to an event that, because of President Obama's poor performance, came close to turning the election: "Obama and Romney, in First Debate, Spar Over Fixing the Economy." The lead paragraph of the story compounds the problem—not just because of a couple of syntactical infelicities, but because it is overstuffed, unfocused, and, despite the use of words such as *deepest* and *invigorate*, the opposite of deep and invigorating. For there is little here that could not have been written before the debate: "Mitt Romney on Wednesday accused President Obama of failing to lead the country out of the deepest economic downturn since the Great Depression, using the first presidential debate to invigorate his candidacy by presenting himself as an equal who can solve problems Mr. Obama has been unable to."[3]

Here, by way of comparison, is how William Kristol began a blog post, written minutes after that debate ended, for the *Weekly Standard:*

> President Obama was right in his closing statement: "This was a terrific debate." So it was. For Mitt Romney.
>
> Mitt Romney stood and delivered the best debate performance by a Republican presidential candidate in more than two decades.[4]

The *Weekly Standard* is unabashedly conservative. Kristol was clearly pleased by the Republican's triumph. But he also caught the meaning of the debate, and his prose is taut, lively, to the point. Writing this terse—it is growing more and more common—will not be required of everyone hired by twenty-first-century journalism organizations: longer sentences have their charms. But there won't be much room for writing that is not lively and to the point. Wisdom journalism benefits from work that is aesthetically as well as intellectually pleasing.

Here, for example, is a nicely balanced and meaningful pair of sentences from ace blogger Andrew Sullivan: "What some on the far right seem not to grasp is that opposition to torture is not about being soft on terrorism. It is about being effective against terrorism."[5]

For investigations—to switch this discussion from writing to reporting—we would want some reporters on the staff of a twenty-first-century journalism organization with experience exposing malfeasance at one or another level of government or business. We would want reporters who know their way around documents and databases, reporters with a sense of whom and what to ask. No change, in other words, from traditional American journalism at its best here. However, this would be a change from current practice at most online news sites, which, with few exceptions, have been laggard so far in their deployment of skilled investigative reporters and particularly in their deployment of teams of skilled investigative reporters. They do, it must be acknowledged, have an excuse: releasing reporters for the periods of time that thorough investigations require is expensive. However, adept use of the new data sources becoming available from online sources might both enrich and quicken such investigations.

For many other varieties of exclusives, some experience in the care and feeding of sources would also be useful—including a familiarity with the meaning of "deep background" and "not for attribution," along with a resistance to overusing them. But a whole range of exclusives nowadays is available mostly to adventurous types—individuals who are alert to the overlooked and prepared to go where they need to go to see, ask, and learn. Katherine Boo is an example and not just for her reporting from a Mumbai slum. Boo has also reported for the *New Yorker* on nurses who help poor mothers in the swamps of Louisiana and on the loss of manufacturing jobs in South Texas.[6] Journalism organizations might want to find and cultivate more such sharp-eyed, lone-wolf, off-the-beaten-track, injustice-sensitive nomads—of a sort not always at home in traditional news organizations.

Boo had worked as a reporter for the *Washington Post* before the *New Yorker*, but such free-range exclusives are also available to individuals without a traditional reporting résumé. Joan Didion lacked one: she got started as an editor at *Vogue* and has also written fiction, film scripts, and, more recently, memoirs. Never having occupied a desk in the pressroom at a city hall has not seemed to impede in any way the flow of journalistic exclusives from Didion—contributed to periodicals and collected in books.

If the main goal of a twenty-first-century journalism organization is to fill its site with wisdom, the hiring practices at most American news organizations have not been changing fast enough—even if the occasional Katherine Boo gets on staff or Joan Didion gets an assignment. Indeed, the career ladder in journalism has often seemed as encrusted with tradition as the stories. It has been hard to let go of the expectation that you should work your way up through a series of beats—from covering a suburban town, say, to covering city politics—before, if you're lucky, making it to Washington or even a foreign posting. The newspapers or broadcast stations, the assumption has been, would grow larger as that career progressed. And if you ascended from rung to rung with sufficient poise and competence, some news analyses or even a column might be waiting as you grayed and tired of jotting down someone else's thoughts.

Experienced practitioners in any field tend to advise or require newcomers to replicate their own career paths. But in journalism, with newspapers and broadcast stations laying off more than hiring, that old path is disappearing. And if this view of where journalism is heading is correct, that path no longer seems to proceed in the right direction, for gathering facts and interpreting them are different activities. And the talents nurtured by allotting the "allegedly's" on the police beat or cozying up to an assistant something-or-other at city hall would not seem to have that strong a relationship to the ability to pen compelling interpretations of current events.

Covering crime or local politics may be of some use to the aspiring wisdom journalist—just as spending some time on a farm or selling produce can't hurt if you want to be a chef. But chefs need to learn to cook. And twenty-first-century journalists need to learn to interpret. Indeed, among the oddities of twentieth-century journalism was its habit of rewarding reporters skilled at suppressing evidence of a point of view with a position—columnist, say—in which a point of view was required.

Moreover, that traditional career ladder was designed to train generalists. Promoting reporters from beat to sometimes unrelated beat or designating them "general-assignment reporters" often left them lacking the level of expertise on any of those beats or assignments needed to move much beyond "he said, she said" reporting. This situation was well captured in a quip by humor columnist Dave Barry in 1995: "We journalists make it a point to know very little about an extremely wide variety of topics; this is how we stay objective."[7]

That strategy may have worked when skill in journalism was measured by an ability to gather a lot of quotes and transcribe or paraphrase them accurately—when journalistic prose was dominated by verbs of attribution. It may have worked when objectivity was as important a goal as truth, insight or understanding. It works less well when the goal is making facts sensible, revealing hidden truths, providing perspective, expanding views of the world, and looking for larger principles. These purposes all tend to benefit from knowing quite a bit about a topic.

≈

"When my young friends consult me as to the conditions of successful journalism," the essayist Leslie Stephen wrote in 1881, "my first bit of advice comes to this: know something really; at any rate, try to know something."[8] It is time for this, once again, to be the "first bit of advice" given to prospective journalists.

And note: Stephen said "know something," not "know everything." Here I admit to diverging a wee bit from the teachings of Benjamin Franklin. Rather than ask that journalists who want to interpret, to make an argument, "be well acquainted with Geography, with the History of the Time, with the several Interests of Princes and States, the Secrets of Courts, and the Manners and Customs of all Nations,"[9] I would recommend that they focus on one area of knowledge—perhaps "the Manners and Customs" and history and geography of just, say, the Arab world or perhaps health policy, the environment, or macroeconomics. We can't all be, like Franklin, masters of a whole lot. But it is important, following Leslie Stephen, for a journalist to master something.

One certainly can disagree with the staunchly liberal and aggressively Keynesian Paul Krugman, a widely read columnist for the *New York Times*, but it would be hard to dispute the benefit that his analyses of the country's and the world's financial perturbations derive from his background as a Nobel Prize–winning Princeton economist. Krugman has—to recall once again Stephen Edelson Toulmin's criteria for a "claim to know" and to put it mildly—"enough experience."[10]

Krugman's undeniable expertise not only provides authority and a facility with the statistics and the math but also enables him to place contemporary debates and theories in contexts—historical or otherwise; it enables him to provide perspectives. Here is another way to say it: Paul Krugman doesn't have to lean too heavily on quotes from experts.

Expertise, even at less than Nobel Prize level, brings something else: ideas. Leslie Stephen's advice to aspiring journalists in 1881 also included this suggestion, "Be the slaves of some genuine idea, or you will be the slaves of a newspaper."[11] This may sound disagreeably doctrinaire to traditional journalists—especially to those with memories of the twentieth century's too rigid ideologies. (The word *slaves* does not help.) And such ideas should always be subject, of course, to amendment or abandonment after the arrival of contrary information. But perhaps we might again be able to see ideas for what they are—honed thoughts. And perhaps we might again be able to see journalism as composed of thoughts— thoughts about current events.

My colleague Jay Rosen, much quoted in this book, asked the following question on Twitter during the 2012 presidential campaign: "Do you need a good theory of what the 2012 election is 'about' to be able to report well on it? Most reporters would say no. I say yes."[12] Most traditional reporters—whether they admit it or not—do ride theories of some sort through their stories. The sluggish lead paragraph to that *Times* article on the first presidential debate did trot out a theory of some sort on what Mitt Romney accomplished—"using the first presidential debate to invigorate his candidacy by presenting himself as an equal"— but it would be hard to maintain that this was a particularly surprising or insightful theory.

Might readers searching for some extra value not appreciate the more frequent flickering of "a good theory" or, as Stephen put it, "some genuine idea?" Isn't having such a theory or idea—in other words, having a robust, evidence-based, thought-through, thought-provoking point of view— akin to having something to say? Aren't journalists who fail to pursue intriguing theories or ideas enslaving themselves to an increasingly unremunerative, unambitious, uninspiring view of what journalism might be?

When it comes to ideas, scholarly journalists who have studied their field at university often have a significant leg up on more traditionally trained journalists: they are conversant with the theories in those disciplines that others have formulated, and they are sufficiently knowledgeable to be able to settle upon, if not actually formulate, their own.

Of course, specialized academics turned journalists have to be able to make their weighty ideas accessible. They need to be able to write at a nonacademic pace—weekly, daily, in some circumstances hourly. They need to employ a nonacademic vocabulary. Scholarship lends itself to private languages—terms of art, jargon. A little of that can quickly exclude the uninitiated and befog prose. And, to be sure, specialized knowledge and a knack for clear writing do not always share the same mind. But if alert to the need for intelligibility, if possessed of a sense of sentences and their rhythms, words and their pleasures, the academic journalist may even have an advantage in translating the jargon—the advantage of understanding. Here is Krugman in 2012 diagnosing (albeit with a small mixed metaphor) one aspect of the European economic crisis—in reasonably colloquial language: "Basically, Spain is suffering the hangover from a huge housing bubble, which caused both an economic boom and a period of inflation that left Spanish industry uncompetitive with the rest of Europe."[13]

Hiring individuals with an academic background in the fields upon which they are commenting seems an obvious move. For a long time it wasn't. Doctorate-bearing scholars were rare in journalism in the last half of the twentieth century.

In the eighteenth century, although advanced degrees were uncommon, the United States, like Europe, had its public intellectuals. Ben Franklin meets many definitions of "scholar"—except the academic ones—and he dived into, even instigated, public debates, as did Daniel Defoe in Britain and Voltaire in France; they were at home in publications intended for broad audiences. John Dickinson had studied law, and his thoughts were of course welcomed into newspapers. In the nineteenth century, Horace Greeley hired Margaret Fuller, a leading Boston intellectual, to write regularly for his *New York Tribune*. But the fact that Henry James's stint at the *Tribune* did not work out later in that century, when Whitelaw Reid was editing the paper, was a sign of things to come in the next century.

In the twentieth century, higher numbers of scholars began accumulating doctorates, but journalism did not accumulate many scholars—at least not with doctorates. Cherished exceptions such as the Harvard paleontologist Stephen Jay Gould, who for decades wrote an entrancing column for the magazine *Natural History*, and Tom Wolfe, who bore a Ph.D. in American studies from Yale, seemed to prove the rule. Journalism did still attract some literary types—Hersey, Baldwin, Mailer, and Didion among them—but their bylines rarely appeared in the news pages of newspapers.

For the most part, the golden age of the public intellectual seemed to have passed by the second half of the twentieth century. Most journalists then were still bedazzled by facts and poorly disposed to the abstract theorizing increasingly occupying professors, especially because many of those theories (the postmodern variety in particular) challenged their beloved realism. Many journalists were as a consequence wandering perilously close to anti-intellectualism. In 1988, when deconstruction was the hottest theory on campus, an article in *Newsweek* began by naming as representative of its spirit Humpty Dumpty and Henry Ford.[14] Meanwhile, scholars were busy ascending their own career ladders in increasingly esoteric and jargon-infested academic departments. Along the way, many seemed to lose whatever urge to comment on current events and whatever talent for winsome prose they may have once possessed. Many academics were also by then becoming pretty suspicious of journalism.

But among the many happy revelations of the Internet has been the realization that the scholarly world is dotted with experts who have no trouble managing the requisite timeliness and readability and seem to enjoy playing the role of journalistic commentator—or, rather, helping reshape the role of journalistic commentator. In economics alone, as I have mentioned, we also have Brad DeLong at Berkeley and Tyler Cowen at George Mason—both of whom can churn out well-written and enlightening analyses on their blogs with appropriate frequency. The *New York Times* may have discovered Princeton professor Paul Krugman's talent for this sort of thing in his writing for an early online publication, *Slate*. And then there's the best-selling, multimedia, "freakonomics" operation captained by Steven D. Levitt at the University of Chicago. We also have, as an example, the journalistic talents demonstrated by Supreme Court lawyers Tom Goldstein and Amy Howe on their *SCOTUSblog*.

Exactly what topics we want scholars to hold forth on varies by discipline. Scientists and doctors are given the privilege of reporting on research in their own fields because that research makes news—from the likely fate of the universe to a new treatment for an old illness. Law professors pen op-ed pieces on new laws or big cases—as many did, on *SCOTUSblog* in particular, following the Supreme Court's health-care decision. Literature professors are often asked to expatiate on books or intellectual life; public interest in literary theory, however, seems considerably less intense.

But when scholars whose fields seem to touch most directly on current events—political scientists, sociologists, and economists—wander into journalism, they are usually asked to speak to current events. This is mostly not the forum in which to go on about Britain's waning economic dominance in the twentieth century—unless there is a lesson there about America's waning economic dominance in the twenty-first. This is mostly not the forum in which to haggle out methodological or technical issues—unless application of those different methods or techniques might affect understandings of our situation today. More than insights on their disciplines, it is insights on the world we want from this selection of emissaries from ivory towers.

And we have begun getting them. The emergence of academics in journalism has brought bigger ideas, longer perspectives, and deeper analyses. It has, in a word, significantly increased journalism's supply of wisdom.

But such wisdom is not just available, of course, to those who hold a professorship or Ph.D. It does not have to be certified by a degree. Indeed, even if the conventions of news reporting still require the staffs of mainstream news organizations to hide behind their sources, those staffs do harbor many journalists who have accumulated the requisite expertise—having not only mastered a beat but thought deeply and originally about that beat.

Steven Pearlstein, a business columnist for the *Washington Post*, won the Pulitzer Prize in 2008 for, as the citation put it, "his insightful columns that explore the nation's complex economic ills with masterful clarity."[15] Pearlstein is now also Robinson Professor of Public and International Affairs at George Mason University, but it was his journalism that earned him the professorship, not the other way around. Indeed, Pearlstein's only degree is a B.A. in American studies. He became a journalist with an expertise in business and economics the traditional way: through a long and varied career as an editor and reporter.

Two of my favorite bloggers, Ezra Klein at the *Washington Post* and Matthew Yglesias at *Slate*, are too young to have learned from or even to have had long and varied careers in journalism. Both make do with only a B.A. Yet, as I noted in chapter 4, Klein manages to supply insights on public policy, and Yglesias on business and economics—both with surprising originality and frequency. They have read intensively, and they have learned from the searching, contentious online conversation of which their work is a part. In other words, Klein and Yglesias have become experts, albeit self-taught. And that's fine. Indeed, another of the happy revelations of the Internet has been that the world is filled with plenty of extremely bright but uncredentialed experts.

A doctoral program is a reasonably efficient way to accumulate expertise, but it is hardly the only way. The argument here is not for the degree, but for the expertise, the specialization. Journalism organizations should increasingly be staffed with individuals who "know something really" in one of the variety of fields that regularly touch on current events.

Such experts can be snatched away from graduate schools or borrowed from university faculties, as the *New York Times* has done with Krugman. They can be found by monitoring blogs—as the *Times* found Brian Stelter. If journalism programs insist that their students master a subject matter, not just techniques—as some programs, my own included, are now doing[16]—then journalism programs can supply candidates. The Nieman Fellowship program at Harvard has long helped journalists deepen their understandings. But the argument here is that we can no longer rely on such experts to be trained, as Pearlstein was, by working their way up through a variety of reporting and editing positions—for two reasons: first, because most of these noninvestigative, nonexpert reporting and editing positions seem unlikely to continue to exist; and, second, because the generalist, beat-to-beat expertise those positions provided often proved—with significant exceptions, as for Steven Pearlstein—inadequate.

Instead of fact-oriented generalists who are dependent upon expert sources, the idea would be to hire idea-oriented specialists who know as much as the expert sources. Instead of a background sparring with mayors and police chiefs, three or four of these hires might bring an expertise in urban policy, for instance, and another few might speak Mandarin or Japanese and be well versed on Asian affairs.

Guaranteeing that audiences will find a thoughtful take on, not a mere account of, the day's most newsworthy events will also require a continued transformation of priorities and procedures at most journalism organizations. News analyses on any but the largest stories too often remain hit or miss, and columnists, op-ed contributors, and editorial writers are not always well coordinated. Steven Pearlstein's analyses of the financial crisis in 2008 and 2009 were welcomed onto the front page of the *Washington Post* on some days during the worst of that crisis. Paul Krugman's analyses, however, remained relegated to the back of the A section in the *New York Times*. In this, the *Times* was perhaps more typical. Interpretation in traditional news organization has sometimes been not only bland, but sporadic and unreliable—an afterthought.

The argument here is that interpretation will be the primary mission of the journalism organization—the front-page mission. "Opinion" will not just be a button on the home page, but a main feature of the home page. Anyone who clicks her way there should expect to find the day's news not so much covered but explained—reliably, systematically. This will require, to put the point of the previous section in blunt terms, that reporting staffs increasingly be replaced—except for those pursuers of investigations or other exclusives—with interpreting staffs.

Will these wisdom journalists still report? Facts still must be checked and double-checked. Some wisdom journalists will continue to chase exclusives and pursue investigations. All will be expected to observe, sniff around, ask questions—preferably in person, preferably where the effects of policies are most directly felt. But their beats will also include academic offices, journals, books, policy papers, and increasingly the Web. And none of these wisdom journalists, unlike their brethren on the wire services, will be responsible for that staple of the twentieth-century reporter: stenography. They will not often be asked to stand, notebook in hand, in the crowd around police chiefs, disaster survivors, or even politicians.

Columnists, charged with coming up with an opinion on something in the news a couple of times a week, might begin to seem anachronistic with the rise of wisdom journalism—unless they offer the focus upon a specialty of a Paul Krugman or a Steven Pearlstein. Once expert arguments begin appearing all over the journalism site, what use would there be for often less expert arguments arrayed together on a page labeled "Opinion"?

How will these wisdom journalists be organized? The beat system, as noted in chapter 4, is a holdover from the pretelevision, not to mention pre-Internet, age. It tends to arrange the world around the locations where news is announced. Wisdom journalists, looking not for news, but for the meanings and consequences of that news, will be less focused on particular buildings—police headquarters, for example—and more focused on how policies travel in and out of various organizations and locales—from think tanks to prisons to the streets. They will be organized, the point is, by subject matters akin to academic disciplines or subdisciplines.[17] On the local level, those subjects might include criminal justice, housing, education, transportation. Many news organizations were already giving their beats a rethink and heading in this direction: adding a beat on commuting, for example. This new approach to journalism offers an opportunity to deepen that reconceptualization.[18]

Physical beats may be cut back sharply. Traditional journalists tended to walk well-trod paths, stick close to familiar locales, and follow time-tested routines. Such procedures made manageable the process of handling a substance as inherently messy and unstable as news. But such procedures as a rule do not lead to original perspectives and are not conducive to the formation of original ideas. They must change.

How will these wider-ranging wisdom journalists be deployed? Editors and producers have long gone to great lengths to make sure they include a report on each of the major stories of the day. Timeliness and comprehensiveness are still important for a journalism organization, but reporting on events that most already know about is not. So editors and producers will now need to be similarly prompt and apply similar diligence in making sure they provide their audiences with an interpretation of—an argument on—each of the major stories of the day. (Often those arguments will go out of their way to include a brief recap—perhaps in a separate box—of what happened for those who had managed to avoid news sites in the intervening hours.)

Each day journalism organizations would therefore assign at least one such interpretive journalist, with the appropriate specialty, to each of the major developments of the day—in the same way news organizations now assign a reporter to each of those news stories. If two people have been shot downtown, a criminal-justice specialist on staff, instead of or in addition to just showing up at the scene, might use statistics to examine whether downtown has been growing more or less dangerous.

The same goes for international stories. If the Israeli prime minister has just said something significant for the peace process, a journalism organization would not want to waste much space transcribing his by then widely available words. It instead would make sure someone conversant with the history of Mideast peace negotiations is given space to evaluate that statement and the state of the peace process.

This means that a large journalism organization will need more than one expert in each area—it will need a small flotilla of urban affairs or foreign affairs analysts, for example, if it sees those matters as within its purview. That way, even if one expert is working on a longer piece, someone else should always be available to wax analytic on breaking news.

Can interpretations be churned out this rapidly—as rapidly as breaking news reports are now produced? We have seen repeated evidence on the Web that they can—on two of the stories discussed in chapter 4, for example: the G-20 summit in London and the Supreme Court's health-care decision.

Will what qualifies as news change as commentary comes to the fore? I suspect it will. Journalists charged with interpreting will look for differ-ent qualities in their raw material than journalists merely charged with recounting. They will favor news that comes surrounded by significance, consequence, and ramification because such stories will help them do their work. And they will be inclined to underplay the merely odd and outsized because such tales of men and women biting dogs tend to con-found the search for meaning.

I am not naive (about news, at least). Journalism will never entirely free itself from what in chapter 4 I called the "screaming anomaly": our interest in the transgressive, the bizarre, the shocking runs deep. A story in October 2012 about a nanny in New York City accused of killing two young children in her care is an example: horrible, frightening, wildly unrepresentative.[19] Such anomalies are, by definition, almost incom-prehensible.[20] They may not prove as attractive to journalists looking to make sensible, to find larger perspectives as they have been to journal-ists whose main function has been to tap us on the back, point, and say, "You're not going to believe what terrible thing just happened!"

Will journalists lose their jobs during such a transition to wisdom journalism? Sadly, some—lacking a serviceable expertise, trained primar-ily to collect facts—might. But journalists are already losing jobs.

And what would be the result of all these changes in focus, staffing, and procedures? Audiences could look forward to journalism sites that *interpret* the news as thoroughly, reliably, and adeptly as newspapers such as the *New York Times* and the *Washington Post* have *reported* the news.

≈

And now a different sort of question, the audience question: Will enough people want to patronize this wiser journalism to support new organiza-tions or transformed old organizations? After all, a thoughtful argument on an issue, perhaps even employing some scholarship, can be more difficult to follow than a straightforward report on an event. It didn't take much effort to comprehend the details and grasp the horror of that nanny story.

Wisdom journalism will, to be sure, leave not just its practitioners but their audiences with increased responsibilities. After all, audiences for art had to work harder after the easily intelligible re-creations of events by Ernest Meissonier and other realists were replaced by impressionism, cubism, abstract expressionism, and all that followed. Readers, listeners, and viewers will be asked to grapple with shifting and sometimes unexpected perspectives upon the news. They will sometimes have to look something up. If they have not been plugged in, they may have to turn elsewhere to brief themselves on who, what, when, or where, while the journalists they favor undertake the what for, what next, and with what consequences. They will often be challenged. They will sometimes disagree.

However, other forms of media—films, television programs, even videogames—have grown increasingly complex, even difficult in recent decades. They more often provide what Steven Johnson calls a "cognitive workout."[21] With videogames such as *Myst* and its successors, in which players have to learn the rules as they play, we have come a long way not only since *Pong*, but since *Monopoly*. With television programs in which viewers are asked to follow multiple and multifaceted plots from episode to episode and across seasons—the *Sopranos, Lost*—we have come a long way not only since *Perry Mason*, but since Edgar Allan Poe. And similar demands are made of the audiences for movies such as *Waking Life, Memento, Inception*, and even *Groundhog Day*.

Education levels have risen dramatically in the United States since the middle of the twentieth century and the heyday of the old just-the-facts, descriptive journalism; now they are rising around the world. General levels of awareness and sophistication have climbed as radio and then, more powerfully, television and then, even more powerfully, the Internet have made it possible to know as much in the country as in the city. And it is now rapidly becoming possible to learn as much on a laptop as in a classroom.

Journalists have at times seemed to write with their least-aware, least-educated, least-sophisticated readers, listeners, or viewers in mind—always going out of their way to recap the background and summarize the basic facts. They have long leaned toward simplicity and straightforwardness: extra clarity, undemanding vocabulary, basic narrative structures, uncontroversial political perspectives, and easily verifiable facts. They sometimes have been guilty of condescension, even of pedantry. Journalists have put so much effort into not turning anyone off that it has become more difficult to turn anyone on. They have in many ways spoon-fed their audiences.

But why shouldn't journalists instead take a page from the book of those videogame, television, and film producers who have found success in recent decades by abandoning the least common denominator and challenging their audiences? Indeed, the pleasure so many Internet users now find in tracking down the latest bit of information or commentary on some obsession of theirs is evidence that journalism consumers are prepared, even eager, to work harder. There is no great satisfaction in being spoon-fed.

This is not to say that journalists should indulge in obtuseness or irrelevance. But they might aim—in this new environment, they must aim—significantly higher. Commercial success may, of course, vary. Wisdom journalism is intended as a journalism plan more than a business plan. But I suspect that audiences, significant audiences, are on the lookout for more stimulating, more challenging fare. Some journalism—like some videogames, TV shows, and movies—may shy away from such "cognitive workouts." The best won't.

Some of the best blogs have increasingly been holding debates on public-policy issues: how entitlement costs might be reduced with the least impact on the less well off, for example, or how the growth of health-care costs might best be slowed. The traditional press once fell back on its most solemn prose when it dared to hazard such subjects. But these bloggers have been demonstrating that it is possible to pursue them not only with numbers and charts, but with wit and even the occasional pop-culture reference. They cite each other. They tease each other. They have, of all things, fun. (Most of the bloggers mentioned in previous chapters are examples.) As a result, although these public-policy issues may not quite be "trending," they are being discussed—on Twitter certainly, on smaller blogs, around water coolers. Audiences are being discovered, if not created. We might even hope that our politicians will find more productive ways of discussing these issues.

This book is not intended to be a utopian screed. Journalism can and must improve, but it is created in hours, not years, and will remain vulnerable to hastiness and the passions of the moment. And journalism is a popular art form: even a renewed commitment to wisdom and high standards will not eradicate sensationalism or transform journalism sites into Oxford tutorials.

And there's always the danger that this new order for journalism, while repairing some of the weaknesses of the old order, might lead to new weaknesses. Wisdom journalists on deadline may be tempted to substitute bloviating for substantiating. In surrendering the obsessive pursuit of details, they may be tempted also to sacrifice an obsessive commitment to accuracy. The license to opine may tempt them to grow deaf to contrary opinions. And they may be reduced to hemming too much and hawing too much should something fresh to say come too slowly.

But we can guard against some of these dangers—as journalists, as journalism critics, as journalism audiences—by becoming more perceptive in our evaluations of interpretative journalism. We can guard against them by spending less time noting that we happen to agree or disagree with an argument and more time searching out whatever weaknesses that argument may display in character, discourse, method, style, evidence, and logic. Thanks to its rapid and crowd-sourced feedback mechanisms, the Web has actually proven quite adept at probing the weaknesses of arguments.

And the potential benefits will be large if our journalists—our best journalists—are increasingly freed from the more "mercantile and clerical" task of news gathering; if they more often assume their responsibilities as, to quote the phrase Jürgen Habermas quotes, "'bearers and leaders of public opinion'";[22] if they are trained for and charged with providing informed, intelligent, interpretive, insightful, and illuminating perspectives on current events. We might hope, in particular, that as competition in journalism turns from who transcribes and summarizes best to who goes deepest and is most astute, our understanding of the workings of government and society will be strengthened.

I also have, in other words, some nonutopian hopes for our politics. Wise interpretive pieces won't prevent politicians from protesting and promising too much, but they can make it easier to analyze their protests and promises. They certainly won't immunize political discourse against distortions and dubious claims, but they can at least make available some antidotes.

Wisdom journalists will be in a better position to check a sound bite against the facts in question or a pledge against the results in question. Indeed, that is already beginning to happen. Freed to weigh in on larger issues, these journalists might less often jump on trivial slipups. Deprived of the crutch of balance, these journalists will have to question more frequently the assumption of equivalence in charge and countercharge. During recent battles in Congress and during the 2012 elections, it was possible to watch journalists goad themselves into doing more and more of this questioning.

We have begun to see, too—and this is even more significant—new ideas begin to flow more regularly once again from journalists to the public and into politics. We may not have seen anything yet of the scale of Rachel Carson's idea on the environment in *Silent Spring* or with the impact of John Dickinson's analysis of the Townshend Acts. But if we try to focus on the wisest journalism of the wisest journalists on the Web— as I have focused on the wisest by the wisest in the history of American journalism—it is possible to notice the emergence not just of some challenging critiques, but of some challenging ideas.

We are watching, in other words, as journalism begins to change. Such transformations are inevitably not only misunderstood, but messy, erratic, unsatisfying: new standards and procedures take time to perfect.

But journalists will get better at playing the role of evaluators and idea generators. And although the more thoughtful journalism they produce won't suddenly get all the kinks out of democracy, it should improve the conversations upon which it is based.

A wiser journalism should lead to wiser citizens and therefore wiser politics. John Dickinson and Rachel Carson altered the trajectory of events by offering their audiences a new perspective on the world. That should be wisdom journalism's highest aspiration. That should be journalism's highest aspiration.

NOTES

INTRODUCTION

1. Bill Keller, "Talk to the Newsroom: Executive Editor," NYTimes.com, January 30, 2009, http://www.nytimes.com/2009/01/30/business/media/02askthetimes.html ?pagewanted=all&_r=0.

2. Pew Research Center's Project for Excellence in Journalism, *The State of the News Media 2013* (Washington, D.C.: Pew Research Center, 2013), http://stateofthemedia .org/2013/overview-5/. These numbers are based on data or estimates through 2012. I have also consulted Pew Research Center's Project for Excellence in Journalism, *The State of the News Media: An Annual Report on American Journalism* (Washington, D.C.: Pew Research Center, 2011), http://stateofthemedia.org/2011/ .

3. Pew Research Center's Project for Excellence in Journalism, *The State of the News Media 2013*. Pew's source here is the American Society of News Editors, *Newsroom Employment Census* (Columbia, Mo.: American Society of News Editors, 2010), but Pew has calculated and added estimates for more recent years.

4. See Jennifer Dorroh, "Statehouse Exodus," *American Journalism Review*, April–May 2009, http://www.ajr.org/article.asp?id=4721. "In 2003, there were more than a thousand foreign journalists covering the war in Iraq," noted then *New York Times* managing editor Jill Abramson in 2010, when foreign troops were still fighting there. "Today that number has dwindled to fewer than one hundred" ("Sustaining Quality Journalism," *Daedalus* 139 [Spring 2010]: 39–44). The 2013 Pew Center report complains of "a continued erosion of news reporting resources" (*The State of the News Media 2013*).

5. See, for example, the 2008 University of California, Berkeley, panel on "the crisis in news" at http://fora.tv/2008/04/26/The_Crisis_in_News_Print_Media.

6. This is the definition I introduced in *A History of News* in 1988. See Mitchell Stephens, *A History of News*, 3rd ed. (New York: Oxford University Press, 2007), 4.

7. For an interesting Heideggerian perspective on technological developments that promote the "live" and the "real time" as well as the distortions they cause for "eventization," see Bernard Stiegler, *Technics and Time*, vol. 1, trans. Richard Beardsworth and George Collins (Stanford, Calif.: Stanford University Press, 1998), 16 and elsewhere.

8. For a discussion of this difficulty, see Slavko Splichal and Colin Sparks, *Journalists for the 21st Century* (Norwood, N.J.: Ablex, 1994), 1–31.

9. See Clay Calvert, "And You Call Yourself a Journalist? Wrestling with a Definition of 'Journalist' in the Law," *Dickinson Law Review*, 103 (Winter 1999): 411–51.

10. For the spread of pay walls, see the discussion of newspapers in Pew Research Center's Project for Excellence in Journalism, *The State of the News Media 2013*, specifically at http://stateofthemedia.org/2013/newspapers-stabilizing-but-still-threatened/.

11. For a discussion of advertising's problems online, see Michael Wolff, "The Facebook Fallacy," *Technology Review*, May 22, 2012, http://www.technologyreview.com/web/40437/?nlid=nldly&nld=2012-05-22.

12. Ross King, *The Judgment of Paris* (New York: Walker, 2006), 2–3, 204–5, 331, 344.

13. Quoted in ibid., 2.

14. Quoted in Constance Cain Hungerford, *Ernest Meissonier: Master in His Genre* (Cambridge: Cambridge University Press, 1999), 39.

15. Quoted in Marc J. Gotlieb, *The Plight of Emulation* (Princeton, N.J.: Princeton University Press, 1996), 165.

16. Quoted in Hungerford, *Ernest Meissonier*, 162, 173.

17. King, *The Judgment of Paris*, 369. For the price, see also Henry James, "The American Purchase of Meissonier's *Friedland*," in *The Painter's Eye* (Madison: University of Wisconsin Press, 1989), 108. Constance Cain Hungerford, however, gives the price as 300,000 francs (*Ernest Meissonier*, 174).

18. Quoted in Hungerford, *Ernest Meissonier*, 162.

19. Marc J. Gotlieb explains that "Muybridge's stills forced the collapse at the end of the nineteenth century of a verist standard of artistic truth that had prevailed in Salon painting for a half-century or more" (*The Plight of Emulation*, 183).

20. Quoted in Hungerford, *Ernest Meissonier*, 205.

21. Ibid., 206.

22. King, *The Judgment of Paris*, 370–71.

23. Keller, "Talk to the Newsroom."

24. Honoré de Balzac, preface to *The Chouans*, trans. Katharine Prescott, electronic ed. (N.p.: MobileReference, 2009), http://books.google.com/books?id=En7jT7K PJvYC&dq=Balzac+%22author+firmly+believes+that+details+alone%22&source =gbs_navlinks_s.

25. The cholera story is well told in Steven Johnson, *The Ghost Map: The Story of London's Most Terrifying Epidemic—and How It Changed Science, Cities, and the Modern World* (New York: Riverhead Books, 2006). David Mindich emphasizes the shift from religious explanations for cholera in the American press to more fact-based

explanations: "What more fitting way is there to enter the age of 'realism' than with a replacement of God with the 'foul effluvia of . . . overflowing privies'" (*Just the Facts* [New York: New York University Press, 1998], 111, quoting the *New York Tribune*; in his book, Mindich connects the effort to prevent cholera to realism in general and to the rise of objectivity in the press in particular).

26. Quoted in Stephens, *A History of News*, 246.

27. Mindich writes: "It is no less than remarkable that years after consciousness was complicated by Freud, observation was problematized by Einstein, perspective challenged by Picasso, writing was deconstructed by Derrida and 'objectivity' was abandoned by practically everyone outside newsrooms, 'objectivity' is still the style of journalism that our newspapers articles and broadcast reports are written in, or against" (*Just the Facts*, 5).

28. Quoted in Mitchell Stephens, *the rise of the image the fall of the word* (New York: Oxford University Press, 1998), 75.

29. Quoted in Michael Doran, ed., *Conversations with Cézanne* (Berkeley: University of California Press, 2001), 124.

30. Virginia Woolf, "Modern Fiction," in *Virginia Woolf Reader* (Orlando, Fla.: Harcourt, 1984), 285–86.

31. For an example of a journalism critic who did question realism, see Robert Karl Manoff, "Writing the News (by Telling the 'Story')," in Robert Karl Manoff and Michael Schudson, eds., *Reading the News* (New York: Pantheon, 1986), 197–229.

32. The "New Journalists" of the last third of the twentieth century waged more of a revolution in writing style than a revolt against the primacy of detail. Indeed, Tom Wolfe, perhaps the most eager of this bunch to debate with journalists, fashioned himself a great partisan of realism: "The introduction of realism into literature by people like Richardson, Fielding and Smollett was like the introduction of electricity into machine technology" ("The New Journalism," in Tom Wolfe and Edward Warren Johnson, *The New Journalism* [New York: Harper Row, 1973], 34). Nonetheless, among the freedoms reintroduced by the "New Journalism" was the freedom to interpret.

33. Walter Lippmann, *Public Opinion* (New York: Harcourt, Brace, 1922) 3–32; on Lippmann and his view, see Mitchell Stephens, "Deconstruction and the Get-Real Press," *Columbia Journalism Review* 30, no. 3 (1991): 38–42.

34. Committee of Concerned Journalists, "Principles of Journalism," reprinted by the Pew Research Center's Project for Excellence in Journalism at http://www .journalism.org/resources/principles. "These [principles] became," this website reports, "the basis for *The Elements of Journalism*, the book by PEJ Director Tom Rosenstiel and CCJ Chairman and PEJ Senior Counselor Bill Kovach"—an influential book by two influential thinkers on journalism.

35. Karl Kraus, *In These Great Times* (1914), trans. Harry Zohn, in Vassiliki Kolocotroni, ed., *Modernism: An Anthology of Sources and Documents* (Chicago: University of Chicago Press, 1998), 204–5.

36. I am not arguing that Walter Cronkite intended his tagline, "And that's the way it is," as some sort of philosophical statement. He stumbled upon it, by his own account. At the time, CBS News president Richard Salant criticized this line for its presumption, a criticism Cronkite understood. But the presumption in question, according to Cronkite, was that the broadcast would prove to have been "mistake" free—not that its perspective on reality was necessarily subjective or limited, let alone that it was making news through its reporting of the news ("Walter Cronkite—on His 'That's the Way It Is' Signoff," 1998 interview, Archive of American Television, http://www.youtube.com/watch?v=NOa4sg2WOEQ; Jeff Alan, *Anchoring America* [Chicago: Bonus Books, 2003], 129–30; see also Karen S. Johnson-Cartee, *News Narratives and News Framing* [Oxford: Rowman & Littlefield, 2005], 114).

37. See Patrick Collier, *Modernism on Fleet Street* (Hampshire, U.K.: Ashgate, 2006), 201. Collier writes: "English newspapers and literature lived happily together for 200 years. . . . So closely tied were literature and journalism that the distinction between them would have made no sense to writers from Daniel Defoe . . . to Matthew Arnold. . . . By the age of modernism, such a productive nexus of literature, journalism and politics seemed unimaginable." Collier is writing of England, but this close tie also existed in America, and its severing, which Collier credits more to quality than to ideology, may have been even more dramatic here. The relationship between Henry James and the *New York Tribune*, discussed at the end of chapter 2, is representative of that tie, its break, and my understanding of what went wrong.

38. Stephens, "Deconstruction and the Get-Real Press."

39. Wolfe, "The New Journalism," 31. See also Tom Wolfe, *The Painted Word* (New York: Picador, 1975), and *From Bauhaus to Our House* (New York, Macmillan, 2009).

40. Wolfe, "The New Journalism," 28–35.

41. Josh Marshall, "Sounds Right," *Talking Points Memo*, January 2, 2012, http://talkingpointsmemo.com/archives/2012/01/sounds_right.php?ref=fpblg.

42. Quoted in King, *The Judgment of Paris*, 226.

43. Abramson, "Sustaining Quality Journalism," 43.

44. In this article, written in 2010, Abramson seems confident of the importance of "quality journalism"—a term she uses eight times. But she sometimes seems to be struggling to settle upon the proper relationship between information and analysis in "quality journalism": "People don't crave just information. They seek judgment from someone they can trust, who can ferret out information, dig behind it and make sense of it. They want analytic depth, skepticism, context and a presentation that honors their intelligence" ("Sustaining Quality Journalism," 43).

45. Journalism criticism has certainly featured earlier acknowledgments of the value of interpretation. "We want more than the facts pleasingly arranged," James W. Carey, for example, wrote in 1986. "We also want to know how to feel about events and what, if anything, to do about them" ("The Dark Continent of American Journalism," in Manoff and Schudson, eds., *Reading the News*, 150). In 2008, Philip Meyer

wrote: "The old hunter-gatherer model of journalism is no longer sufficient. Now that information is so plentiful, we don't need new information so much as help in processing what's already available. . . . We need someone to put it into context, give it theoretical framing and suggest ways to act on it" ("The Elite Newspaper of the Future," *American Journalism Review*, October–November 2008, http://www .ajr.org/article.asp?id=4605).

46. Baron's speech is reprinted in Jim Romenesko, "*Boston Globe* Editor: Newspapers Are Badly Bruised, but Not Beaten," Jim Romenesko.com, September 17, 2012, http://jimromenesko.com/2012/09/17/boston-globe-editor-newspapers-are -badly-bruised-but-we-are-not-beaten/#more-24850.

47. Robert Weisman, "Martin Baron, Editor of *The Boston Globe*, to Become Editor of *The Washington Post*," *Boston Globe*, November 13, 2012, http://www.boston .com/businessupdates/2012/11/13/martin-baron-editor-the-boston-globe-become -editor-the-washington-post/ycJWyd1XOsuvpQAQ3LMStI/story.html.

48. In his thoughtful discussion of the civic consequences of the twenty-first-century crisis in journalism, Alex S. Jones distinguishes between the "news of assertion" and "fact-based news" or the "news of verification," and he notes that "traditional journalists have long believed that this form of fact-based accountability news is the essential food supply of democracy" (*Losing the News: The Future of the News That Feeds Democracy* [New York: Oxford University Press, 2011], 3). I am arguing, in part, for the "news of assertion."

1. "PRINCIPLES, OPINIONS, SENTIMENTS, AND AFFECTIONS"

1. Bill Keller, "Talk to the Newsroom: Executive Editor," NYTimes.com, January 30, 2009, http://www.nytimes.com/2009/01/30/business/media/02askthetimes .html?pagewanted=all&_r=0.

2. Thomas Jefferson to Edward Carrington, January 16, 1787, in *Jefferson: Political Writings*, ed. Joyce Appleby and Terence Ball (Cambridge: Cambridge University Press, 1999), 153.

3. Keller, "Talk to the Newsroom."

4. See Mitchell Stephens, *A History of News*, 3rd ed. (New York: Oxford University Press, 2007), 205–13.

5. Ibid., 131–43.

6. "The new tydings out of Italie are not yet com" (first line used as title), reproduced in Stephens, *A History of News*, 140.

7. Carlota S. Smith, *Modes of Discourse* (Cambridge: Cambridge University Press, 2003).

8. Letter in *Boston News-Letter*, April 17–24, 1704, reprinted in William W. Wheildon, *Curiosities of History: Boston, 1630–1880* (Boston: Lee and Shepard, 1880), 87, http://archive.org/details/curiositiesofhis1880whei.

9. Jürgen Habermas, "The Public Sphere: An Encyclopedia Article," in Douglas M. Kellner and Meenakshi Gigi Durham, eds., *Media and Cultural Studies: Key Works* (Malden, Mass.: Blackwell, 2006), 76.

10. Frank Luther Mott, *American Journalism* (New York: Macmillan, 1941), 15–17.

11. *New England Courant*, first issue, August 7, 1721, http://www.ushistory.org/franklin/courant/issue1.htm.

12. "Silence Dogood, No. 4," *New-England Courant*, May 14, 1722, in *Benjamin Franklin: Writings*, ed. J. A. Leo Lemay (New York: Library of America, 1987), 10–13.

13. Smith, *Modes of Discourse*, 13, 155–83.

14. Walter Isaacson, *A Benjamin Franklin Reader* (New York: Simon & Schuster, 2005), 9–10.

15. Benjamin Franklin, *The Autobiography and Other Writings* (New York: Signet Classic, 1961), 29.

16. "The Printer to the Reader," *Pennsylvania Gazette*, October 23, 1729, http://franklinpapers.org/franklin/framedVolumes.jsp.

17. Benjamin Franklin, "A Thunderstorm," *Pennsylvania Gazette*, September 25, 1734, in *Benjamin Franklin*, ed. Lemay, 233.

18. Walter Isaacson, *Benjamin Franklin: An American Life* (New York: Simon & Schuster, 2003), 132–33.

19. Stephens, *A History of News*, 7–15.

20. Benjamin Franklin, "Apology for Printers," *Pennsylvania Gazette*, June 10, 1731, in *Benjamin Franklin*, ed. Lemay, 171–77.

21. Benjamin Franklin, "Rattle-Snakes for Felons," *Pennsylvania Gazette*, May 9, 1751, in ibid., 359–61.

22. Benjamin Franklin, "Proposals and Queries to Be Asked the Junto," 1732, in ibid., 208–12.

23. Benjamin Franklin, "On Literary Style," *Pennsylvania Gazette*, August 2, 1733, http://franklinpapers.org/franklin/framedVolumes.jsp.

24. Benjamin Franklin, "The Printer to the Reader," *Pennsylvania Gazette*, October 2, 1729, in *Benjamin Franklin*, ed. Lemay, 136–37.

25. *New-England Courant*, first issue, August 7, 1721, http://www.ushistory.org/franklin/courant/issue1.htm.

26. "Wisdom journalism" may also bring to mind the efforts of certain governments or religions and their supporters to fill the press with homilies. I see wisdom journalism—restless, penetrating, insightful—as instead challenging such paternalistic propaganda or pat calls to "virtue." Horst Pöttker is particularly alert to the problem of condescension ("A Reservoir of Understanding," *Journalism Practice* 5, no. 5 [2011]: 520–47).

27. Merrill Jensen, ed., *Tracts of the American Revolution, 1763–1776* (Indianapolis: Hackett, 2003), 127.

28. John Dickinson, "Letters from a Farmer in Pennsylvania to the Inhabitants of the British Colonies in America," letter 2, Online Library of Liberty, http://

oll.libertyfund.org/?option=com_staticxt&staticfile=show.php%3Ftitle=690&cha
pter=102299&layout=html&Itemid=27.

29. Charles Janeway Stillé, *The Life and Times of John Dickinson 1732–1808* (Philadelphia: Lippincott, 1891), 81.

30. Jay Rosen, "I'm There, You're Not, Let Me Tell You About It: A Brief Essay on the
Origins of Authority in Journalism," *PressThink*, March 27, 2012, http://pressthink
.org/2012/03/im-there-youre-not-let-me-tell-you-about-it/.

31. Isaiah Thomas, no article title, *Massachusetts Spy*, May 3, 1775, http://www
.teachushistory.org/node/333.

32. See George A. Kennedy, *A New History of Classical Rhetoric* (Princeton, N.J.:
Princeton University Press, 1994).

33. Andrew R. Cline's website, the Rhetorica Network (http://rhetorica.net/meter
.htm), has undertaken the task of applying rhetorical theory to journalism and
contemporary public discourse.

34. Aristotle, *On Rhetoric*, trans. George A. Kennedy (New York: Oxford University
Press, 1991), 37–38 (1.2.2, 1.2.4).

35. *New-England Courant*, no. 18, November 27 to December 4, 1721, http://www
.ushistory.org/franklin/courant/issue18.htm.

36. See Mott, *American Journalism*, 15–21.

37. Aristotle, *On Rhetoric*, 38 (1.2.4).

38. Ibid., 121 (2.1.5).

39. Dickinson, "Letters from a Farmer in Pennsylvania to the Inhabitants of the
British Colonies in America," letter 2.

40. "The longer I've studied it," Jay Rosen writes, "the more I've come to see that
'objectivity' as practiced by the American press is a form of persuasion. It tries to
persuade all possible users of the account that the account can be trusted because
it is unadorned" ("Objectivity as a Form of Persuasion," *PressThink*, July 7, 2010,
http://archive.pressthink.org/2010/07/07/obj_persuasion.html).

41. Max Hamburger, *Morals and the Law: Aristotle's Legal Theory* (New York: Biblo and
Tannen, 1965), 90.

42. I owe this point to Thomas Patterson; I return to it in chapter 5.

43. Ortwin Renn and Thomas Webler, *Fairness and Competence in Citizen Participation*
(Dordrecht, Netherlands: Kluwer, 1995), xviii, http://books.google.com/books?id
=i6osqwfcy3wC&dq=habermas+fairness&source=gbs_navlinks_s.

44. Stephen Edelston Toulmin, *The Uses of Argument* (Cambridge: Cambridge University Press, 1999), 60.

45. For an earlier effort to think about what we might mean by a "journalistic method,"
see Stephens, *A History of News*, 216–17.

46. Stillé, *The Life and Times of John Dickinson*, 21–30.

47. Aristotle, *On Rhetoric*, 30, 38 (1.1.5, 1.2.5).

48. The Center for Journalism Ethics at the University of Wisconsin offers this
advice, for example: "Emotional stories should not dominate the news coverage

and overshadow critical analysis. Vignettes of people caught up in tragedy bring the story home to viewers. But when over-used they lead to compassion fatigue or divert editorial resources away from the big picture" (Steven J. A. Ward, "Emotion in Reporting: Use and Abuse," Center for Journalism Ethics, School of Journalism and Mass Communication, University of Wisconsin, Madison, August 23, 2010, https://ethics.journalism.wisc.edu/2010/08/23/emotion-in -reporting/).

49. Dickinson, "Letters from a Farmer in Pennsylvania to the Inhabitants of the British Colonies in America," letters 1–3.

50. Aristotle, *On Rhetoric*, 235 (3.7.1).

51. See Stephens, *A History of News*, 100–104.

52. Toulmin, *The Uses of Argument*, 30–35.

53. Thomas, *Massachusetts Spy*, May 3, 1775.

54. Dickinson, in "Letters from a Farmer in Pennsylvania to the Inhabitants of the British Colonies in America," letter 2.

55. John B. Blake, "The Inoculation Controversy in Boston: 1721–1722," *New England Quarterly* 25, no. 4 (1952): 489–506.

56. John R. Searle, *Mind, Language, and Society* (New York: Basic Books, 1999), 148–50.

57. Thomas, *Massachusetts Spy*, May 3, 1775.

58. Searle, *Mind, Language, and Society*, 142.

59. Aristotle, *On Rhetoric*, 187 (2.22.4).

60. Thomas, *Massachusetts Spy*, May 3, 1775.

61. City of New York v Grosfeld Realty Co., 570 NYS2d 61, 62 (2nd Dep't 1991). This case from New York State refers in particular to defeating "a motion for summary judgment," but the legal principle involved is accepted enough to be considered part of black-letter law.

62. *Federal Rules of Evidence*, Rule 801 (c), 802.

63. My researcher, Darcy Boynton, helped develop these categories.

64. Thomas, *Massachusetts Spy*, May 3, 1775.

65. Ibid.

66. "Evidence is relevant," the *Federal Rules of Evidence* explains, "if (*a*) it has any tendency to make a fact more or less probable than it would be without the evidence; and (*b*) the fact is of consequence in determining the action" (Rule 401).

67. Quoted in Dickinson, "Letters from a Farmer in Pennsylvania to the Inhabitants of the British Colonies in America," letter 2.

68. Aristotle, *On Rhetoric*, 190–204 (2.23).

69. Ibid., 196–97 (2.23.12).

70. Dickinson, "Letters from a Farmer in Pennsylvania to the Inhabitants of the British Colonies in America," letters 1 and 2.

71. Aristotle, *On Rhetoric*, 40–41 (1.2.8–10).

72. Ibid., 40–41 (1.2.8–10), 44 (1.2.19); see also 181 (2.20.9).

73. No article title, *New-England Courant*, no. 1, August 7, 1721, http://www.ushistory
.org/franklin/courant/issue1.htm. The author did present a second example of a
fever stemming from inoculation: that of the son of the doctor championing
inoculation.

74. This is not on Aristotle's list of rhetorical fallacies, and it is not clear here to what
extent he is attacking a style of argument or attacking teachers of rhetoric (*On
Rhetoric*, 30 [1.1.3]).

75. Ibid., 204–10 (2.24).

76. Ibid., 207 (2.24.4).

77. "Absinthium," *New-England Courant*, December 11–18, 1721, http://www.masshist
.org/online/silence_dogood/img-viewer.php?item_id=632&img_step=1&tpc=&pid
=&mode=transcript&tpc=&pid=.

78. Ibid.

79. Aristotle, *On Rhetoric*, 209 (2.24.10).

80. For a relatively recent effort to examine journalistic fallacies based on the work of
Frans H. van Eemeren and Rob Grootendorst, see John Wilson, Ahmed Sahlane,
and Ian Somerville, "Argumentation and Fallacy in Newspaper Op/Ed Coverage
of the Prelude to the Invasion of Iraq," *Journal of Language and Politics* 11, no. 1
(2012): 1–31. The authors lay out seven fallacies and apply them to journalistic work:
(1) straw man fallacy, (2) argumentum ad hominem, (3) argumentum ad conse-
quentiam, (4) argumentation by (faulty) analogy, (5) inappropriate "relations of
concomitance," and (6) presupposition. The journalistic illustrations they choose,
however, are not always persuasive.

81. Thomas Paine, *Common Sense* (1776; reprint, Mineola, N.Y.: Dover, 1997), 33.

82. Quoted in Mott, *American Journalism*, 128.

83. Stephens, *A History of News*, 179.

84. Thomas Jefferson to John Norvell, June 14, 1807, in *The Letters of Thomas Jefferson:
1743–1826*, http://www.let.rug.nl/usa/P/tj3/writings/brf/jefl179.htm.

85. Thomas Jefferson to the Marquis de La Fayette, November 4, 1823, in *Memoirs,
Correspondence, and Private Papers*, ed. Thomas Jefferson Randolph, vol. 3 (London:
Henry Colburn and Richard Bentley, 1829), 393, also in Online Library of Liberty,
http://oll.libertyfund.org/?option=com_staticxt&staticfile=show.php%3Ftitle=808
&chapter=88459&layout=html&Itemid=27.

86. James Madison, "Public Opinion," *National Gazette*, December 19, 1791, in *The
Writings of James Madison*, ed. Gaillard Hunt, vol. 6 (New York: Putnam, 1906),
70, also in Online Library of Liberty, http://oll.libertyfund.org/?option=com
_staticxt&staticfile=show.php%3Ftitle=1941&chapter=124390&layout=html&Ite
mid=27.

87. Committee of Concerned Journalists, "Principles of Journalism," 2006–2013,
reprinted by the Pew Research Center's Project for Excellence in Journalism at
http://www.journalism.org/resources/principles.

88. John Adams to H. Niles, February 13, 1818, http://teachingamericanhistory.org/library/index.asp?document=968.

2. "YESTERDAY'S DOINGS IN ALL CONTINENTS"

1. See Mitchell Stephens, *A History of News*, 3rd ed. (New York: Oxford University Press, 2007).

2. The word *journalist*, according to the *Oxford English Dictionary*, made the transition earlier. Voltaire, for example, used it in 1737 to mean "contemporary historian" ("On History: Advice to a Journalist," in Fritz Stern, ed., *The Varieties of History: From Voltaire to the Present* [New York: Meridian Books, 1956], 36–45). But it was still widely used to describe someone who kept a journal; see *Spectator # 323*, in Joseph Addison, *The Works of Joseph Addison*, vol. 2 (New York: Harper Brothers, 1864), 16.

3. "Journalism," *Westminster Review* 18 (January–April 1833): 195–208, translated from the article "Du Journalism," *Revue Encyclopédique*, September 1832. Horst Pöttker's distinction between "the orientation function" and "the news function" parallels, to some extent, this distinction between "opinion" and "intelligence" ("A Reservoir of Understanding," *Journalism Practice* 5, no. 5 [2011]: 520–37).

4. In a YouTube video reported and edited by Kelly Kettering, recorded at the 2010 Schuneman Symposium, http://www.youtube.com/watch?v=G_kAhw96-cM.

5. Frank Luther Mott, *American Journalism: A History of Newspapers in the United States* (New York: Macmillan, 1941), 115–16.

6. *The Dispatches and Letters of Vice Admiral Lord Viscount Nelson*, vol. 2: *1795 to 1797* (London: Henry Colburn, 1845), 251.

7. T. W. M. Marshall, *Christian Missions: Their Agents and Their Results*, vol. 2, 2d ed. (London: Longman, Green, Longman, Roberts and Green, 1863), 313.

8. *Notes and Queries*, Ninth Series, 5 (January–June 1900), 517. This quote is attributed to the *Century Dictionary*.

9. *The Debates and Proceedings in the Congress of the United States. Fifth Congress. May 15, 1797 to March 3, 1799* (Washington, D.C.: Gales and Seaton, 1851), 1289–90 (March 1798). Isaac Pitman's book on shorthand is entitled *The Reporter: Or, Phonography Adapted to Verbatime Reporting* (Bath, U.K.: Isaac Pitman: 1846).

10. For a history of reporting, see Stephens, *A History of News*, 205–39.

11. Whitelaw Reid, "The Practical Issues in a Newspaper Office" (1879), in *American and English Studies*, vol. 2 (New York: Charles Scribner's Sons, 1913), http://www.ebooksread.com/authors-eng/whitelaw-reid/american-and-english-studies-volume-2-die/page-14-american-and-english-studies-volume-2-die.shtml.

12. Ibid.

13. Stephens, *A History of News*, 215.

14. Quoted in Mott, *American Journalism*, 403.

15. Horace Greeley, "The Prayer of the Twenty Millions," *New York Tribune*, August 19, 1862, http://www.civilwarhome.com/lincolngreeley.htm.

16. Stephens, *A History of News*, 225, 234.

17. Richard Grant White, "The Morals and Manners of Journalism," *The Galaxy* 8, no. 6 (1869), 840, American Periodicals Series. Thanks to Brooke Kroeger for bringing this article to my attention.

18. John Adams to H. Niles, February 13, 1818, http://teachingamericanhistory.org/library/index.asp?document=968.

19. See Mitchell Stephens, *the rise of the image the fall of the word* (New York: Oxford University Press, 1998), 26–39.

20. Charles Dickens, *American Notes for General Circulation*, vol. 2 (London: Chapman and Hall, 1842), 296.

21. "Editor's Study," ed. Henry Mills Alden, Frederick Lewis Allen, Lee Foster Hartman, Thomas Bucklin Well, *Harper's New Monthly Magazine* 77 (June–November 1888): 314–15.

22. White, "The Morals and Manners of Journalism," 6.

23. Ibid. Horst Pöttker, perhaps reflecting a different cultural tradition, is resistant to the idea of journalists as "educationalists." He gives two reasons: "respect [for] the maturity of their public" and a distaste for "explaining the world with a schoolmaster's pointing finger" ("A Reservoir of Understanding," 520–37). However, Dallas Liddle notes that this view of "the role of the Victorian press as public instructor" was a familiar one at the time ("Who Invented the 'Leading Article'? Reconstructing the History and Prehistory of a Victorian Newspaper Genre," *Media History* 5, no. 1 [1999]: 5–18).

24. White, "The Morals and Manners of Journalism," 6.

25. Jürgen Habermas, "The Public Sphere: An Encyclopedia Article," in Douglas M. Kellner and Meenakshi Gigi Durham, eds., *Media and Cultural Studies: Key Works* (Malden, Mass.: Blackwell, 2006), 73–78.

26. Leslie Stephen, "The Duties of Authors," in *Social Rights and Duties*, vol. 2 (London: Sonnenschein, 1896), 154–56.

27. Whitelaw Reid, "Journalism as a Career" (1872), in *American and English Studies*, vol. 2.

28. This does not mean that Reid's own *New York Tribune* was always scrupulous in avoiding partisanship, at least from the perspective of a twenty-first-century observer. Such revolutions take time.

29. Interview with Whitelaw Reid, in Charles Frederick Wingate, ed., *Views and Interviews on Journalism* (New York: F. B. Patterson, 1875), 25.

30. Habermas, "The Public Sphere," 76, quoting Karl Bücher in the first quote.

31. Reid, "Journalism as a Career." In my discussion here, I have benefited from reading David Paul Nord, "Benjamin Franklin and Journalism," in David Waldstreicher, ed., *A Companion to Benjamin Franklin* (New York: Wiley, 2011), 290–307.

32. Habermas, "The Public Sphere," 76.

33. Reid, "The Practical Issues in a Newspaper Office."

34. Stephens, *A History of News*, 184, 188.

35. Mott, *American Journalism*, 303; "News Paper Spires," Skyscraper Museum, http://www.skyscraper.org/EXHIBITIONS/SPIRES/spires.htm. To be fair, much of the height of the *Tribune* building was in its clock tower.

36. "News Paper Spires"; Mott, *American Journalism*, 546.

37. Reid, "The Practical Issues in a Newspaper Office."

38. Reid, "Journalism as a Career."

39. For the rise of "independent" journalism in the United States and its accomplishments, see Matthew Gentzkow, Edward L. Glaeser, and Claudia Goldin, *The Rise of the Fourth Estate: How Newspapers Became Informative and Why It Mattered*, National Bureau of Economic Research (NBER) Working Paper no. 10791 (Cambridge, Mass.: NBER, 2004), http://www.nber.org/papers/w10791 or http://faculty.chicagobooth.edu/matthew.gentzkow/research/fourthestate.pdf.

40. Interview with Whitelaw Reid, in Wingate, ed., *Views and Interviews on Journalism*, 38.

41. Ibid., 39.

42. William Johnston, "England as It Is, Political, Social, and Industrial in the Middle of the Nineteenth Century," in George Boyce, James Curran, and Pauline Wingate, eds., *Newspaper History: From the Seventeenth Century to the Present Day* (London: Constable, 1978), 184.

43. Quoted in Stephen J. A. Ward, *The Invention of Journalism Ethics* (Quebec: McGill-Queen's University Press, 2004), 188.

44. James W. Carey was interesting on this subject (as on most subjects): "How and why are the most problematic aspects of American journalism: the dark continent and invisible landscape. Why and how are what we most want to get out of a news story and are least likely to receive or what we must in most cases supply ourselves," he writes ("The Dark Continent of American Journalism," in Robert Karl Manoff and Michael Schudson, eds., *Reading the News* [New York: Pantheon, 1986], 149).

45. Quoted in David T. Z. Mindich, *Just the Facts: How "Objectivity" Came to Define American Journalism* (New York: New York University Press, 1998), 118.

46. Ibid., 5, 8, 13, 118. In using the term *naive empiricism*, Mindich is quoting Michael Schudson, *Discovering the News* (New York: Basic Books, 1978), 7.

47. Quoted in Daniel W. Pfaff, *Joseph Pulitzer II and the "Post-Dispatch": A Newspaperman's Life* (University Park: Pennsylvania State University Press, 1991), 62.

48. Reid, "Journalism as a Career."

49. Ibid.

50. See Mindich, *Just the Facts*, 1.

51. See Stephens, *A History of News*, 246–51, for these explanations and others regarding the move toward facts and objectivity. Matthew Yglesias has also discussed the economic value of impartiality ("Objectivity as a Business Strategy," *ThinkProgress*, June 29, 2010, http://thinkprogress.org/media/2010/06/29/184603/objectivity-as

-a-business-strategy/; "Partisan Media: An Economic Analysis," *Slate*, February 7, 2012, http://www.slate.com/blogs/moneybox/2012/02/07/partisan_media_an _economic_analysis.html).

52. Lincoln Steffens, *The Autobiography of Lincoln Steffens* (New York: Harcourt, 1931), 285–91.

53. See Edward Jay Epstein, *News from Nowhere: Television and the News* (Chicago: Ivan R. Dee, 2000).

54. See John Hersey, "Hiroshima," *New Yorker*, August 31, 1946, and *Hiroshima* (New York: Knopf, 1946).

55. War reporting gained cachet earlier in the nineteenth century with dashing reporters such as William Howard Russell, Richard Harding Davis, and Stephen Crane. However, they were known for their literary and interpretive abilities and for their courage more than for their adeptness with facts.

56. See Schudson, *Discovering the News*, 145–55.

57. Jonathan Dee, "John Hersey," in George Plimpton, ed., *Writers at Work: The Paris Review Interviews*, vol. 8, no. 92 (New York: Penguin, 1988), 99–136, http://www .theparisreview.org/interviews/2756/the-art-of-fiction-no-92-john-hersey.

58. For an important discussion of Theodore Roosevelt's use of the press, see David Greenberg, "Theodore Roosevelt and the Image of Presidential Activism," *Social Research: An International Quarterly* 78, no. 4 (2011): 1057–88.

59. Harold B. Hinton, "M'CARTHY ACCUSES KEYSERLINGS AGAIN," *New York Times*, April 22, 1952, http://query.nytimes.com/mem/archive/pdf?res=9D0 CE7DD133BE23BBC4A51DFB2668389649EDE. Mary Dublin Keyserling was cleared of these charges and went on to serve in the Labor Department under President Lyndon B. Johnson. For a discussion of facts behind this case, see Landon R. Y. Storrs, "Red Scare Politics and the Suppression of Popular Front Feminism: The Loyalty Investigation of Mary Dublin Keyserling," *Journal of American History* 90, no. 2 (2003): 491–524.

60. "Infiltration Figures Given," *New York Times*, June 10, 1966, http://query.nytimes .com/mem/archive/pdf?res=9904EEDF133DE43BBC4852DFB066838D679EDE.

61. Fyodor Dostoevsky, *The Brothers Karamazov*, trans. Constance Garnett (New York: Macmillan, 1922), 256.

62. Reprinted a few years later in Henry James, *Portraits of Place* (Boston: Houghton Mifflin, 1883), 142–43.

63. Royal Cortissoz, *The Life of Whitelaw Reid*, vol. 1 (New York: Scribner's, 1921), 306–9.

3. "CIRCULATORS OF INTELLIGENCE MERELY"

1. Alternatively, you could place the beginning of this era with the first significant signs of change in the 1830s, when the Hoe press arrived, reporting started to catch

on, and cheap newspapers began accumulating large circulations. And you could place the end in the 1990s, with appearance of two large signs of trouble for professional journalists' monopoly on news: the debut of the World Wide Web and the *Drudge Report*'s work in breaking the Monica Lewinsky scandal. Horst Pöttker measures this era as lasting a century, beginning in the 1880s with the arrival of the inverted pyramid ("A Reservoir of Understanding," *Journalism Practice* 5, no. 5 [2011]: 520–37).

2. Frank Luther Mott, *American Journalism: A History of Newspapers in the United States* (New York: Macmillan, 1941), 405.

3. Robert L. Bishop, Katherine Sharma, and Richard J. Brazee, "Determinants of Newspaper Circulation: A Pooled Cross-Sectional Time-Series Study in the United States, 1850–1970," *Communication Research* 7, no. 1 (1980): 3–22, http://deepblue .lib.umich.edu/bitstream/2027.42/67057/2/10.1177_009365028000700101.pdf.

4. For the question of who was first to transmit full sound, not Morse code, see James E. O'Neal, "Fessenden: World's First Broadcaster?" *Radio World*, October 25, 2006, http://www.rwonline.com/article/fessenden-world39s-first-broadcaster/15157.

5. Davis broadcasts described in James E. Brittain, "Scanning the Past," *Proceedings of the IEEE* 80, no. 12 (1992), http://ieee.cincinnati.fuse.net/reiman/02_2002.html; Davis quoted in Mitchell Stephens, "Radio: From Dots and Dashes to Rock and Larry King," *New York Times*, November 20, 1995, http://www.nyu.edu/classes/stephens/ Radio%20history%20page.htm, and Mitchell Stephens, *A History of News*, 3rd ed. (New York: Oxford University Press, 2007), 268–69.

6. Edwin Emery and Michael Emery, *The Press and America*, 5th ed. (Englewood Cliffs, N.J.: Prentice-Hall, 1984), 448–49.

7. Alexander J. Field, "Communications," in *Historical Statistics of the United States: Millennial Edition Online*, http://hsus.cambridge.org/HSUSWeb/indexes/ indexEssayPath.do?id=Dg.ESS.01; Alfred McClung Lee, *The Daily Newspaper in America*, vol. 1 (London: Routledge and Thoemmes Press, 2001), 72–74; Jameson Otto, Sara Metz, and Nathan Ensmeger, "Sports Fans and Their Information-Gathering Habits: How Media Technologies Have Brought Fans Closer to Their Teams Over Time," in William H. Aspray and Barbara M. Hayes, eds., *Everyday Information: The Evolution of Information Seeking in America* (Cambridge, Mass.: MIT Press, 2011), 191; William H. Young and Nancy K. Young, *The 1930s* (Westport, Conn.: Greenwood Press, 2002), 163.

8. "Daily and Sunday Newspaper Circulation as % of Households, 1940–2010," in "Sixty Years of Daily Newspaper Circulation Trends," discussion paper, Communications Management, Inc., May 6, 2011, http://media-cmi.com/downloads/ Sixty_Years_Daily_Newspaper_Circulation_Trends_050611.pdf; Robert D. Putnam, *Bowling Alone: The Collapse and Revival of American Community* (New York: Simon & Schuster, 2000), 218; Newspaper Association of America, "Newspaper Circulation Volume," last updated September 4, 2012, http://www.naa.org/en/ Trends-and-Numbers/Circulation-Volume/Newspaper-Circulation-Volume.asp.

9. "Modern newspapers . . . are, by almost any measure, far superior to their 1960s counterparts: better written, better looking, better organized, more responsible, less sensational, less sexist and racist, and more informative and public-spirited than they are often given credit for" (Carl Sessions Stepp, "State of the American Newspaper, Then and Now," *American Journalism Review*, September 1999, http://www.ajr.org/Article.asp?id=3192).

10. Newspapers' increased respectability came in part because the audiences they were left to serve—after television—tended to be older and better educated.

11. Newspaper Association of America, "Newspaper Circulation Volume."

12. "Daily and Sunday Newspaper Circulation as % of Households, 1940–2010"; Putnam, *Bowling Alone*, 218; Newspaper Association of America, "Newspaper Circulation Volume."

13. I initially conducted such a study for Mitchell Stephens, "Beyond the News," *Columbia Journalism Review* 45, no. 5 (2007), http://www.cjr.org/feature/beyond_the_news.php, then for Mitchell Stephens, "Beyond News: the Case for Wisdom Journalism," Joan Shorenstein Center on the Press, Politics, and Public Policy, Discussion Paper Series, June 2009, http://shorensteincenter.org/wp-content/uploads/2012/03/d53_stephens.pdf.

14. David T. Z. Mindich alerted me to *Wikipedia*'s role as a news medium.

15. That day my researcher, Angela Flores, and I set out to monitor a broad swath of news coverage.

16. I took this information from the Technorati blog, http://technorati.com, but this site is long gone.

17. Mark Landler and David E. Sanger, "World Leaders Pledge $1.1 Trillion to Tackle Crisis," *New York Times*, April 3, 2009, http://www.nytimes.com/2009/04/03/world/europe/03summit.html.

18. Field, "Communications."

19. See Brian Stelter, "Copyright Challenge for Sites That Excerpt," *New York Times*, March 1, 2009, http://www.nytimes.com/2009/03/02/business/media/02scrape.html; Jonathan Bailey, "Excerpts, Scraping, and Fair Use," *Plagiarism Today*, March 3, 2009, http://www.plagiarismtoday.com/2009/03/03/excerpts-scraping-and-fair-use/.

20. For complications in this relationship, see Greg Beato, "Bizarre Love Triangle: Breitbart, Reuters, and the *Drudge Report*," *Gawker*, November 5, 2009, http://gawker.com/5398176/bizarre-love-triangle-breitbart-reuters-and-the-drudge-report.

21. Pew Research Center, *State of the News Media 2012* (Washington, D.C.: Pew Research Center, 2012), http://stateofthemedia.org/2012/mobile-devices-and-news-consumption-some-good-signs-for-journalism/?src=prc-section.

22. Felix Salmon, finance blogger for Reuters, tells the tale of a blogger from Australia with a Blogspot account whose exposé on a Chinese travel company traded on the New York Stock Exchange went viral and caused that stock to drop 20 percent of its value in one day ("Blogonomics: Moving Markets," Reuters, September

15, 2010, http://blogs.reuters.com/felix-salmon/2010/09/15/blogonomics-moving
-markets/; "Teaching Journalists to Read," Reuters, September 17, 2010, http://blogs
.reuters.com/felix-salmon/2010/09/17/teaching-journalists-to-read/). (That blogger shorted the stock before blogging about it, which would, of course, have been an
ethical violation at most news organizations.) For the financial blog post that went
viral, see Bronte Capital, "Traveling Through China . . .," September 15, 2010, http://
brontecapital.blogspot.com/2010/09/travelling-through-china-with-universal
.html.

23. John Herrman, "How 18-Year-Old Morgan Jones Told the World About the
Aurora Shooting," *BuzzFeed*, July 20, 2012, http://www.buzzfeed.com/jwherrman/
how-18-year-old-morgan-jones-told-the-world-about.

24. Jill Abramson, "Sustaining Quality Journalism," *Daedalus* 139, no. 2 (2010): 42.

25. A favorite example of such trigger-fast feedback: After David Carr wrote a *New
York Times* column criticizing the *Washington Post* business model, Rick Edmonds
on the Poynter website complained that Carr had left out of his analysis the substantial income the *Post* receives from its "cable and broadcasting units." David
Carr then quickly and nobly tweeted a link to Edmonds's critique: "@rickedmonds
says i missed WashPo's underlying muscle" (Rick Edmonds, "Pot Calls Kettle
Black in *New York Times* Piece on *Washington Post* Business Troubles," *Poynter.org*,
November 20, 2012, http://www.poynter.org/latest-news/business-news/the-biz
-blog/196028/pot-calls-kettle-black-in-new-york-times-piece-on-washington
-post-business-troubles/#.UKubrbunTlR.twitter; David Carr, "*Washington Post*'s
Chief Falters Anew," *New York Times*, November 18, 2012, http://www.nytimes
.com/2012/11/19/business/media/at-washington-post-katharine-weymouth
-struggles-for-surer-footing.html).

26. Whitelaw Reid, "Journalism as a Career" (1872), in *American and English Studies*, vol. 2 (New York: Scribner's, 1913), http://www.ebooksread.com/authors-eng/
whitelaw-reid/american-and-english-studies-volume-2-die/page-14-american
-and-english-studies-volume-2-die.shtml.

27. Jürgen Habermas, "The Public Sphere: An Encyclopedia Article," in Douglas M.
Kellner and Meenakshi Gigi Durham, eds., *Media and Cultural Studies: Key Works*
(Malden, Mass.: Blackwell, 2006), 73–78.

28. Horst Pöttker puts the point about the new playing field this way: "The ties
between journalism and the news function have loosened since external non-
journalistic communicators and communicator organizations have started to gain
prominence and make use of the working techniques and presentational forms
developed by news journalism" ("A Reservoir of Understanding," *Journalism Practice* 5, no. 5 [2011]: 522).

29. David Taintor, "Ana Marie Cox: 'GOP Doesn't "Hate" Women, but Gender Gap Is
Real,'" *Talking Points Memo (TPM)*, June 22, 2012, http://2012.talkingpointsmemo
.com/2012/06/ana-marie-cox-interview.php.

30. Quoted in Abramson, "Sustaining Quality Journalism," 41.

31. The saying that journalists "should comfort the afflicted and afflict the comfortable" is often attributed to H. L. Mencken, but according to Ralph Keyes it was used much earlier by Finley Peter Dunne (Ralph Keyes, *The Quote Verifier* [New York: St. Martin's Press, 2006], 34).

32. In this case, there were a surprising number of leaks afterward about the deliberative process. See, for example, Jan Crawford, "Discord at Supreme Court Is Deep and Personal," CBSnews.com, July 8, 2012, http://www.cbsnews .com/8301-3460_162-57468202/discord-at-supreme-court-is-deep-and-personal/.

33. Quoted in Sarah Kliff, "How Will You Know if Obamacare Still Stands Tomorrow? Probably from Lyle," *Wonkblog* (*Washington Post*), June 27, 2012, http://www .washingtonpost.com/blogs/ezra-klein/wp/2012/06/27/how-will-you-know-if -obamacare-still-stands-tomorrow-probably-from-lyle/; Melissa Block, "Blog Sees Success in Supreme Court Focus," NPR, June 26, 2012, http://www.npr .org/2012/06/26/155792586/blog-sees-success-in-supreme-court-focus; Staci D. Kramer, "*SCOTUSblog*: After a Decade, an Overnight Sensation," *paidContent*, June 29, 2012, http://paidcontent.org/2012/06/29/scotusblog-after-a-decade-an-overight -sensation/?utm_source=feedburner&utm_medium=feed&utm_campaign =Feed:+pcorg+(paidContent)&utm_content=Google+Reader.

34. The on-air timings and quotes are from "The Supreme Court's Obamacare Ruling—CNN & Fox News Report," *The Daily Show*, Comedy Central, June 28, 2012, http://www.thedailyshow.com/watch/thu-june-28-2012/cnn-fox-news -report-supreme-court-decision. Other quotes are from David Taintor, "CNN, Fox News Bungle Supreme Court Coverage," *Talking Points Memo (TPM)*, June 28, 2012, http://tpmdc.talkingpointsmemo.com/2012/06/cnn-fox-news-supreme -court-coverage.php; and Aaron Blake, "CNN, Fox Jump the Gun on Supreme Court Health Care Decision," *Washington Post*, June 28, 2012, http://www .washingtonpost.com/blogs/the-fix/post/networks-jump-the-gun-mistakenly -report-that-supreme-court-struck-down-mandate/2012/06/28/gJQAmsa98V _blog.html. NPR, *Time* magazine, and the *Huffington Post* also sent out incorrect tweets announcing the decision, as reported in Adam Peck, "In a Rush to Be First, CNN, FOX, *Huffington Post*, and *TIME* Get Supreme Court Story Exactly Wrong," *ThinkProgress*, June 28, 2012, http://thinkprogress.org/media/2012/06/28/508072/ in-a-rush-to-be-first-cnn-fox-huffington-post-and-time-get-supreme-court -story-exactly-wrong/?mobile=nc.

35. By far the most thorough account of these events was written by Tom Goldstein himself: Tom Goldstein, "We're Getting Wildly Differing Assessments," *SCOTUSblog*, July 7, 2012, http://www.scotusblog.com/2012/07/were-getting -wildly-differing-assessments. I wrote my own account of the dissemination of this story before I saw Goldstein's story and have stuck with my timing of the sequence of events, but I have used Goldstein's account to check and correct facts. Goldstein credits a *Bloomberg* alert at 10:07 that morning—"OBAMA'S HEALTH-CARE OVERHAUL UPHELD BY U.S. SUPREME COURT"—with beating

SCOTUSblog with an accurate report on the decision. This detail would be very useful and important to stock traders; however, there is no doubt that it was *SCOTUSblog*'s initial report fifty-eight seconds later that would spread around the political and journalistic world.

36. Quoted in Kat Stoeffel, "Supreme Court Health Care Decision Really Confusing, CNN and Fox News Discover," *New York Observer*, June 6, 2012, http://observer.com/2012/06/supreme-court-health-care-decision-really-confusing-cnn-and-fox-news-discover/.

37. John H. Cushman Jr., "Supreme Court Allows Health Care Law Largely to Stand," *New York Times*, 10:26 a.m., June 29, 2012, http://elections.nytimes.com/2012/live-coverage/scotus-healthcare. The complete early version of this story is no longer available on the *Times* website

38. As reported in Kliff, "How Will You Know If Obamacare Still Stands Tomorrow?"; Block, "Blog Sees Success in Supreme Court Focus"; Kramer, "*SCOTUSblog*"; "The Supreme Court's Obamacare Ruling."

39. Goldstein, "We're Getting Wildly Differing Assessments."

40. Nate Silver, "*FiveThirtyEight* to Partner with *New York Times*," *FiveThirtyEight*, June 3, 2010, http://www.fivethirtyeight.com/2010/06/fivethirtyeight-to-partner-with-new.html.

41. Julie Bosman, "The Kid with All the News About the TV News," *New York Times*, November 20, 2006, http://www.nytimes.com/2006/11/20/business/media/20newser.html?pagewanted=all; "Meet Brian Stelter," Towson University, n.d., http://www.towson.edu/main/discovertowson/brianstelter.asp, accessed August 17, 2013; Michael Calderone, "New York Times Hires TVNewser Blogger Stelter," *New York Observer*, June 12, 2007, http://observer.com/2007/06/inew-york-timesi-hires-tvnewser-blogger-stelter/.

42. Quoted in Menaham Blondheim, *News Over the Wires* (Cambridge, Mass.: Harvard University Press, 1994), 37.

43. For these headlines, see "Supreme Court Health Care Ruling: Newspaper Front Pages Report Affordable Care Act Decision," *Huffington Post*, June 29, 2012, http://www.huffingtonpost.com/2012/06/29/supreme-court-health-care-ruling-newspaper-front-pages_n_1637175.html#slide=1163613.

44. Pöttker, "A Reservoir of Understanding," 522.

45. Abramson, "Sustaining Quality Journalism," 39.

46. David Carr, "A Vanishing Journalistic Divide," *New York Times*, October 10, 2010, http://www.nytimes.com/2010/10/11/business/media/11carr.html?pagewanted=all.

47. Paul Krugman, "Scoop Dupes," NYtimes.com, October 30, 2012, http://krugman.blogs.nytimes.com/2012/10/30/scoop-dupes/?smid=tw-NytimesKrugman&seid=auto.

48. Nina Bernstein, "Immigrant Detainee Dies, and a Life Is Buried, Too," *New York Times*, April 3, 2009.

49. Felix Salmon has this hesitation about journalists' habitual nostalgia for the golden age of investigation: "Even in those halcyon days when investigative reporters could spend years on an investigation, the number of readers that investigation

reached was tiny: you needed to fortuitously be a reader of the right newspaper on the right day when it appeared, and you needed to be interested in the subject. Today, investigations are much more likely to reach a broad and influential audience, because they are easily available, in perpetuity, no matter where you are in the world" ("Teaching Journalists to Read," Reuters, September 17, 2010, http://blogs .reuters.com/felix-salmon/2010/09/17/teaching-journalists-to-read/).

50. Quoted in Stephens, "Beyond the News."

51. See Brendan Watson, "Bloggers' Reliance on Newspaper, Online, and Original Sources in Reporting on Local Subjects Ignored by the Press," paper presented at a meeting of the Association for Education in Journalism & Mass Communication, St. Louis, August 2011. "This study of 100 blogs found that contrary to media assertions and prior research, local public affairs bloggers do not rely on newspapers for a majority of their sources. Bloggers in this study were more likely to use original sources and original reporting than rely on media sources, particularly when writing about local topics (e.g. historic preservation) the news media frequently ignore." For a brief discussion of Watson's paper, see Jack Shafer, "Bloggers Not Parasites," *Slate*, August 10, 2011, http://www.slate.com/articles/news_and_politics/ press_box/2011/08/bloggers_not_parasites.html.

52. Salmon, "Teaching Journalists to Read."

53. Quoted in Blondheim, *News Over the Wires*, 37.

4. "BYE-BYE TO THE OLD 'WHO-WHAT-WHEN-WHERE' "

1. Jonathan Cohn, "Supreme Court Rules, Obamacare Can Go Forward," *New Republic*, June 28, 2012, http://www.tnr.com/blog/plank/104445/the-supreme-court-has -ruled-health-care-reform-constitutional. I am working with the updated version of this 10:26 A.M. post and can confirm only that the first sentence quoted here was definitely part of that post.

2. Ezra Klein, "In 5–4 Decision, Supreme Court Rules for the Uninsured," *Washington Post*, June 28, 2012, http://www.washingtonpost.com/blogs/ezra-klein/ wp/2012/06/28/in-5-4-decision-supreme-court-rules-for-the-uninsured/.

3. Jonathan Chait, "John Roberts Saves Us All," *New York* magazine, June 28, 2012, http://nymag.com/daily/intel/2012/06/john-roberts-saves-us-all.html. This post, too, was updated; the wording I have quoted may have been changed since its "original publication" at 11:33 A.M.

4. Andrew Sullivan, "Live-Blogging SCOTUS's ACA Ruling: Broccoli Wins!" *Daily Beast*, June 28, 2012, http://andrewsullivan.thedailybeast.com/2012/06/live -blogging-scotus-healthcare-ruling.html.

5. Megan McArdle, "ObamaCare Is Constitutional, Sun Still Shining. News at 11," *Daily Beast*, June 28, 2012, http://www.thedailybeast.com/articles/2012/06/28/ obamacare-stays-for-now.html.

6. Laurence Tribe, "Chief Justice Roberts Comes Into His Own and Saves the Court While Preventing a Constitutional Debacle," *SCOTUSblog*, June 28, 2012, http://www.scotusblog.com/2012/06/chief-justice-roberts-comes-into-his-own-and-saves-the-court-while-preventing-a-constitutional-debacle/.

7. Jonathan Adler, "Lose the Battle, Win the War?" *SCOTUSblog*, June 28, 2012, http://www.scotusblog.com/2012/06/lose-the-battle-win-the-war/.

8. "Special Feature: Post-decision Health Care Symposium," *SCOTUSblog*, June 29, 2012, http://www.scotusblog.com/category/special-features/post-decision-health-care-symposium/page/2/.

9. "A Report on Senator Joseph R. McCarthy," *See it Now*, CBS-TV, March 9, 1954, archived online by the Media Resources Center, Moffitt Library, University of California, Berkeley, http://www.lib.berkeley.edu/MRC/murrowmccarthy.html.

10. Carlota S. Smith, *Modes of Discourse* (Cambridge: Cambridge University Press, 2003), 155–83.

11. A. M. Sperber, *Murrow: His Life and Times* (New York: Fordham University Press, 1998), 431.

12. D. D. Guttenplan, *American Radical: The Life and Times of I. F. Stone* (Evanston, Ill.: Northwestern University Press, 2012), 285.

13. David Brooks, "Pessimism Without Panic," *New York Times*, June 18, 2006, http://www.nytimes.com/2006/06/18/opinion/18brooks.html?_r=1; the Charlie Rose interview of Burns is quoted in this article.

14. Email from John Burns in Baghdad to Mitchell Stephens, October 6, 2006.

15. Thomas E. Ricks, *Fiasco: The American Military Adventure in Iraq* (New York: Penguin, 2007).

16. Farnaz Fassihi, "From Baghdad: A *Wall Street Journal* Reporter's E-mail to Friends," *Common Dreams*, September 30, 2004, http://www.commondreams.org/views04/0930-15.htm.

17. See, for example, Katherine Fink and Michael Schudson's evidence of an increase in "contextual journalism" in newspapers in their article "The Rise of Contextual Journalism, 1950s–2000s," *Journalism*, February 17, 2013, http://lbr.jrn.columbia.edu:1234/system/documents/703/original/Fink-Schudson-ContextualJournalism.pdf.

18. "G-Force," Economist.com, April 2, 2009, http://www.economist.com/node/13415746; Dean Baker, "G20: Why Support the IMF," Guardian.co.uk, April 2, 2009, http://www.guardian.co.uk/commentisfree/cifamerica/2009/apr/02/g20-agreement-imf-tax-havens; Ezra Klein, "IMF FTW," Prospect.org, April 2, 2009, http://prospect.org/article/imf-ftw; Steven Pearlstein, "A Rare Triumph of Substance at the Summit," *Washington Post*, April 3, 2009.

19. Harry Jaffe, "Flash: Front Page of Washington Newspaper Contains No News," *Capital Comment Blog*, Washingtonian.com, March 6, 2009, http://www.washingtonian.com/blogs/capitalcomment/post-watch/flash-front-page-of-washington

-newspaper-contains-no-news.php. Jaffe, to be fair, had interesting, nuanced views of the *Post*'s situation. Thanks to Maralee Schwartz for directing me to this story.

20. Sheryl Gay Stolberg, "After Recess, Health Talk Steps Lively," *New York Times*, September 9, 2009. The jaunty headline for this piece is not reflective of its content. Online headlines are, of course, different.

21. Helene Cooper, "On Big Stage, an Overture," *New York Times*, April 3, 2009.

22. For a different reading of historical coverage of presidential messages to Congress, see Michael Schudson, "The Politics of Narrative Form: The Emergence of News Conventions in Print and Television," *Daedalus* 111, no. 4 (1982): 97–112.

23. Thomas E. Patterson found something similar in a content analysis of the *New York Times*: "Between 1960 and 1992, the proportion of interpretive reports on its front page increased tenfold, from 8 percent to 80 percent" ("Bad News, Bad Governance," *Annals of the Academy of Political and Social Science* 546 [July 1996]: 102).

24. "Traditional objectivity insists that reports should contain *only* facts and exclude the reporter's opinion and interpretation" (Stephen J. A. Ward, *Invention of Journalism Ethics: The Path to Objectivity and Beyond* [Quebec: McGill-Queen's University Press, 2004], 20).

25. Quoted in "Brauchli Responds to Jaffe 'No News' Claim," *FishbowlDC*, mediabistro .com, March 6, 2009, http://www.mediabistro.com/fishbowldc/brauchli-responds -to-jaffe-no-news-claim_b15221.

26. Global Editors Network, "Global Editors Network," "About Us," and "Manifesto," n.d., http://www.globaleditorsnetwork.org/manifesto/, accessed August 8, 2013. Some of the ways this organization describes itself on its website have changed since I wrote this material in 2012. However, the list of "dimensions" of "quality journalism" it presents in its manifesto—the focus of my criticism—had not changed as of August 8, 2013.

27. In a YouTube video reported and edited by Kelly Kettering, recorded at the 2010 Schuneman Symposium, http://www.youtube.com/watch?v=G_kAhw96-cM.

28. See Mitchell Stephens, *A History of News*, 3rd ed. (New York: Oxford University Press, 2007), 205–17.

29. Debby Woodin, "Joplin City Council to Hear Comments on Grant Proposals," *Joplin Globe*, August 19, 2012, http://www.joplinglobe.com/local/x257410972/ Joplin-City-Council-to-hear-comments-on-grant-proposals.

30. See John R. Searle, *Mind, Language, and Society* (New York: Basic Books, 1999), 148–50; Mitchell Stephens, with Beth M. Olson, *Broadcast News*, 4th ed. (Belmont, Calif.: Thomson Wadsworth, 2005); Jerry Lanson and Mitchell Stephens, *Writing and Reporting the News*, 3rd ed. (New York: Oxford University Press, 2008).

31. Quoted in Cooper, "On Big Stage, an Overture."

32. Quoted in Sridhar Pappu, "Washington's New Brat Pack Masters Media," *New York Times*, March 25, 2011, http://www.nytimes.com/2011/03/27/fashion/ 27YOUNGPUNDITS.html?_r=1&pagewanted=all.

33. Mark Landler and David E. Sanger, "World Leaders Pledge $1.1 Trillion to Tackle Crisis," *New York Times*, April 3, 2009.

34. Quoted in Howard Kurtz, "*Huffington* Snags *N.Y. Times* Star," *Washington Post*, September 21, 2010, http://voices.washingtonpost.com/howard-kurtz/2010/09/huffington_snags_ny_times_star.html.

35. Rem Rieder, "A Matter of Interpretation," *American Journalism Review*, December–January 2011, http://ajr.org/Article.asp?id=4975.

36. Stolberg, "After Recess, Health Talk Steps Lively."

37. Susan Rasky and Brad DeLong, "Twelve Things Journalists Need to Remember to Be Good Economic Reporters," *Nieman Watchdog*, June 13, 2006, http://www.niemanwatchdog.org/index.cfm?fuseaction=background.view&backgroundid=0093.

38. CNN Wire Staff, "Walmart Shooting Followed Fight at Party, Police Say," August 20, 2012, http://www.cnn.com/2012/08/20/us/texas-walmart-shooting/index.html?hpt=hp_t2.

39. Dalia Sussman, "Times/CBS News Poll: The Recession's Profound Impact," *The Caucus*, NYtimes.com, December 14, 2009, http://thecaucus.blogs.nytimes.com/2009/12/14/timescbs-news-poll-the-recessions-profound-impact/. The lead was somewhat improved, at least in its second sentence, when it appeared the next morning atop the newspaper's front page: "More than half of the nation's unemployed workers have borrowed money from friends or relatives since losing their jobs. An equal number have cut back on doctor visits or medical treatments because they are out of work" (Michael Luo and Megan Thee-Brenan, "Poll Reveals Trauma of Joblessness in U.S.," *New York Times*, December 14, 2009, http://www.nytimes.com/2009/12/15/us/15poll.html).

40. See Stephens, *A History of News*, 116–28.

41. Kevin Vaughan and Burt Hubbard, "Analysis: Most Gun Deaths in Colorado Are Suicides," *Steamboat Today*, March 10, 2013, http://www.steamboattoday.com/news/2013/mar/10/analysis-most-gun-deaths-colorado-are-suicides/.

42. Ezra Klein, "Do the News Media Spend Too Much Time on News?" *Washington Post*, June 22, 2010, http://voices.washingtonpost.com/ezra-klein/2010/06/does_the_news_media_spend_too.html.

43. Pappu, "Washington's New Brat Pack Masters Media."

44. Matthew Yglesias, "Nancy Pelosi Calls for Constitutional Abrogation of the Debt Ceiling," *Slate*, June 20, 2012, http://www.slate.com/blogs/moneybox/2012/06/20/pelosi_says_14th_amendment_makes_the_debt_ceiling_unconstitutional.html; Yglesias's tweet is at https://twitter.com/mattyglesias/status/215520251033554944.

45. Quoted in Pappu, "Washington's New Brat Pack Masters Media."

46. Felix Salmon, "Teaching Journalists to Read," Reuters, September 17, 2010, http://blogs.reuters.com/felix-salmon/2010/09/17/teaching-journalists-to-read/.

47. Nate Silver, "Swing Voters and Elastic States," *New York Times*, May 21, 2012, http://fivethirtyeight.blogs.nytimes.com/2012/05/21/swing-voters-and-elastic-states/.

48. Nate Silver, "Journalism Day Henry Pringle Lecture," Columbia University, May 17, 2011, http://www.journalism.columbia.edu/system/documents/478/original/nate_silver.pdf.

49. In Joshua Benton, "Q & A with Ana Marie Cox," Nieman Journalism Lab, October 27, 2008, http://www.niemanlab.org/2008/10/ana-marie-cox-asking-the-audience-to-pay-for-journalism/.

50. Quoted in "*Independent* Goes Red as Bono Edits," *BBC News*, May 16, 2006, http://news.bbc.co.uk/2/hi/uk_news/4984864.stm.

51. Simon Kelner, interviewed by the author, October 2006; Mitchell Stephens, "Beyond the News," *Columbia Journalism Review* 45, no. 5 (2007), http://www.cjr.org/feature/beyond_the_news.php; Roy Greenslade, "The Kelner Years—How the Viewspaperman Survived Despite Falling Sales," *Guardian*, July 1, 2011, http://www.guardian.co.uk/media/greenslade/2011/jul/01/simon-kelner-theindependent.

52. France's daily *Libération* might be another model of such a magazine-like boldness and focus.

53. "The Foxification of News," *The Economist*, July 7, 2011, http://www.economist.com/node/18904112?fsrc=rss&story_id=18904112.

54. Horst Pöttker reports on some success for a more interpretive model of journalism in Germany: "As opposed to the general trend of the continual decline in the circulation of daily newspapers, it is—at least in Germany—weekly newspapers such as *Die Zeit* and the *Frankfurter Allgemeine Sonntagszeitung* with their sophisticated reflection, thorough investigation and literary quality which enjoy considerable increases in circulation" ("A Reservoir of Understanding," *Journalism Practice* 5, no. 5 [2011]: 523).

55. Quoted in Stephens, "Beyond the News."

56. The article is quoted in ibid.; Tim Logan and John Doherty, "The Promised Land," *Times Herald-Record*, January 29, 2006.

57. Christine Young, "Mike Levine, *Record* Editor, Dead," *Times Herald-Record*, January 14, 2007, http://www.recordonline.com/apps/pbcs.dll/article?AID=/20070114/NEWS/70114010.

5. "MUCH AS ONE MAY TRY TO DISAPPEAR FROM THE WORK"

1. Email from John Burns in Baghdad to Mitchell Stephens, October 6, 2006.

2. Brian Stelter, "Two Takes at NPR and Fox on Juan Williams," *New York Times*, October 21, 2010, http://www.nytimes.com/2010/10/22/business/media/22williams.html?_r=2. NPR's quasi-public status has, in fairness, contributed to the organization's sensitivity on such matters, but it has not made this news organization unique in that sensitivity.

3. Thomas Bowles, "Clap, Clap Goodbye," *Frontstretch*, February 28, 2011, http://www.frontstretch.com/tbowles/32940/; the representative quoted in "Sports Illustrated

Responds to Freelancer Fired After Daytona 500," *Inside Line*, March 2, 2011, http://www.insideline.com/car-news/sports-illustrated-responds-to-freelancer-fired-after-daytona-500.html. *Sports Illustrated* did not confirm that this clapping incident was the sole reason Thomas Bowles was let go. But "a high-ranking *SI* official" did say that it "was the final straw," according to *Inside Line*. Here are a couple of additional examples: Joe Williams, *Politico*'s White House correspondent, suspended in 2012 for comments made on MSNBC accusing then Republican presidential candidate Mitt Romney of being more "comfortable" with "white folks" (Erik Wemple, "*Politico* Suspends Reporter," *Washington Post*, June 22, 2012, http://www.washingtonpost.com/blogs/erik-wemple/post/politico-suspends-reporter/2012/06/22/gJQAvvf8uV_blog.html); and *Washington Post* blogger Dave Weigel, who was writing about the conservative movement, resigned after emails he wrote attacking conservatives were leaked (Andy Alexander, "Blogger Loses Job; *Post* Loses Standing Among Conservatives," *Washington Post*, June 25, 2010, http://voices.washingtonpost.com/ombudsman-blog/2010/06/blogger_loses_job_post_loses_s.html).

4. Stephen Ward, "Pragmatic News Objectivity: Objectivity with a Human Face," Discussion Paper D-37, May 1999, Joan Shorenstein Center on the Press, Politics, Public Policy, Harvard University.

5. Jonathan Dee, "John Hersey," in George Plimpton, ed., *Writers at Work: Paris Review Interviews* 8, no. 92 (New York: Penguin, 1984), 130, http://www.theparisreview.org/interviews/2756/the-art-of-fiction-no-92-john-hersey.

6. Carlota S. Smith, *Modes of Discourse* (Cambridge: Cambridge University Press, 2003), 155–83.

7. Stephen Ward locates this change more in the second half of the twentieth century ("Pragmatic News Objectivity"), but I believe this placement understates the disruptions of modernism and physics in the first half of that century.

8. Thomas Nagel, *The View from Nowhere* (Oxford: Oxford University Press, 1986), 26.

9. "Interview: Len Downie," *Frontline*, April 19, 2006, http://www.pbs.org/wgbh/pages/frontline/newswar/interviews/downie.html. Recall Aristotle's celebration of fair-mindedness (*epieikeia*), noted in chapter 1.

10. Jay Rosen adds some other terms that traditional journalists substitute for the now mostly discredited word *objectivity*: "They may talk of the 'tradition of non-partisan news coverage,' or put neutrality in place of objectivity. 'No axe to grind.' 'No vested interest.' 'Straight reporting.' Different call letters, same station" ("Objectivity as a Form of Persuasion: A Few Notes for Marcus Brauchli," *PressThink*, July 7, 2010, http://archive.pressthink.org/2010/07/07/obj_persuasion.html).

11. Ezra Klein, "A Not-Very-Truthful Speech in a Not-Very-Truthful Campaign," *Washington Post*, August 30, 2012, http://www.washingtonpost.com/blogs/ezra-klein/wp/2012/08/30/a-not-very-truthful-speech-in-a-not-very-truthful-campaign/.

12. This effort to avoid excessive partisanship is a venerable one. Among Cicero's basic rules of history is that an author "shall be free of all prepossession of all pique" (*De Oratore*, trans. William Guthrie [Boston: R. P. and C. Williams, 1822], II, 15, 126).

13. David Mindich examines the word *detachment* (*Just the Facts* [New York: New York University Press, 1998], 15–39).

14. "Post Newsroom Leader to Retire," *Washington Post*, June 25, 2008, transcript of conversation with readers, http://www.washingtonpost.com/wp-dyn/content/discussion/2008/06/24/DI2008062401047.html.

15. Matthew Yglesias, "What Is Hidden and What Is Revealed," *ThinkProgress*, June 26, 2010, http://thinkprogress.org/yglesias/2010/06/26/197694/what-is-hidden-and-what-is-revealed/.

16. Russell Baker, "Now Even Rockets Have Spokespersons," *Eugene Register-Guard*, October 14, 1986, http://news.google.com/newspapers?nid=1310&dat=19861014&id=otwzAAAAIBAJ&sjid=hOEDAAAAIBAJ&pg=3982,3433596.

17. Andrew Sullivan, "How Objectivity Breeds Extremism," *Daily Dish*, June 8, 2010, http://www.theatlantic.com/daily-dish/archive/2010/06/how-objectivity-breeds-extremism/186122/.

18. Baker, "Now Even Rockets Have Spokespersons."

19. "M'CARTHY BENTON EXCHANGE CHARGES," *New York Times*, July 4, 1952, http://query.nytimes.com/mem/archive/pdf?res=9F06EEDF153AE23BBC4C53DFB1668389649EDE.

20. Brad DeLong, "Journalism Education: Finding New Leaders for Changing Times," November 17, 2011, http://delong.typepad.com/sdj/2011/11/what-should-the-next-berkeley-journalism-dean-do-who-should-the-next-berkeley-journalism-school-dean-be.html.

21. "CNN Leaves It There," *The Daily Show*, Comedy Central, October 12, 2009, http://www.thedailyshow.com/watch/mon-october-12–2009/cnn-leaves-it-there.

22. Jay Rosen, "He Said, She Said Journalism: Lame Formula in the Land of the Active User," *PressThink*, April 12, 2009, http://archive.pressthink.org/2009/04/12/hesaid_shesaid.html.

23. "Arpaio: Obama Birth Record 'Definitely Fraudulent,'" Associated Press, July 17, 2012, http://news.yahoo.com/arpaio-obama-birth-record-definitely-fraudulent-010211250.html.

24. Molly Ivins, *Molly Ivins Can't Say That, Can She?* (New York: Vintage Books, 1992), 231. Ivins is referring to the example in Baker's column "Now Even Rockets Have Spokespersons."

25. Jay Rosen, "We Know What Our Journalists Believe About the Debt Crisis," *Quote and Comment*, July 31, 2011, http://jayrosen.tumblr.com/post/8317838361/we-know-what-our-journalists-believe-about-the.

26. Joan Didion, "The Deferential Spirit," *New York Review of Books*, September 19, 1996, http://www.nybooks.com/articles/archives/1996/sep/19/the-deferential-spirit/?pagination=false.

27. "Why the Supercommittee Is About to Fail," *Washington Post*, live Q and A, host: Paul Kane, November 21, 2011, http://live.washingtonpost.com/why-the-super-committee-is-about-to-fail-111121.html.

28. Stephen Edelston Toulmin, *The Uses of Argument* (Cambridge: Cambridge University Press, 1999), 60.

29. Dianna Parker, "*Wash. Post* Again Reported GOP Criticism of Reconciliation, but Not That GOP Repeatedly Used Process," *Media Matters*, April 9, 2009, http://mediamatters.org/research/2009/04/09/wash-post-again-reported -gop-criticism-of-recon/149030.

30. "*Post* Politics: Cap-and-Trade Delays, Appointee Confirmations, More," *Post Politics Hour with Paul Kane, Washington Post*, April 9, 2009, transcript, http://www .washingtonpost.com/wp-dyn/content/discussion/2009/04/08/DI2009040802992. html?hpid=discussions.

31. Matthew Yglesias, "*Post* Reporter Says It's Not His Job to Check the Accuracy of People He's Quoting," *ThinkProgress*, April 9, 2009, http://thinkprogress.org/ media/2009/04/09/184375/post_reporter_says_its_not_his_job_to_check_the _accuracy_of_people_hes_quoting/?mobile=nc.

32. Alec MacGillis, "It's All Fair Game," *New Republic*, July 26, 2012, http://www.tnr .com/blog/plank/105429/its-all-fair-game.

33. *Meet the Press*, NBC, October 22, 2006, transcript, http://www.msnbc.msn.com/ id/15304689/ns/meet_the_press/t/mtp-transcript-oct/#.UFtOvtDhe_A. See also Matthew Yglesias, "Journalism as Sadism," *Atlantic*, November 11, 2007, http:// www.theatlantic.com/politics/archive/2007/11/journalism-as-sadism/46981/.

34. For an explication of coverage of President Obama's gaffe and its implications, see Ezra Klein, "Politicians Don't Take Questions: Can You Blame Them?" *Washington Post*, June 22, 2012, http://www.washingtonpost.com/blogs/ezra-klein/ wp/2012/06/22/politicians-dont-take-questions-can-you-blame-them/.

35. Jay Rosen, "The View from Nowhere: Questions and Answers," *PressThink*, November 2010, http://pressthink.org/2010/11/the-view-from-nowhere-questions -and-answers/.

36. Jeff Zeleny and Jim Rutenberg, "Romney Adopts Harder Message for Last Stretch," *New York Times*, August 25, 2012, http://www.nytimes.com/2012/ 08/26/us/politics/mitt-romneys-campaign-adopts-a-harder-message.html; David Lauter, "Rick Santorum Repeats Inaccurate Welfare Attack on Obama," *Los Angeles Times*, August 28, 2012, http://articles.latimes.com/2012/aug/28/news/ la-pn-santorum-welfare-obama-20120828. See also James Fallows, "False-Equivalence Watch: A Positive Sign," *Atlantic*, August 2012, http://www.theatlantic.com/ politics/print/2012/08/false-equivalence-watch-a-positive-sign/261581, and "Bit by Bit It Takes Shape: Media Evolution for the 'Post-Truth' Age," *Atlantic*, August 2012, http://www.theatlantic.com/politics/print/2012/08/bit-by-bit-it-takes-shape -media-evolution-for-the-post-truth-age/261741/.

37. "Nicholas Lehman: Can Journalists Be Objective?" *Big Think*, February 6, 2008, interview transcript, http://bigthink.com/ideas/2883.

38. Jay Rosen published a book called *What Are Journalists For?* (New Haven, Conn.: Yale University Press, 2001). His answer is in essence political: furthering

democracy—a worthy goal. But I look at the question in terms of furthering varieties of knowledge.

39. Carl Bernstein, "How to Be a Great Journalist," *Big Think*, August 10, 2010, interview transcript, http://bigthink.com/ideas/21732.

40. John R. Searle, *Mind, Language, and Society* (New York: Basic Books, 1999), 142.

41. Aristotle, *On Rhetoric*, trans. George A. Kennedy (New York: Oxford University Press, 1991), 187 (2.22.4).

42. Carl Bernstein and Bob Woodward, "Woodward and Bernstein: 40 Years After Watergate: Nixon Was Far Worse Than We Thought," *Washington Post*, June 8, 2012, http://www.washingtonpost.com/opinions/woodward-and-bernstein-40-years -after-watergate-nixon-was-far-worse-than-we-thought/2012/06/08/gJQAlsio NV_story.html.

43. Bob Woodward and Carl Bernstein, "GOP Security Aide Among Five Arrested in Bugging Affair," *Washington Post*, June 19, 1972, http://www.washingtonpost.com/ politics/gop-security-aide-among-five-arrested-in-bugging-affair/2012/06/07/ gJQAYTdzKV_story.html.

44. Howard Kurtz, "*Huffington* Snags *New York Times* Star," *Washington Post*, September 21, 2010, http://voices.washingtonpost.com/howard-kurtz/2010/09/huffington _snags_ny_times_star.html. Howard Kurtz himself, as Rem Rieder notes, soon made a similar move from the *Washington Post* to the *Daily Beast* (Rem Rieder, "A Matter of Interpretation," *American Journalism Review*, December–January 2011, http://www.ajr.org/Article.asp?id=4975).

45. Peter S. Goodman, "Goldman's Victory: Don't Blame Prosecutors," *Huffington Post*, August 10, 2012, http://www.huffingtonpost.com/peter-s-goodman/goldman-sachs -regulation_b_1764295.html.

46. Felix Salmon, "Teaching Journalists to Read," Reuters, September 17, 2010, http:// blogs.reuters.com/felix-salmon/2010/09/17/teaching-journalists-to-read/.

47. Thomas Paine, "The Crisis," December 23, 1776, reprinted at http://www.ushistory .org/paine/crisis/c-01.htm; Émile Zola, "J'Accuse!" *L'Aurore*, January 13, 1898, reprinted in *Wikipedia*, http://en.wikipedia.org/wiki/File:J_accuse.jpg.

48. David Bornstein has been leading the crusade for more "solutions journalism." See, for example, his article "Why 'Solutions Journalism' Matters, Too," *New York Times*, December 20, 2011, http://opinionator.blogs.nytimes.com/2011/12/20/ why-solutions-journalism-matters-too/.

49. Peter S. Goodman, "On Education, Strive Partnership Offers Useful Template," *Huffington Post*, June 11, 2012, http://www.huffingtonpost.com/peter-s-goodman/ strive-partnership_b_1582573.html.

50. Lincoln Steffens, *The Shame of the Cities* (New York: Hill and Wang, 1967), 12.

51. Ibid., 2.

52. Quoted in Jim Romenesko, "AP Warns Staff About Expressing Opinions on Social Networks," *Poynter*, July 7, 2011, http://www.poynter.org/latest-news/ mediawire/138288/ap-warns-staff-about-expressing-opinions-on-social-networks/.

53. Jim Naureckas, "Leaked Reuters Memo Suggests Reporters Should Keep Ideas to Themselves," *FAIR*, July 6, 2010, http://www.fair.org/blog/2010/07/26/leaked-reuters-memo-suggests-reporters-should-keep-their-ideas-to-themselves/.

54. Quoted in Margaret Sullivan, "After an Outburst on Twitter, *The Times* Reinforces Its Social Media Guidelines," *New York Times*, October 17, 2012, http://publiceditor.blogs.nytimes.com/2012/10/17/after-an-outburst-on-twitter-the-times-reinforces-its-social-media-guidelines/.

55. Quoted in Karl E. Meyer, "Introduction," in Karl E. Meyer, ed., *Pundits, Poets, and Wits: An Omnibus of American Newspaper Columns* (New York: Oxford University Press, 1990), xxxvii.

56. Tom Wolfe, "The New Journalism," in Tom Wolfe and Edward Warren Johnson, *The New Journalism* (New York: Harper and Row, 1973), 17–18.

57. Minha Kim, "News Objectivity and Political Conversation: An Experimental Study of Mad Cow Disease and Candlelight Protest," *Development and Society* 41, no. 1 (2012): 56. Kim is citing William E. Jackson Jr., "Save Democracy from Civic Journalism: North Carolina's Odd Experiment," *Harvard International Journal of Press/Politics* 2, no. 3 (1997): 102–17, and Louise Woodstock, "Public Journalism's Talking Cure: An Analysis of the Movement's 'Problem' and 'Solution' Narratives," *Journalism* 3, no. 1 (2002): 37–55. See also Dylan Byers, "Against Objectivity, Toward Opinion," *Politico*, July 25, 2012, http://www.politico.com/blogs/media/2012/07/against-objectivity-toward-opinion-130087.html.

58. I owe this point to Thomas Patterson.

59. Rosen, "The View from Nowhere."

6. "THE WORLD'S IMMEASURABLE BABBLEMENT"

1. Walter Lippmann, "Force and Ideas," *New Republic*, November 7, 1914, reprinted in *The Early Writings* (New Brunswick, N.J.: Transaction, 1970), 3. I discuss the extraordinary music of these two sentences in Mitchell Stephens, *Journalism Unbound* (New York: Oxford University Press, forthcoming).

2. Quoted in Karl E. Meyer, "Introduction," in Karl E. Meyer, ed., *Pundits, Poets, and Wits: An Omnibus of American Newspaper Columns* (New York: Oxford University Press, 1990), xxxvii.

3. Chris Matthews, *Hardball*, MSNBC, September 14, 2012, http://hardballblog.msnbc.com/_news/2012/09/14/13868379-matthews-american-leadership-is-holding-together-getting-stronger?lite.

4. Aristotle, *On Rhetoric*, trans. George A. Kennedy (New York: Oxford University Press, 1991), 209 (2.24.9).

5. Ibid., 207 (2.24.4).

6. "One Year Ago: Barack Obama Declared Peace in Our Time at the United Nations," *Rush Limbaugh Show*, transcript, September 14, 2012, http://www

.rushlimbaugh.com/daily/2012/09/14/one_year_ago_barack_obama_declared
_peace_in_our_time_at_the_united_nations.

7. Aristotle, *On Rhetoric*, 207 (2.24.4). Limbaugh also probably "amplified" the significance of the wave of attacks by radical Islamists in September 2012.

8. Judith Miller's April 30, 2012, article on FoxNews.com, although somewhat confused, includes evidence that the Obama administration had in fact rebuked
a State Department official for saying the "war on terror is over" ("Is the War
on Terror Over?" FoxNews.com, April 30, 2012, http://www.foxnews.com/
opinion/2012/04/30/is-war-on-terror-over/.

9. Aristotle, *On Rhetoric*, 207 (2.24.4).

10. See, for example, "Bernanke Sees the Coming Collapse," *Rush Limbaugh Show*,
transcript, September 14, 2012, http://www.rushlimbaugh.com/daily/2012/09/14/
bernanke_sees_the_coming_collapse. For the argument that Democrats also used
the word *regime* to describe the Bush administration, see Mark Whittington,
"Chris Matthews, Rush Limbaugh, and 'the Regime,'" Yahoo, April 4, 2010, http://
voices.yahoo.com/chris-matthews-rush-limbaugh-regime-5773566.html.

11. "14-Year-Old Radio Host: Obama and Biden Are 'Making Kids Gay,'" *Think-
Progress*, June 6, 2012, http://thinkprogress.org/lgbt/2012/06/06/495860/14-year-old
-radio-host-obama-and-biden-are-making-kids-gay/?mobile=nc; "Caiden Cowger,
Conservative Teen Radio Host, Slams President Obama for 'Making Kids Gay,'"
Huffington Post, June 6, 2012, http://www.huffingtonpost.com/2012/06/06/caiden
-cowger-teen-radio-host-gay-obama_n_1574524.html; "Bill Maher Slams GOP:
'You Act Exactly Like 14-Year-Old Boys,'" *Huffington Post*, June 23, 2012, http://
www.huffingtonpost.com/2012/06/23/bill-maher-slams-gop-you-act-like-14-year
-old-boys_n_1621182.htm. See also *Caiden Cowger Show*, http://www.caidencowger
program.com/stations.html.

12. Aristotle, *On Rhetoric*, 30 (1.1.5).

13. Stephen Edelston Toulmin, *The Uses of Argument* (Cambridge: Cambridge University Press, 1999), 60.

14. "Bill O'Reilly: Mitt Romney, the Truth, and the Folks," *O'Reilly Factor*, Fox
News Channel, September 18, 2012, transcript, http://www.foxnews.com/on-air/
oreilly/2012/09/19/bill-oreilly-mitt-romney-truth-and-folks#ixzz271rJWjH6.

15. See, for example, Floyd Norris, "As the U.S. Borrows, Who Lends?" *New York Times*,
September 21, 2012, http://www.nytimes.com/2012/09/22/business/economy/
as-the-us-borrows-who-lends.html.

16. "Bernanke Sees the Coming Collapse," *Rush Limbaugh Show*, transcript,
September 14, 2012, http://www.rushlimbaugh.com/daily/2012/09/14/bernanke
_sees_the_coming_collapse.

17. I. F. Stone, "There Should Have Been a Court Martial, Not a Reprisal," *I. F.
Stone's Weekly*, February 15, 1965, http://www.ifstone.org/weekly/IFStonesWeekly
-1965feb15.pdf.

18. Toulmin, *The Uses of Argument*, 60.

19. See, for example, Binyamin Appelbaum, "Cautious on Growth, Bernanke Offers No Hint of New Action," *New York Times*, July 17, 2012, http://www.nytimes .com/2012/07/18/business/economy/bernanke-testifies-before-senate-panel .html?_r=0.

20. Niall Ferguson, "Hit the Road, Barack: Why We Need a New President," *Newsweek* and *Daily Beast*, August 19, 2012, http://www.thedailybeast.com/ newsweek/2012/08/19/niall-ferguson-on-why-barack-obama-needs-to-go.html.

21. Jay Rosen, "The View from Nowhere: Questions and Answers," *PressThink*, November 2010, http://pressthink.org/2010/11/the-view-from-nowhere-questions -and-answers/.

22. I have relied here primarily on the following critiques of Ferguson's article: James Fallows, "As a Harvard Alum, I Apologize," *Atlantic*, August 20, 2012, http://www .theatlantic.com/politics/archive/2012/08/as-a-harvard-alum-i-apologize/261308/; Ezra Klein, "The Worst Case Against the Obama Administration," *Washington Post*, August 20, 2012, http://www.washingtonpost.com/blogs/ezra-klein/ wp/2012/08/20/the-worst-case-against-the-obama-administration/; and Paul Krugman, "Unethical Commentary, *Newsweek* Edition," *New York Times*, August 19, 2012, http://krugman.blogs.nytimes.com/2012/08/19/unethical-commentary -newsweek-edition/. For Neill Ferguson's response to his critics, see "Niall Ferguson Defends *Newsweek* Cover: Correct This, Bloggers," *Daily Beast*, August 21, 2012, http://www.thedailybeast.com/articles/2012/08/21/niall-ferguson-defends -newsweek-cover-correct-this-bloggers.html, and "Ferguson's *Newsweek* Cover Rebuttal: Paul Krugman Is Wrong," *Daily Beast*, August 20, 2012, http://www.the dailybeast.com/articles/2012/08/20/newsweek-cover-rebuttal-paul-krugman-is -wrong.html.

23. Sarah Kliff, "Health Reform at 2: Why American Health Care Will Never Be the Same," *Washington Post*, March 24, 2012, http://www.washingtonpost.com/blogs/ ezra-klein/post/health-reform-at-2-why-american-health-care-will-never-be -the-same/2012/03/22/gIQA7ssUVS_blog.html.

24. Aristotle, *On Rhetoric*, 187 (2.22.4). See also Paul Krugman, "Kinds of Wrong," *New York Times*, August 21, 2012, http://krugman.blogs.nytimes.com/2012/08/21/ kinds-of-wrong/.

25. John R. Searle, *Mind, Language, and Society* (New York: Basic Books, 1999), 142, 148–50.

26. Quoted in Michael O'Brien, "GOP: Fed Action a Sign of Weak Economy Under Obama," NBCnews.com, September 13, 2012, http://nbcpolitics.nbcnews .com/_news/2012/09/13/13847770-gop-fed-action-a-sign-of-weak-economy-under -obama?lite.

27. "QE3: Bernanke's Obama Bailout," *Rush Limbaugh Show*, transcript, September 13, 2012, http://www.rushlimbaugh.com/daily/2012/09/13/qe3_bernanke_s _obama_bailout.

28. Did I. F. Stone have the evidence in 1965 that "the South Vietnamese regime is one we have tried to impose on its people against their will"? The American press by then had reported on a series of disputes between the Americans and their South Vietnamese allies, leading in at least one case to the South Vietnam military leader's insisting that he would not "carry out the policy of any foreign power" (quoted in Peter Grose, "He Defies Taylor," *New York Times*, December 23, 1964, http://select.nytimes.com/gst/abstract.html?res=FA0B1EFB355F147A93C1AB1789D95F408685F9). Stone did not quote this statement; however, it certainly was part of the background for his assertion a couple of months later. And in earlier issues of his *Weekly*, he presented some quotes from a foreign critic of the war and from some antiwar senators supporting his view—not impartial sources, but significant at a time when few officials dared speak out against the war. Stone also included some anecdotal evidence: a letter home from an American soldier the day before he was killed, quoted in the *Washington Evening Star*, saying, "These people don't even want us here," along with a report, also in the *Star*, on an event in which reparations were paid to Vietnamese for children or animals killed during American operations—an event during which, according to that article, "almost every [recipient's] face registered hate" (I. F. Stone, "The Truth About the Vietnamese War in a Dead U.S. Soldier's Pathetic Last Letter Home" and "The War's No End of Fun in Saigon, but Not So Jolly in the Villages," *I. F. Stone's Weekly*, February 8, 1965, http://www.ifstone.org/weekly/IFStonesWeekly-1965feb08.pdf). These examples are at best paradigmatic—not proof, but they do enter the ledger as evidence.

29. Mike Levine, interviewed by the author, September 25, 2006.

30. Michael Slackman, "Voices of Peace Muffled by Rising Mideast Strife," *New York Times*, July 14, 2006, http://www.nytimes.com/2006/07/14/world/middleeast/14assess.html; Matthai Chakko Kuruvila, "Papal Gaffe Was Setback for Religious Dialogue," *San Francisco Chronicle*, September 24, 2006, http://www.sfgate.com/news/article/NEWS-ANALYSIS-Papal-gaffe-was-setback-for-2487772.php; Duke Helfand, "For Mayor, Opportunity and Daunting Challenges," *Los Angeles Times*, August 31, 2006, http://articles.latimes.com/2006/aug/31/local/me-mayor31.

31. Mobutu Sese Seko, "Barack Obama Is Libya's Al-Qaida Chief for Hawaii," *Gawker*, September 14, 2012, http://gawker.com/5943334/barack-obama-is-libyas-al+qaida-chief-for-hawaii?tag=america.s-screaming-conscience.

32. Richard Hofstadter, *The Paranoid Style in American Politics, and Other Essays* (Cambridge, Mass.: Harvard University Press, 1965).

33. Quoted in Andrew Kirell, "Rush Limbaugh: Al-Qaeda 'Gave Up Osama Bin Laden' to Make 'Obama Look Good,'" *Mediaite*, September 13, 2012, http://www.mediaite.com/tv/limbaughs-new-theory-al-qaeda-gave-up-osama-bin-laden-to-make-obama-look-good/.

34. A. J. Liebling, *The Press* (New York: Ballantine Books, 1964), 30.

35. Aristotle, *On Rhetoric*, 182 (2.21.1).

36. Liebling's suggestion was that newspapers, like universities, be supported by endowments (*The Press*, 23–24).

37. Louis Menand, "Foreword," in Edmund Wilson, *To the Finland Station* (New York: New York Review of Books, 2003), xi.

38. Lincoln Steffens, *The Shame of the Cities* (New York: Hill and Wang, 1967), 2.

39. James Baldwin, "Autobiographical Notes," in *Notes of a Native Son* (Boston: Beacon Press, 1984), 5–6.

40. James Baldwin, "Nobody Knows My Name," in *The Price of the Ticket: Collected Nonfiction, 1948–1985* (New York: Macmillan, 1985), 189.

41. Katherine Boo, *Behind the Beautiful Forevers* (New York: Random House, 2012), ix.

42. Tom Wolfe, "Radical Chic: That Party at Lenny's," *New York* magazine, June 8, 1970, http://nymag.com/news/features/46170/.

43. I. F. Stone, "It's Been a Faked Class B Movie from the Beginning," *I. F. Stone's Weekly*, January 25, 1965, http://www.ifstone.org/weekly/IFStonesWeekly-1965jan25.pdf.

44. Norman Mailer, *The Time of Our Time* (New York: Random House, 1998), 880. Leslie Savan directed me to this quotation.

45. See Norman Mailer, *Armies of the Night* (New York: New American Library, 1968), and *The Executioner's Song* (1979; New York: Grand Central, 2012).

46. Rachel Carson, *Silent Spring* (1962; New York: Houghton Mifflin Harcourt, 2002), 5.

47. Those tweets from Nate Silver are available at https://twitter.com/fivethirtyeight/status/249118414663188481, https://twitter.com/fivethirtyeight/status/249118835528048641, and https://twitter.com/fivethirtyeight/status/249119160381091840.

48. Quoted in John Maxwell Hamilton, *Journalism's Roving Eye: A History of American Foreign Reporting* (Baton Rouge: Louisiana State University Press, 2009), 269–70.

49. Baldwin, "Nobody Knows My Name," 185.

50. Joan Didion, *Salvador* (New York: Vintage, 1994), 17.

51. Joan Didion, "Some Dreamers of the Golden Dream," in *Slouching Toward Bethlehem* (New York: Macmillan, 1968), 4.

52. Quoted in Dallas Liddle, "Who Invented the 'Leading Article'? Reconstructing the History and Prehistory of a Victorian Newspaper Genre," *Media History* 5, no. 1 (1999): 11.

53. This cartoon is reproduced at http://www.theatlantic.com/daily-dish/archive/2008/11/toles-flawless-response/208985/.

54. Liddle, "Who Invented the 'Leading Article'?" 14.

55. "A Report on Senator Joseph R. McCarthy," *See it Now*, CBS-TV, March 9, 1954, archived online by the Media Resources Center, Moffitt Library, University of California, Berkeley, http://www.lib.berkeley.edu/MRC/murrowmccarthy.html.

56. Quoted in Liddle, "Who Invented the 'Leading Article'?" 13.

7. "SHIMMERING INTELLECTUAL SCOOPS"

1. David Carr, "Journalists Dancing on the Edge of Truth," *New York Times*, August 20, 2012, http://www.nytimes.com/2012/08/20/business/media/journalists-plagiarism -jonah-lehrer-fareed-zakaria.html?_r=0.

2. Whitelaw Reid made the argument that journalism should cover ideas, even as he was arguing that journalism should emphasize facts in its coverage, although the example he used has proven controversial: "As a matter of news, Herbert Spencer's great ideas are as important, because likely to affect future philosophy, as George H. Pendleton's plan of paying the national debt in greenbacks was, because likely to affect the action of the Democratic party" (interview with Whitelaw Reid in Charles Frederick Wingate, ed., *Views and Interviews on Journalism* [New York: F. B. Patterson, 1875], 26). I have made attempts to report on ideas. See, for example, my articles "Jacques Derrida," *New York Times Magazine*, January 23, 1994, http://www.nyu.edu/ classes/stephens/Jacques%20Derrida%20-%20NYT%20-%20page.htm; "The Theologian of Talk: Jurgen Habermas," *Los Angeles Times Magazine*, October 23, 1994, http://www.nyu.edu/classes/stephens/Habermas%20page.htm; "To Thine Own Selves Be True (Postmodern Psychology)," *Los Angeles Times Magazine*, August 23, 1992, http://www.nyu.edu/classes/stephens/Postmodern%20psych%20page.htm; and "The Professor of Disenchantment (Stephen Greenblatt and the New Historicism)," *West*, March 1, 1992, http://www.nyu.edu/classes/stephens/Greenblatt%20page.htm.

3. Jeff Zeleny and Jim Rutenberg, "Obama and Romney, in First Debate, Spar Over Fixing the Economy," *New York Times*, October 4, 2012, http://www .nytimes.com/2012/10/04/us/politics/obama-and-romney-hold-first-debate .html?pagewanted=all.

4. William Kristol, "A Terrific Debate," *Weekly Standard*, October 3, 2012, http://www .weeklystandard.com/blogs/terrific-debate_653528.html.

5. "The *Daily Dish* by Andrew Sullivan," in "25 Best Blogs of 2009," *Time*, February 17, 2009, http://www.time.com/time/specials/packages/completelist/0,29569 ,1879276,00.html.

6. Katherine Boo, "Swamp Nurse," *New Yorker*, February 6, 2006, http://www.new yorker.com/archive/2006/02/06/060206fa_fact_boo?mobify=0, and "The Churn: Creative Destruction in a Border Town," *New Yorker*, March 29, 2004, http://www .newyorker.com/archive/2004/03/29/040329fa_fact?currentPage=all.

7. Dave Barry, "Ok, Who Stole the Universe?" *Chicago Tribune*, January 29, 1995, http:// articles.chicagotribune.com/1995-01-29/features/9501290129_1_astronomers -distant-galaxy-dormitory-environment.

8. Leslie Stephen, "The Duties of Authors," in *Social Rights and Duties*, vol. 2 (London: Sonnenschein, 1896), 156.

9. Benjamin Franklin, "The Printer to the Reader," *Pennsylvania Gazette*, October 2, 1729, in *Benjamin Franklin: Writings*, ed. J. A. Leo Lemay (New York: Library of America, 1987), 136–37.

10. Stephen Edelston Toulmin, *The Uses of Argument* (Cambridge: Cambridge University Press), 60.

11. Stephen, "The Duties of Authors," 156.

12. Jay Rosen, Twitter feed, February 27, 2012, @JayRosen_NYU, https://twitter.com/jayrosen_nyu/status/174281714112270337.

13. Paul Krugman, "Europe's Austerity Madness," *New York Times*, September 27, 2012, http://www.nytimes.com/2012/09/28/opinion/krugman-europes-austerity-madness.html?partner=rssnyt&emc=rss.

14. See Mitchell Stephens, "Deconstruction and the Get-Real Press," *Columbia Journalism Review* 30, no. 3 (1991): 38–42.

15. "Commentary," *The Pulitzer Prizes*, http://www.pulitzer.org/bycat/Commentary.

16. For example, my own program, New York University's Arthur L. Carter Institute of Journalism, now offers specialized master's programs in, among other subjects, science, health and environmental journalism, cultural reporting, global journalism, and business and economic journalism. And all undergraduate journalism majors are required to complete another major in the liberal arts.

17. For another take on alternatives to beats, see Gideon Lichfield, "On Elephants, Obsessions, and Wicked Problems: A New Phenomenology of News: Goodbye to the Beat," *News Thing*, September 16, 2012, http://newsthing.net/2012/09/16/quartz-obsessions-phenomenology-of-news/.

18. For an example of an organization focusing on subject matters rather than beats, see "Our Current Obsessions," *Quartz*, n.d., http://qz.com/about/our-current-obsessions-2/.

19. Wendy Ruderman and Marc Santora, "2 Siblings Killed in New York City; Nanny Arrested," *New York Times*, October 25, 2012, http://www.nytimes.com/2012/10/26/nyregion/fatal-stabbings-on-upper-west-side-nanny-is-arrested.html?pagewanted=all.

20. On the attractions and limitations of such anomalies, see Mitchell Stephens, *A History of News*, 3rd ed. (New York: Oxford University Press, 2007), 116–28.

21. Steven Johnson, *Everything Bad Is Good for You* (New York: Penguin, 2006), 14.

22. Jürgen Habermas, "The Public Sphere: An Encyclopedia Article," in Douglas M. Kellner and Meenakshi Gigi Durham, eds., *Media and Cultural Studies: Key Works* (Malden, Mass.: Blackwell, 2002), 76, quoting Karl Bücher.

ACKNOWLEDGMENTS

This book—a call for more interpretation in journalism—is itself, of course, a work of interpretation. I have had the privilege of trying out many of its arguments before thoughtful and accomplished journalism scholars, critics, and practitioners—most notably while a fellow at the Joan Shorenstein Center on the Press, Politics, and Public Policy at Harvard's Kennedy School in spring 2009. Much of the research for this book was completed there, and I benefited tremendously from the Shorenstein Center's marvelous resources and from the comments and assistance of those I worked with there, including Alex S. Jones, Thomas E. Patterson, James O'Shea, Maralee Schwartz, Michael Traugott, Nancy Parker, and Edith Holway.

In addition, I have presented these ideas and received numerous valuable suggestions and criticisms at conventions of the Association for Education in Journalism in 2009 and 2010, at the Joint Journalism Historians Conference in New York in 2011, and at the conference "Technologies, Media, and Journalism" in Saarbrücken, Germany, in 2013.

My students and colleagues at the Arthur L. Carter Journalism Institute at New York University have continually tested and strengthened my ideas on journalism and its future. Thanks, too, to Jerry Lanson at Emerson College for allowing me to try to convince him (I've made some progress) and for important suggestions on how I might better convince others and to David Mindich at St. Michael's College for various stimulating panels and conversations—the latter sometimes while on bicycles. Bruce Weaver, formally at Albion College, looked over and improved my excursion into his field, rhetoric. My theoretical understandings have also been broadened by discussions with Jeanette McVicker at the State University of New York, Fredonia.

Two anonymous reviewers helped improve the manuscript and my thinking. And I had the benefit of an editor at Columbia University Press, Philip Leventhal, with considerable talent for playing the devil's advocate. The book's points were sharpened and its logic often strengthened in response to his queries.

I was fortunate to work with a number of talented student researchers on this project, beginning with the scholarly, thoughtful, and ever inquisitive John Sillings, who, in the spirit of the book, contributed important ideas as well as facts. Luisa Rollenhagen and Darcy Boynton also improved these discussions. Kristin Kelleher helped with the notes, and Katie Ryder came in at the end to save me from errors. Those errors that remain are, of course, my own, as are any weaknesses in these arguments.

I have written previously about news, its history, its importance, and its limitations. This book has borrowed some points and examples from *A History of News* (the third edition was published by Oxford University Press in 2007), but its main argument has been quite different. I have not been questioning the centrality or ubiquity of news here, but I have been asserting that the best journalism in the twenty-first century must, as it did before the nineteenth century, find a more ambitious role for itself than just telling news.

While working on this book, I also completed a guide to producing new forms of journalism, *Journalism Unbound* (forthcoming from Oxford University Press). Readers of both books will note that they share some points and a handful of examples. But that book is a broader how-to guide for new kinds of twenty-first-century journalism. It is intended for journalists and prospective journalists. This is a more focused argument about twenty-first-century journalism, intended for those who think about as well as practice it.

Since this book presumes to say something about the future, I have had in mind my children Lauren, Seth, and Noah Stephens-Davidowitz, one of whom currently writes journalism, but all of whom have done journalism and have heard these ideas out and weighed in on them. My largest debt, however, is to the two working journalists with whom I have lived: my wife, Esther Davidowitz, and my late father, Bernard Stephens, a labor newspaper editor and my first and best editor.

INDEX